KT-148-650

INTERVENING IN CHILD SEXUAL ABUSE

INTERVENING IN CHILD SEXUAL ABUSE

Edited by

KATHLEEN MURRAY and

DAVID A. GOUGH

with a Foreword by

Professor SANFORD N. KATZ

SCOTTISH ACADEMIC PRESS

Published by
Scottish Academic Press Ltd,
139 Leith Walk
Edinburgh EH6 8NS

ISBN 7073 0566 7 hbk
ISBN 7073 0565 9 pbk

British Library Cataloguing in Publication Data
Intervening in child sexual abuse.
1. Children. Sexual abuse by adults. Prevention
I. Murray, Kathleen II. Gough, David A.
362.76

Typeset by Trinity Typesetting, Edinburgh
Printed in Great Britain by
Thomson Litho Ltd, East Kilbride, Scotland

CONTENTS

THE CONTRIBUTORS

Judith V. Becker
Professor of Clinical Psychology, College of Physicians and Surgeons, Columbia University, and Director of the Sexual Behavior Clinic, New York Psychiatric Institute, New York, U.S.A.

Lucy Berliner
Assistant Clinical Professor of Social Work, College of Social Work, University of Washington, and Research Director, Harborview Sexual Assault Center, Seattle, Washington, U.S.A.

Harry M. Elias
Deputy District Attorney, Chief, Child Abuse Division, County of San Diego, California, U.S.A.

David Finkelhor
Co-director of the Family Research Laboratory and the Family Violence Research Program, University of New Hampshire, U.S.A.

Rhona Flin
Lecturer in Psychology, Business School, Robert Gordon's Institute of Technology, Aberdeen, Scotland.

Esther Gillies
Director of the Southern California Training Center for Child Sexual Abuse Treatment, Children's Institute International, Los Angeles, California, U.S.A., and formerly Member of the Board of Directors of Parents United International.

David A. Gough
Research Fellow, Social Paediatric and Obstetric Research Unit, University of Glasgow, Scotland.

Astrid H. Heger
Director, Child Sexual Abuse Clinic, Pediatrics Department, University of Southern California School of Medicine, Los Angeles, California, U.S.A.

David P. H. Jones
Consultant Child Psychiatrist, Park Hospital for Children, Oxford, and Clinical Lecturer, University of Oxford, England.

Kee MacFarlane
Director, Child Sexual Abuse Diagnostic Center, Children's Institute International, Los Angeles, California, U.S.A.

Kathleen Murray
Research Fellow, Department of Social Administration and Social Work, University of Glasgow, Scotland.

John E. B. Myers
Professor of Law, University of the Pacific, McGeorge School of Law, Sacramento, California, U.S.A.

Gordon Nicholson QC	Sheriff Principal of Lothian and Borders, Scotland, and formerly member of the Scottish Law Commission, Edinburgh, Scotland.
John R. Spencer	Tutor in Law, Selwyn College, University of Cambridge, England.
Patricia A. Toth	Director, National Center for the Prosecution of Child Abuse, American Prosecutors Research Institute, Virginia, U.S.A.

PREFACE

It is hard to believe that a mere ten years ago the sexual abuse of children was perhaps society's most closely guarded secret and virtually went unrecognised by health and social work practitioners. In the past few years, however, public and professional awareness of child sexual abuse has increased markedly. Health, welfare and law enforcement agencies have been preoccupied with an explosive growth in the number of referrals in which sexual abuse is a major factor. The Cleveland Inquiry, the widespread and highly emotive attention given by the media, and the plethora of conferences, books and other publications on the subject are further indication of increasing recognition of the problem.

This book has been developed from papers that were first presented at a major conference held in Glasgow in June 1988, organised by the University of Glasgow in association with the Children's Institute International, Los Angeles. This joint venture, which grew out of a study visit in the United States by Kathleen Murray, led to an exchange of ideas and experience about intervening in child sexual abuse in our respective countries, at a time when the problem in the United Kingdom had moved to centre stage.

Compared with the United Kingdom, American experience of child sexual abuse is longer-standing, is on a much greater scale, and covers a broader range of approaches and philosophies. Its lessons are highly relevant to the issues currently being raised in the United Kingdom where the social, clinical and legal complexities of the problem have more recently emerged. Of course American experience of intervention strategies is not replicable elsewhere, nonetheless it does help to establish a number of fundamental and generally acceptable principles that are equally relevant to the development of policy and practice in a very different cultural and legal context. Our contributors and we as editors have tried to present an account of the present state of knowledge in such areas as interviewing, physical examination, gathering legal evidence, legal reforms to enable children to testify, various approaches to prevention and treatment as well as some examination of critical issues in policy and practice.

Many of our contributors have been closely identified with the development of theoretical knowledge and professional expertise in the area of child sexual abuse, the majority have worked within clinical or legal settings and several others have been engaged in training and academic research. They represent the range of backgrounds commonly associated with the management of social problems, although in child sexual abuse there is a heightened importance attached to mutual understanding and collaboration.

Our main purpose has been to provide a text which would be of value in the training of specialist workers in the field. We believe too that across Britain there is sufficient demand for information and knowledge in the rapidly developing field of child sexual abuse to justify a volume containing commentaries on American experience. We hope it will serve the further purpose of stimulating critical discussion of proposed approaches in policy and practice both social and legal.

The chapters of the book have been grouped under four main sections and it may be helpful briefly to indicate the scope of each. The first deals with the value of prevalence studies, the purpose, content and style of interviewing children and families, and the strengths and limitations of medical evaluation in the assessment process. In section II are brought together accounts of the legal frameworks of Scotland and England where cases of child sexual abuse are likely to appear. Included is an American perspective on what is involved in making a complete and effective investigation in a sexual abuse case, and the uses and limitations of expert testimony in the event of a trial. Section III examines both theoretically and in their practical application a number of special issues arising within the legal process: the pros and cons of diversion in the criminal justice system, the impact of the court on the competence and credibility of the child witness, and the use of videotechnology and other means of making it easier for children to give evidence in the criminal courts. The fourth section is concerned with different methods of intervening, whether preventive or reactive. In a final chapter we review some of the lessons to be learned from the American experience. We speculate on the policy and practice issues that will need to be resolved and where the course of future development lies, drawing particularly on material provided in the foregoing chapters, partly on the findings of research and largely on our own judgment.

Throughout the collection we have adopted the attitude that our authors should be allowed to speak for themselves; therefore we have reduced our editing to a strict minimum. We should like to express our great thanks for their generosity in updating and rewriting their conference papers. A number of colleagues in addition to the named authors have helped to make the enterprise possible. We have very much appreciated the assistance of Irene Young who typed successive drafts of chapters; also Janet Watson for clerical support. The book arose from the 1988 Glasgow conference and we therefore owe much gratitude to those who made the conference possible, in particular, Dr Andrew Boddy, Professor Fred Stone and Professor Rex Taylor of the University of Glasgow for their advice and guidance on the conference planning committee; to Bridget Rothwell who provided essential administrative assistance to the conference; and to the Child and Family Trust who contributed underwriting support for that event.

However, the book itself has been a separate exercise for which only the respective authors and we as editors bear any responsibility.

Kathleen Murray and David Gough

Glasgow, November 1990

FOREWORD

BY

SANFORD N. KATZ
PROFESSOR OF LAW, BOSTON COLLEGE LAW SCHOOL

ALMOST THIRTY YEARS ago, I participated in a meeting of professionals called by the Children's Bureau of the United States Department of Health, Education, and Welfare to review the findings of the Los Angeles Police Department along with other research on abusive parental conduct toward children carried out by behavioural scientists. The police department had begun to piece together reports from various Los Angeles hospitals regarding inexplicable injuries to children. The information from the police department reports and the innovative and important research findings of Dr C. Henry Kempe[1] of Colorado were the impetus for a model child abuse reporting law discussed at that meeting and later drafted by the federal government in 1963.

By 1967, every American state and the District of Columbia had enacted mandatory child abuse reporting laws requiring certain professionals to report suspected child abuse cases to social service or law enforcement agencies.[2] The purpose of these laws was to protect children. Their effect was to allow the state to intrude into the normally private parent-child relationship — a very important change in American family law and policy.[3] Early legislation was directed at physicians, who were considered most likely to recognise evidence of abuse. Later, many statutes were expanded to include other professionals such as teachers, social workers, police officers, and child care workers.[4] Increasingly, states have required all persons to report suspected incidents of child abuse where, for example, they have 'reasonable cause to believe' abuse has occurred.[5] These statutes generally include penalties for failure to report and grant immunity for false reports made in good faith.[6]

The model child abuse reporting law was drafted a century after the 'battered child syndrome' was first described by Ambroise Tardieu,[7] a professor of legal medicine in Paris. Coincidentally, the year Tardieu discussed the autopsy findings of 32 children battered to death by whipping and burning in Paris, Athol Johnson at the Hospital for Sick Children of London described cases of children who had repeated bone fractures unrelated to rickets.[8]

During the early 1960s, two major studies were published that laid the foundation for much of the future work in the field of child abuse and neglect. Dr Herta Riese's *Heal the Hurt Child*[9] pointed the way for others to work for the redirection of social policies in the United States to protect children. Riese recognised that a home deprived of the normal objects in a child's life threatens that child's psychological balance, and that merely surviving on the bare necessities of life — a roof over one's head, three meals a day, a mother in attendance — leads to dullness in children. She concluded that social disorder and mental disorder are interconnected, with persistent social disorganisation ultimately leading to mental disorganisation. Riese discussed the importance of stimulation and nurturing in a child's life, comparing this ideal with the voidness experienced by black children in Richmond, Virginia.

While Riese's study was a primer for policy-makers, Dr Leontine Young's book, *Wednesday's Children*,[10] educated clinicians, lawyers and judges. It defined child abuse and neglect more precisely than had been the case in the past. To Young, child abuse and neglect were complicated. How one classified parental misconduct was a key to the approach one took toward parents, socially, psychologically and legally.

Young described the 'severely neglected' child as one who is starved, chained to a bed, caged like an animal or found in a cellar, secluded and malnourished. Parents of 'severely neglected' children were indifferent. While they may have acted unintentionally, they had little capacity to do better if they tried. Their lives were chaotic and their conduct unpredictable. 'Moderately neglected' children differed from the 'severely neglected' in that their parents understood what was needed for survival. Still, their parents had no regard for cleanliness or adequate medical attention.

In contrast, 'severely abused' children were tortured by their parents. They were beaten, and burned by lighted cigarettes, scalding water, and hot stoves. Parents twisted their children's limbs until they were broken, destroyed their children's loved pets, used abusive language and threatened their children with death. The frequency of abuse differentiated 'moderately abused' children from 'severely abused' ones. To Young, abusive parents' actions were deliberate, calculated, consistent and tortuous, in other words, cold blooded, rather than normal parental reactions to a child's behaviour.

Young's study involved 300 American families in which abuse or neglect had occurred. The cases, typical of those currently found in social services agencies, were supplied by both public (state) and private (voluntary) agencies. The case records, the source of all the information in the studies, followed the families from periods of one to 20 years.

Young's classifications remain important for determining the timing, degree and manner of state intervention into family life, a problem that has sparked debate for the past 20 years in the United States.[11] The starting point for this debate has been the premise that the family is a social unit that should function independently of all but the most limited intrusions. However, a price is paid for the concept of family privacy — perhaps too high a price. Thousands of cases of child abuse and neglect may go undetected because of the view that parents ought to raise their children as they see fit.

A troubling question that officials face today is: at what point should the public intrude into the family? If a case involves a child who is 'severely abused' according to Young's classification, there are few who would question the legality and justification for the intervention. A difficult problem arises when authorities are faced with the issue of whether they should intervene before there is a manifest outbreak of pathology in the child, for example, when public authorities seek to place a newborn child under wardship because its mother is a drug addict and the likelihood of her newborn being affected is high.[12] An even more difficult question is whether a court should support a public authority's decision to place a child yet to be born under the public authority's jurisdiction? When the child is born, should it be taken from the mother and placed in foster care? Is coercive intervention justified in order to further the unborn child's best interests once the child is born? This is an unusual case. But it raises questions about the state's responsibility in protecting children, even those yet to be born.

What we would label child abuse in 1990 might have been called appropriate discipline in 1950. Parents had extraordinary powers over their children, and they could use physical force either to punish them or to instil respect for parental authority. This licence to use force can be traced to colonial times when a child could be put to death for 'disobeying a father's voice'.[13] Later, only when parents went beyond 'reasonable force' — usually, that meant death of the child — could they be subjected to criminal prosecution.

The 1960s were a high water mark in recognising child abuse and neglect as a legal problem, creating new definitions and fashioning different legal responses.[14] During this period, American states began to examine their processes whereby children were removed from their homes either temporarily or permanently.

Perhaps the most radical change that occurred during this time was the realisation that no matter how much time and energy as well as financial resources are invested in certain parents, their parenting skills will not change. For these parents, termination of parental rights is the only solution. While such an outcome might seem right and proper today, arriving at such a decision in American courts was no simple event. Attempting to make the process fair and reasonable has been an enormous undertaking.

We have called such a process 'permanency planning.'[15] The term derives in part from social scientists, especially Drs Joseph Goldstein, Anna Freud, and Albert Solnit,[16] whose work influenced policy-makers that permanent dispositions were best for children, based on principles of child development. Permanency planning balances parents' rights to rear their children with the state's interest in children's well-being, taking into account such matters as a child's sense of time, and the importance of maintaining continuity of care, minimising separations and expediting the intervention process. It allows for intervention to occur, while letting parents know what in their parenting was offensive to their children's well-being; making a plan for the parents; giving them time to rehabilitate themselves — often with agency help — and, if rehabilitation has occurred, reuniting them with their children. For those parents who are unable or unwilling to participate in the plan, termination of parental rights occurs.

Permanency planning has been attacked by some as being too intrusive, that is, that it does not allow enough time for parents to rehabilitate themselves. However, time is of the essence for young children. While the decision to terminate a parent's right to the custody of his or her child is painful, in many cases it is the only just outcome where the goal is to further a child's overall well-being.

The American Humane Association estimates that in the United States the number of child abuse and neglect reports rose from 669,000 to 1,928,000 between 1976 and 1985. Estimates of childhood sexual abuse based on numerous surveys range from 3 to 15 per cent of boys and 12 to 38 per cent of girls.[17] Since people may be reluctant to admit to having been victims of such abuse, the actual percentages may be much higher. In the Commonwealth of Massachusetts alone there were approximately 2,000 reported cases of childhood sexual abuse in 1987 compared to 130 in 1983. No one seems to have an answer as to why there has been an increase in the number of reported cases. Some have suggested that the increased publicity of child sexual abuse incidents has heightened public awareness of the issue and encouraged the reports. Thus, the taboo against talking about private family matters may have been lifted.

It has already been noted that the 1960s were a high water mark in acknowledging child abuse and neglect. During the 1980s the same could be said of child sexual abuse, the problems of which are the subject of this book. Perhaps the most prevalent emerging problem in the United States concerns the phenomenon of allegations of sexual abuse in divorce and custody cases. A number of theories have been suggested regarding the reason for the large numbers of accusations in these proceedings.[18] On the one hand, the emotionally charged atmosphere of a divorce or custody proceeding may cause one parent to misinterpret the child's account of a stay with the other parent, leading to an unfounded accusation. This emotional setting may also encourage parents to make false accusations in order to gain or retain custody rights, to prevent the other spouse from exercising visitation rights or simply to be malicious. On the other hand, there is strong agreement that the emotional strain of divorce proceedings produces a potent breeding ground for child molestation by parents. Thus, as marital trust evaporates, spouses may notice abuse, where they would not have before. Similarly, the breakdown in marital trust may enable a parent to see that sexual abuse had occurred during the marriage.

Several studies have been concluded regarding the veracity of allegations of sexual abuse.[19] Those that have distinguished between 'unsubstantiated' accusations, (i.e., accusations which lack conclusive evidence) and 'false' accusations (i.e., those accusations which evidence suggests have been fabricated) suggest that the number of fictitious accusations is low relative to the large number of cases reported.[20] This distinction is particularly important in the context of divorce and custody proceedings where a number of factors — the secretive nature of sexual abuse, the uncertain credibility of children's testimony, the conflicting motives of the parties — make it difficult to prove sexual abuse.

The issue of proving sexual abuse of children in the context of divorce and custody proceedings becomes more complicated in light of the results of several studies reported by Myers and his colleagues, which suggest that false allegations of abuse are more likely in connection with these proceedings than in other contexts.[21] One recent study of allegations of child sexual abuse in custody litigation attributed the increase in the number of reports to greater parental awareness of the warning signs.[22] It stated that since the early 1980s the number of reports filed has leveled off. As to the veracity of the claims, the study concluded that it was rare for spouses falsely to accuse an ex-spouse of child abuse in order to influence the custody decision.

Myers and his colleagues state that while false allegations of sexual abuse certainly do occur in divorce and custody proceedings, the fact that many allegations are indeed true makes it necessary for courts to exert caution before accepting or rejecting the accusation.[23] It is not unusual they said that the children will disclose abuse for the first time during the breakup of the family. This results from the inability of the abusing parent to pressure the child to remain silent during periods of separation. They note that the distrust associated with many custody and divorce proceedings increases the inclination of parents to suspect child abuse.

Why child abuse? Although the phenomenon has been with civilised societies for centuries, no one has presented a convincing and comprehensive explanation for its origins.[24] There are, of course, many psychological and sociological explanations. Perhaps we shall never establish one correct answer. However, those who have studied the problem seriously and passionately have been saying for decades that one cause for all types of abuse is the societal tolerance for violence and the misuse of power, evidenced, for example, by the widespread acceptance of war and capital and corporal punishment, and the belief that its control is not always desirable.[25] In fact the roots of this statement go back to Jeremiah: 'The fathers have eaten sour grapes, And the children's teeth are set on edge.' It will take generations of retraining to change this mind set. But the struggle for change is worth the effort. It is a cliché to say that the proper care of children is our insurance for a better world. Yet the statement is worth repeating in the context of child protection. If we can improve the care we give to children, we will have a future world that is worth having.

NOTES

1. *See* C. H. Kempe, F. N. Silverman, B. Steele, W. Droegelmueller and H. K. Silver, The Battered Child Syndrome, 181 *Journal of the American Medical Association* 17

(1962). Dr Kempe and his colleagues were the first American physicians to redefine child abuse as a medical diagnosis. *See The Battered Child,* Chicago: University of Chicago Press, R. E. Helfer and C. H. Kempe (Eds.), 1968. This book has undergone a number of revisions since its first publication.

2. J. Myers, A Survey of Child Abuse and Neglect Reporting Statutes, 10 *Journal of Juvenile Law* 1, 2 (1986) [hereinafter cited as Myers]. In 1974 the U.S. Congress passed the Child Abuse Prevention and Treatment Act (PL 93-247). This act defined child abuse more broadly than most state statutes. It included 'physical or mental injury' and 'sexual abuse'. Mental injury and sexual abuse were missing in the early statutes.
3. D. Besharov, The Legal Aspects of Reporting Known and Suspected Child Abuse and Neglect, 23 *Villanova Law Review* 458, 464 (1977).
4. *Id.* at 467-68.
5. Myers, *supra,* n. 2 at 4.
6. *Id.*
7. A Tardieu, Etude Medico — Legale Sur L'enfanticide (Paris 1968), cited in Kempe, *Child Abuse,* 5 (1978) [hereinafter cited as *Child Abuse*].
8. A. A. W. Johnson, Lectures on the Surge of Childhood, cited in *Child Abuse, supra* n. 7 at 5.
9. Chicago: University of Chicago Press, 1962.
10. New York: McGraw-Hill Book Company, 1964. Unfortunately this excellent and useful study is out of print. My discussion here of Dr. Young's findings as well as those of Dr. Riese are more fully expanded in my review, S. Katz, Book Review 1965 *Duke Law Journal* 208.
11. *See* S. Katz, *When Parents Fail: The Law's Response to Family Breakdown* (Beacon Press, 1971); M. Wald, State Intervention on Behalf of Neglected Children: A Search for Realistic Standards, 27 *Stanford Law Review* 985 (1975); M. Wald, State Intervention on Behalf of Neglected Children: Standards for Removal of Children from their Home, Monitoring the Status of Children in Foster Care, and Termination of Parental Rights, 28 *Stanford Law Review* 625 (1976).
12. *See, e.g. Matter of Baby X,* 293 N.W. 2d 736 (Mich. App. 1980) which held that a newborn who suffers from narcotics withdrawal symptoms as consequences of prenatal maternal drug addiction was properly considered a neglected child within the Michigan probate court's jurisdiction. For a full discussion of this problem, *see* B. I. Robin-Vergeer, The Problem of the Drug-Exposed Newborn: A Return to Principled Intervention, 42 *Stanford Law Review* 745 (1990).
13. The death penalty could be imposed for violation of the Stubborn Child Law, enacted in Massachusetts in 1654 to punish 'diverse children and servants [who] behave themselves too disrespectively, disobediently and disorderly toward their parents, masters and governors.' *See,* N. Shurtleff, *Records of the Governor and Company of Massachusetts Bay Colony in New England,* Vol. 3, 355 (1853-54). For a collection of American colonial laws dealing with the punishment of children *See Children and Youth in America,* Vol. 1, 37-39, Cambridge: Harvard University Press, (R. H. Brenner Ed., 1970).
14. For a bibliography of books and articles on the legal and psychological aspects of child abuse and neglect during the 1960s and 1970s, *see* S. Katz, M. McGrath and R. A. W. Howe, *Child Neglect in America,* 367-372 (Chicago: American Bar Association Press, 1976).
15. *See* S. Katz, 'The Model Act to Free Children for Permanent Placement,' printed in *Family Violence: An International and Interdisciplinary Study,* Toronto: Butterworths, 537 (J. Eekelaar and S. Katz, Eds. 1978) which embodies this principle; *see also* R. A. W. Howe, 'Development of a Model Act to Free Children for Permanent Placement: A Case Study in Law and Social Planning,' 13 *Family Law Quarterly* 257, 281-283 (1979). For a discussion of permanency planning, *see* M. Hardin and A. Shalleck, Children Living Apart from their Parents in *Legal Rights*

of Children 371-377 (R. Horowitz and H. Davidson, Eds. 1984).

16. *See* J. Goldstein, A. Freud and A. Solnit, *Beyond the Best Interests of the Child*, New York: The Free Press (1973); *Before the Best Interests of the Child*, New York: The Free Press (1979); J. Goldstein, A. Freud, A. Solnit and S. Goldstein, *In the Best Interests of the Child*, New York: The Free Press (1986).
17. *See* D. Finkelhor, *Sexually Victimized Children*, New York: Free Press, 1979; A. C. Kinsey, W. Pomeroy, C. Martin and P. Gebhard, *Sexual Behaviour in the Human Female*, Philadelphia: Saunders, 1953; D. E. H. Russell, 'The Incidence and Procedure of Intrafamilial and Extrafamilial Sexual Abuse of Female Children,' *Child Abuse and Neglect*, 133-145 (1983), cited in H. Dubowitz and E. Newberger, 'Paediatrics and Child Abuse,' in *Child Maltreatment: Theory and Research on the Causes and Consequences of Child Abuse and Neglect*, Cambridge: Cambridge University Press 81 (D. Cicchetti and V. Carlson, Eds. 1989) [hereinafter cited as *Child Maltreatment*]. For example, Finkelhor's 1979 survey of 796 college students found that 19 per cent of the women surveyed and 9 per cent of the men were victims of childhood sexual abuse. Russell's 1982 survey in San Francisco found that 28 per cent of the women surveyed were sexually abused before age 17. C. R. Hartman and A. W. Burgess, 'Sexual Abuse of Children: Causes and Consequences,' in *Child Maltreatment*, 98. A 1985 nationwide poll by the *Los Angeles Times* found that 22 per cent of those surveyed had been sexually abused before age 18. *See* A. Heger, 'Child Sexual Abuse: The Medical Evaluation,' in *Sexual Abuse Allegations in Custody and Visitation Cases: A Resource Book for Judges and Court Personnel* (E. B. Nicholson and J. Bulkley, Eds. 1988) [hereinafter cited as *Sexual Abuse Allegations*].
18. *See*, D. Corwin, L. Berliner, G. S. Goodman, J. Goodwin and S. White, Child Sexual Abuse and Custody Disputes, 2 *Journal of Interpersonal Violence* 91 (1987) [hereinafter cited as Corwin].; F. Sink, Studies of True and False Allegations: A Critical View, in *Sexual Abuse Allegations*, *supra* n. 17 at 42-44 [hereinafter cited as Sink].
19. *See*, N. Thoennes and J. Pearson, Summary of Findings from the Sexual Abuse Allegation Project in *Sexual Abuse Allegations* 1, 4, 16, 17.
20. *See* Corwin, *supra*, n. 18 at 94-95, citing a 1983 study which found that of 576 cases of child sexual abuse reported to the Denver Department of Social Services, only eight per cent were probably fictitious. *See also*, Sink, *supra* n. 18 at 40-41.
21. J. Myers, J. Bays, L. Berliner, D. Corwin and K. Saywitz, Expert Testimony in Child Sexual Abuse Litigation 68 *Nebraska Law Review* 1 (1989). This excellent article from which I have benefitted greatly in preparing this Foreword, presents a full discussion of child sexual abuse litigation and a review of the literature in the field.
22. *Id.* at 114-115.
23. *Id.*
24. For an excellent historical perspective on child maltreatment, *see* J. Giovannoni and R. Becerra, *Defining Child Abuse*, New York: The Free Press, 1979. *Also see*, J. Giovannoni, 'Definitional Issues in Child Maltreatment' in *Child Maltreatment*, *supra* n. 17 at 3-37.
25. *See, e.g.*, E. Zigler and N. W. Hall, 'Child Abuse in America,' in *Child Maltreatment*, *supra* n. 17 at 55, quoting one commentator who calls child abuse 'a swatch from the fabric of a violent and abusive society'. As evidence of society's tolerance of violence the article cites National Association for Better Broadcasting statistics that the average child aged 5 to 15 watches the violent destruction of more than 13,400 people on television.

1

THE SCOPE OF THE PROBLEM

DAVID FINKELHOR

OVER THE LAST few years there have been various attempts in North America and elsewhere to estimate the extent of the sexual abuse of children in our communities. It is clear from a number of surveys of both the general population and clinical samples that sexual abuse is a very widespread and serious problem. There are variations in the methodology and results of the surveys and so there is no exact information on prevalence. However, now that we know the degree to which sexual abuse occurs, the exact extent of the problem is not that important for the purposes of research or of practice. What is of more scientific concern than prevalence is the nature of the problem, its causes and effects and the ways that we can intervene to reduce its occurrence and its effect.

The question of prevalence, however, has been extremely important from the standpoint of public policy. One of the most important accomplishments in the last ten years has been informing the public and the professional community in North America who now, for the most part, agree that sexual abuse is extremely widespread. There are a number of reasons for making the dissemination of this knowledge an important priority. It captures media interest and brings attention to the problem. It is useful in mobilizing physical and human resources to attend to the problem and take it seriously. It assists in the reporting of instances of abuse; as people realise that it is widespread they begin to consider the possibility of sexual abuse and look more diligently for cases. It also stimulates spontaneous prevention strategies as many parents and others who have contact with children learn about the prevalence of sexual abuse and then take measures on their own initiative to try to inform children and try to protect them. Finally, and maybe most importantly, the dissemination of this knowledge is important in counteracting some of the impact of sexual abuse. Victims growing up today realise that they are in the company of many many others who have also been victimised. They are thus less isolated than those growing up with this particular experience a generation ago.

This accomplishment in raising public awareness about the scope of sexual abuse has been complicated and many factors have contributed to it.

There has been a cycle of increasing reports leading to increasing awareness, but research and data collection have been particularly influential in this cycle.

Since 1976, the United States has had a national reporting system for collecting child abuse statistics in which most, but not all, of the states participate. It has consistently shown increases of over ten per cent per year in the number of cases of sexual abuse being reported. Although this has been influential, more could have been achieved if the reporting system had been more systematic, with more detail, more careful attention to the data collected, and with greater national participation. There was an unfortunately large amount of resistance on the part of individual states to the system of national reporting, probably because workers and administrators in the field did not fully appreciate the importance of collecting and disseminating comprehensive data.

In addition to the numbers of reported cases, in the ten year period between 1975 and 1985, there have been nine general community epidemiological-type surveys which provided data about the prevalence of sexual abuse in the population at large. One of these was a national survey (Lewis, 1985), and the others were regional surveys displaying considerable variation in their quality. A couple were undertaken by television stations or newspapers; half a dozen were general surveys of large student populations and there was also Diana Russell's (1986) important study. The surveys were important because the figures that emerged were impressive and their meaning was readily grasped by both professional and lay people. This effort has now been expanded at the international level with a number of other countries besides the United States also attempting to undertake such community surveys. These are summarised below.

INTERNATIONAL COMPARISON OF PREVALENCE OF CHILD SEXUAL ABUSE

Country	*Sample Size & Type*	*Rate %*	
		Males	*Females*
Australia (Goldman & Goldman, 1988)	338 M / 603 F College students	9%	28%
Canada (Bagley et al., 1984)	1002 M / 1006 F National Sample	13%	31%
Holland (Draijer, 1989)	1054 F National Sample	–	33%
New Zealand (Mullen et al., 1988)	2000 F National Sample	–	10%
Sweden (Ronstrom, 1985)	501 M / 501 F National Sample	1%	7%
U.K. (Baker & Duncan, 1985)	2019 M and F National Sample	8%	12%
U.S. (Lewis, 1985)	1252 M / 1374 F National Sample	16%	27%

There has been considerable debate about the reasons for the differential results reported by different studies. My own conclusion, from reviewing the range of studies is that the most important factor affecting the rates is the number of different interview questions that probe a possible history of sexual abuse. Thus, a survey that asks a series of questions such as — 'Did you ever have unwanted intercourse when you were a child?' and 'Did someone from your family ever have sexual contact with you when you were growing up?' produce larger prevalence estimates than the many surveys that simply ask — 'Were you ever sexually abused as a child?' The advantages of the multiple question survey are at least four-fold. Firstly, they act to convince respondents that the interviewer has a serious interest in whether they had such a history and it is not just an off-hand question. Secondly, it allows for the fact that people store memories about these experiences in conjunction with very different kinds of cues. Sexual abuse may not be the category or concept where it is stored. Instead it may be stored in a memory about their relationship with their brother or father. Alternatively, a respondent might not categorise such an experience as sexual abuse but as unwanted intercourse or unwanted fondling. If interview questions do not explore the different areas in which abuse could occur then the surveys are likely to under-report abuse. Thirdly, multiple questions allow respondents time to recall. People need to scan their memories, particularly if the experience of sexual abuse is something that the respondent prefers not to recall or think about. Finally, there is undoubtedly a great deal of embarrassment and discomfort arising from these questions. Offering people multiple opportunities to disclose gives respondents time to overcome what initial embarrassment they may feel as a result of being asked. These advantages are, of course, equally relevant to clinical work which requires questioning about histories of sexual abuse.

Although prevalence surveys are very important for public policy they are unlikely to have much broader scientific importance unless they address more specific issues as well. Currently there are at least three such issues requiring attention. Firstly, epidemiological studies can be used to explore unreported cases of abuse that never come to public attention and to determine how these differ from reported cases that are seen by clinicians. Secondly, the epidemiological studies can inform us about risk factors associated with the occurrence of abuse that might put certain individuals at a vulnerability to be victimised. Thirdly, and maybe most importantly, the studies can indicate which aspects of the abuse and its sequelae are associated with long-term effects for the victims of the abuse. It is in these three areas that the North American studies have been particularly productive. For example, they have clearly demonstrated that there is, even today, a mass under-reporting of the abuse of boys. These surveys consistently show one boy to be abused for about every two girls whereas in the reporting system the ratio is about one boy for every four or five girls. The surveys have also shown that there is still under-reporting of the abuse that occurs to very young children since the proportion of very young victims identified in community surveys is larger than that shown in the reporting system.

Prevalence studies have also provided important knowledge about risk factors (Finkelhor and Baron, 1986). In spite of the fact that cases that come to the attention of the reporting system have a clear bias towards deprived and lower socio-economic status, the surveys have demonstrated that there seems to be no relationship between social class background and the risk of being a victim of child sexual abuse. The surveys have also revealed other important risk factors such as poor relationships with parents, broken families, and the presence of a step-father. The fact of having a step-father increases a child's risk of sexual abuse by about a factor of six or seven.

Surveys have also made an important contribution to our knowledge of the long-term impact of abuse. Recent studies by Briere and Runtz (1988), Bagley and Ramsay (1985), and Stein and colleagues (1988) have demonstrated that the association reported by many clinicians between a history of having been abused and later psychological and social problems, is not simply an artefact of retrospective studies of clinical populations. An examination of the general population of individuals who have been sexually abused, most of whom have never sought help, reveals that the risk for mental health impairment in this group is significantly higher, often two to three times higher, than for others in the population. The risk is particularly great for outcomes such as depression, alcohol and drug abuse, anxiety disorders, sexual problems, and suicidal behaviour. The studies have also demonstrated that victims of sexual abuse are about two to four times more likely to experience later additional sexual assaults as adults compared to people who have not been abused.

While research surveys that ask about the prevalence of abuse do in these instances have insights to offer scientific enquiry and clinical practice, before we complete more surveys, there is a need for a better and more complete understanding of the implications of the prevalence findings that we already have. It may not seem difficult to appreciate the implications that the prevalence findings have for the size of the problem, the seriousness of the problem, and public policy. There are, however, several specific implications that have not been adequately attended to.

Firstly, the extent of the sexual abuse of children is not yet fully appreciated by people involved in clinical work in a wide variety of related fields such as paediatrics, psychology and psychiatry, nursing and education. That professionals in the ordinary course of their work are not discovering many cases of sexual abuse indicates that they are simply not asking the right questions nor creating situations where people feel comfortable in talking about their abuse. This is supported by recent research by John Briere and Lisa Zaidi (1988) in a psychiatric out-patient unit. Briere and Zaidi reviewed 200 records of recently seen patients and found that about 8 per cent of the women visiting this out-patient unit had disclosed a history of sexual abuse. They then systematically asked all the clinicians routinely to ask one question about a possible history of sexual abuse in their initial interviews with their next 200 women patients. Reported incidence of sexual abuse rose by a factor of eight from 8 per cent to 64 per cent demonstrating how very simple changes in the extent that people systematically enquire about abuse can produce dramatic results. Under-reporting may be more of a problem in the United States because so many American medical and mental health professionals are operating in the private sector where there is a reluctance to act in ways that might embarrass or possibly alienate their clients. In the British National Health Service it may be easier to be assertive in asking about abuse and to take on board the risks involved in this type of work.

The second way in which the scope of child sexual abuse is also not fully appreciated is among field workers involved in case finding for child protection. Survey data suggest that there are probably three-quarters of a million children in the United States being molested every year in contrast to national reporting of 150,000 cases. Thus, three to five cases are still not being reported for every case that is reported, despite ten years of intensive consciousness raising and of mandatory reporting laws.

A third way in which the scope issue is not fully appreciated concerns researchers themselves. Researchers often suggest that the high incidence of sexual abuse in particular populations that they are studying indicates some causative association. For example, the studies which show that over 20 per cent of the mothers of victims of sexual abuse were themselves victimised are used to suggest causative links, even though these rates of incidence are not that different from other special populations or even from prevalence figures in the population at large. Researchers need control samples or other means of providing baseline information to determine whether a prevalence of sexual abuse in a particular sub-sample of the population is unusually large or not.

Fourthly, the implications of the effects of the prevalence of sexual abuse on the mental health of the population have not been sufficiently addressed. There were methodological problems with many of the first studies interpreting the prevalence of histories of sexual abuse in clinical populations, but it is now clear from controlled studies that child sexual abuse is an important risk factor for later mental health impairment. Identifying sexual abuse therefore offers an extremely efficient way of targeting mental health services to reducing the amount of mental health morbidity in the population. Two research findings arising from a study by Chris Bagley (Bagley and Ramsay, 1985) are particularly relevant. Bagley has shown that the sex differences in mental health morbidity studies showing that women tend to score as having more problems than men disappear when a history of sexual abuse is controlled. The implication is that if women were not sexually abused to a greater extent than men, then the observed difference in morbidity would probably not exist. By extrapolating these findings with other data it is possible to estimate that rates of psychopathology are between two to three times greater amongst victims of abuse than amongst other members of the community. If it were possible to prevent the development of psychopathology in all the victims of child sexual abuse, then a reduction in psychopathology in the total population of between 33 per cent to 44 per cent would be predicted.

A fifth way in which the scope of the problem has not been fully appreciated has been in the theoretical perspectives taken to examine the problem. The theoretical perspective underlying much work in this area has emphasized the psychopathology of perpetrators and the pathological effects on the victims. This has been a productive approach, but it is also necessary to go beyond individual psychological explanations and to look for social psychological explanations to understand why sexual abuse is so prevalent in our societies. The most striking sociological variable is undoubtedly gender. The prevalence studies show that men are much more likely to sexually abuse children than women. This is not a disparity seen in other forms of child abuse. In physical abuse, either greater or equal amounts of abuse is committed by women although physical violence is not a characteristic usually associated with women, any more is than sexual exploitation.

The gender disparity in perpetrators in child sexual abuse may be related to the socialisation process in our society. There are at least three aspects to this. Firstly, there is a sexualisation of emotional expression. Men in our society seem to have difficulty in distinguishing between affection that takes place in a sexual context from that which takes place in a non-sexual context. This may arise in early child rearing where young boys are not encouraged to seek nurturance or get their tender emotional needs met. From an early age they are told to be independent, not to be weak or cry or seek help or comfort or ask for physical nurturance. They are only given the opportunity to fulfil these emotional needs at a later stage as adolescents and young adults *within sexual relationships*, so it is no wonder that sexual relationships come to take on such an importance for men. It is within these sexual relationships that all these other emotional needs are met. Unfortunately, this can also affect men when they interact with children. Children are spontaneous in their search for and need for physical affection and they evoke in men a desire to be close and intimate. Many men deal with this kind of discomfort in wholly rational ways. They recognise it in themselves, they realise that it is inappropriate to be sexual with a child and are able to put it aside. Other men, however, are discomforted by it enough to feel that they have to distance themselves from children. This is evident in the reports from many young girls who say that their fathers simply disappear, are no longer around, or are no longer affectionate to them when they become adolescents. For some other men these fantasies or feelings become overwhelming and they sexualise their relationships with children.

The second important part of the socialisation process concerns the sexualisation of subordination. Men are encouraged to find their appropriate sexual partner amongst those who are younger, smaller and less powerful. We raise women to find their sexual partners among persons who are older, larger and more powerful than themselves. Children are part of such an attraction gradient for men. Children are young, small and weak and therefore they have the characteristics that men are raised to see as being sexually attractive. This creates trouble for men in many situations, not simply with children. Men sexualise relationships with their patients when they are doctors, with their clients when they are therapists, with their secretaries when they are bosses. Some argue that this is simply a question of having the power and being able to get away with it. There may be some truth in this, but it is also necessary to consider whether being in a hierarchical situation of power has inherent elements of sexual arousal for men.

Finally, there is the exemption that men are given from the responsibilities for the care and the well-being of children. Men are not taught, as are women, that it is part of their responsibility in later life to know about children, to be identified with children, and to have responsibility for children's needs and children's welfare. As a result, men have a rather difficult time in having empathy with children, in understanding what children's needs are, and in appreciating what it is that frightens them and what it is that makes them uncomfortable. This can be seen in the statements that many offenders make about why they offend. They cannot understand why everyone makes such a fuss about the sexual abuse. They do not see it as violent but as friendly touching. The men do not recognise that their friendly touching could be very disturbing, confusing, upsetting, frightening to the child. They fail to empathise with the children.

The importance of involvement with children is supported by recent research showing that incestuous fathers are more likely to have been out of the household during the first few years of their child's development and much less likely than comparison groups of fathers to have spent time involved in actual care giving. Some theorists have suggested that there may be a bio-social process which inoculates most parents against finding their children to be sexually attractive. It may be that tactile contact with the skin of a young child or the need to diaper and take care of the children's genitalia creates a different connotation to the children's bodies. Similarly, there may be something about experiencing the child as a highly dependent, highly needy, very young creature that innoculates adults against finding that child at a later date to be sexually stimulating. It certainly helps to explain the finding that step-fathers who are not involved with children at that early age are more likely to become sexually involved with their children.

The sociological or social cultural perspective provides a way to understand why sexual abuse is so prevalent in our societies and therefore also a way forward to address the issue of prevention. However, it is still necessary to explain individual differences in sexually abusive behaviour, including the fact that many men do not abuse children in this way. Sociological mechanisms are unlikely to be able to explain all of this and studies of individual mechanisms of background, personality and family situation will also inform interventions.

From this brief review of questions related to the scope of sexual abuse it is clear that there is still much that we need to learn in order to understand and to intervene effectively with this problem. However, maybe the most important lesson to be learnt is one of humility. There has been a scientific discipline concerning childhood and children and mental health for close on a hundred years. Millions of professionals have been trained in these various disciplines over the course of generations and yet it was not until just a few years ago that it was recognised that sexual abuse occurred to so many children and that it had such a profound effect on them. Such myopia would be understandable for some remote and very unusual group of people but all of us were children once upon a time and even that experience was somehow not enough to alert us, even with all scientific expertise and knowledge and tools that we had been taught. It indicates the degree to which all of us are cut off from our own experience of being a child, the degree to which all of us somehow in the process of getting to be adults jettison memories and awareness and ability to empathise. It is almost as though people are eager to get rid of all the associations of the earlier state of childhood. This is a mistake. Maybe if we can as adults connect with that experience of the child within ourselves, we will all be better advocates and better practitioners in working with the children who so badly need our help.

REFERENCES

Badgley, R., Allard, H., McCormick, N., Proudfoot, P., Fortin, D., Ogilvie, D., Rae-Grant, Q., Gelinas, P., Pepin, L., and Sutherland, S. [Committee on Sexual Offenses Against Children and Youth] (1984). *Sexual Offenses Against Children* (Vol. 1). Ottawa: Canadian Government Publishing Centre.

Bagley, C., and Ramsay, R. (1985). 'Disrupted childhood and vulnerability to sexual assault: Long-term sequels with implications for counselling.' *Social Work and Human Sexuality*, 4, 33-48.

Baker, A., and Duncan, S. (1985). 'Child sexual abuse: A study of prevalence in Great Britain.' *Child Abuse & Neglect*, 9, 457-467.

Briere, J., and Runtz, M. (1988). 'Post sexual abuse trauma.' In G. Wyatt and G. Powell (eds.), *Lasting effects of child sexual abuse.* Newbury Park, CA: Sage.

Briere, J., and Zaidi, L. (1988). *Sexual abuse histories and sequelae in psychiatric emergency room patients.* Paper presented at the American Psychological Association, Atlanta, GA.

Draijer, N. (1989). Personal communication.

Finkelhor, D. (1979). *Sexually victimized children.* New York: Free Press.

Finkelhor, D., and Baron, L. (1986). 'High-risk children.' In D. Finkelhor and Associates (eds.), *A sourcebook on child sexual abuse.* Beverly Hills, CA: Sage.

Goldman, R., and Goldman, J. (1988). *Show me yours: Understanding children's sexuality.* Victoria, Australia: Penguin Books.

Lewis, I. A. (1985). [*Los Angeles Times Poll* #98]. Unpublished raw data.

Mullen, P., Romans-Clarkson, S. E., Walton, V. A., and Herbison, G. P., (1988). 'Impact of sexual and physical abuse on women's mental health.' *The Lancet*, Saturday, 16 April, 841-845.

Ronstrom, A. (1985). *Sexual abuse of children in Sweden: Perspectives on research, interventions and consequences.* Unpublished manuscript. (Radda Barnen, Box 27320, Stockholm, Sweden).

Russell, D. (1986). *The secret trauma: Incest in the lives of girls and women.* New York: Basic Books.

Stein, J. A., Golding, J. M., Siegel, J.M., Audrey Burnham, M., and Sorenson, S. B., (1988). "Long-term psychological sequelae of child sexual abuse: The Los Angeles Epidemiologic Catchment Area Study". In G. Wyatt and G. Powell (Eds.), *Lasting effects of child sexual abuse.* Newbury Park, CA: Sage.

2

INTERVIEWING CHILDREN

DAVID P. H. JONES

OVER THE YEARS, much has been written in the fields of social work, psychology and psychiatry about sensitive interviewing and talking to children, especially those children who are in a state of embarrassment, fear or distress. It is therefore interesting to speculate about the reasons for the sudden concern about talking to children who might have been sexually abused. In many ways the knowledge that has been developed about interviewing troubled children generally is directly applicable to interviewing children about the possibility of sexual abuse. However, in the context of heightened public and professional awareness of the range and scope of child sexual abuse, there is a danger that well-tried methods are overshadowed by an emphasis on 'new' techniques of interviewing children.

Features of sexual abuse interviews

One important distinguishing feature of interviews concerned with sexual abuse simply is the recent history of increased awareness and the substantial rise in the number of investigated cases, which has resulted in a corresponding increase in the process of talking to children about difficult and sensitive issues. Not only are more sexually abused children being interviewed, but because of the greater number of cases, the interviews are being carried out by many professionals who were previously unaccustomed to talking to children. This is particularly important, since often it is through the interview that it becomes clear whether or not a child has been sexually abused.

A further important distinguishing feature of these interviews is that sexual abuse is itself sexual. Complex feelings are aroused in the interviewer that are likely to resonate with all the various sexual experiences which the interviewer has had as a child and adult. Furthermore, professionals may have to justify their action to the media, to the courts, and to their colleagues. Many professionals recount stories of children they have missed, and there may be a sense of collective guilt about having overlooked cases of sexual abuse for so long in the past. As a result of current knowledge, professionals are increasingly aware of the need to ask about sexual abuse, because if a child with something to say is not enabled to talk, inadvertently he or she might be left in an abusive situation. On the other hand, some of the serious consequences that can accrue from identifying abuse are that children may be subjected to physical examinations, to separation from their family and to the possible criminal prosecution of their parents. Hence, there has been a significant increase in the pressures and consequences for professionals of talking or not talking to children.

The additional pressures on staff that come from personal vilification and being sued in the courts, may prompt them to elicit a disclosure from a child in a single interview. Unfortunately, this pressure, which is wholly unnecessary and based upon an over-simplistic view of sexual abuse as a clear-cut unitary phenomenon requiring a single focused assessment, is transferred to the child. In reality, the considerable variation in the types of cases requires a similar variation in approach. Many cases of abuse are not clear-cut and may require monitoring and assessment over a considerable period to determine what is happening in the family and what is best for the child.

Conte *et al.*, (1986) found that twenty-four per cent of cases were single instances of abuse, forty-three per cent had occurred over a limited period of time and twenty-five per cent of the children had been chronically abused. We found a similar range (Goodman, *et al.*, 1989). Cases differ also in the delay between the time of the most recent sexual assault and the time of victim report. Both Conte, *et al.*, (1986) and ourselves (1989), showed a spread over time from within 48 hours to more than six months and, in some cases, several years before a report was made. Furthermore, in both studies, abusers ranged from strangers, through neighbours to family members. They held varying degrees of closeness of relationship with the child. The children themselves held a wide range of beliefs as to what would happen if they told someone about the abuse, ranging from being believed to being rejected. In both studies only about seven to eight per cent felt that they would be believed. Forty per cent of the children were coerced into sexual activity and twenty to forty per cent were not told not to tell in the two studies. On disclosure of the abuse, approximately seventy per cent of mothers in both studies believed and were supportive of their children. These results are somewhat contrary to current myths. The important point for this discussion is that since the children were in very different situations and had different pressures upon them, the interviewing strategies should vary accordingly. Taking this perspective it is unlikely that a single interview or a single type of interview will be appropriate for all cases.

Issues in interviewing

This chapter briefly examines only some of the more important issues in interviewing. First, the *setting* of the interview or interviews. Most people agree about the need for a safe, relaxed setting with relatively little interruption. However, some people argue for the use of a specially equipped interview room whilst others prefer a safe setting that is known to the child such as the child's home, or a neutral place such as a church or a school. In some circumstances, returning to the original place of victimization, provided this does not impose too great an emotional or psychological pressure on the child, can have advantages in terms of cueing the child's memory about past experiences.

Another major issue concerns *consent*. There is general agreement that consent should be obtained before talking to children although very few authors actually discuss this in detail. The problem is what to do if consent is refused. The police, who are under an obligation to determine whether a crime has been committed, do not experience a problem. On the other hand, intervention by social services departments is not mandatory except when a child is in immediate danger. Health professionals are likely to require consent. Whether children who are subject to a place of safety order should be interviewed with enabling techniques is currently under debate. A related issue is the relevance of *prior information*: what staff need to know about a case before undertaking an interview. Many authors and practitioners feel that prior information about the family is essential in preparing the approach to the interview with the child. However, White and colleagues (1987) argue against obtaining prior knowledge, particularly before an interview using anatomically correct dolls.

My own view is that reviewing the prior information is essential to educate the approach and to assess competing possibilities as to the origin of the possibility of child sexual abuse. Bias is an ever present snare but shielding oneself from prior information does little to remove this danger. At least there is no proven benefit of *not* knowing.

Another controversial issue is *video-recording*. MacFarlane (1985) has discussed some of the costs and benefits of video-taping, including its therapeutic value. The present writer and his colleagues are currently working with several children who have been able to deposit their 'record' of their experiences. We become the holders of the child's record. It has proved very useful both to have it 'in store' and occasionally, at some later date, to review it with the child. Very little research has been done on whether the presence of a videotape or video camera in any way restricts the child's spontaneity or expression of feeling. One problem is that a child often talks unexpectedly about possible sexual abuse so that the camera may well be unavailable at the relevant moment.

A further issue is whether the child's parent *should be present* during the interview with the child. Most authors argue that the child should be alone with the interviewer, and, White *et al.* (1987) stand at one end of the spectrum, stating that a 'doll' interview should not occur if the parent is present. Others, including the present author, believe that when child and parent cannot be separated, it is reasonable to interview the child, with a parent perhaps seated behind and out of sight of the child so that non-verbal and verbal cues between them are minimised. However, it is unrealistic to suppose that subtle communications between child and parent can be totally prevented. If a parent has been pressurizing a child, it may be more fruitful to observe such interaction rather than miss the possibility of witnessing it.

The *gender* of the interviewer is a particularly contentious issue. Some suggest that all interviewers of children should be female, or at least that the male interviewer should be accompanied by a female colleague (Vizard and Tranter, 1988). They are concerned that the interview itself recreates the context of the abusive situation, especially as most abusers are male. This author would emphasize the over-riding importance of the interviewer's ability and skill in relation to his or her verbal and non-verbal communications which could be misconstrued by the child. These actions may be more important than gender per se. Additionally, when interviewing the child, we do not know,

(a) if he/she has been abused at all or, if so,

(b) whether it was by a male, female or both.

Our clinical experience is widening our sense of possibilities and as we cannot predict the outcome of the interview, it is perhaps best to stress the importance of avoiding ambiguous messages in communicating with embarrassed and stressed children rather than placing excessive emphasis on gender of the interviewer. Lastly, if at all possible the child's choice may be the most important deciding factor, as it is usually possible for a male or female to have a person of the opposite gender in attendance in order to allay the child's concerns.

Purposes and goals of interviews

The stance taken on many of the above issues can be evaluated only after considering the purposes and goals of the interview. The purpose of an investigative interview may be to see if the child needs protecting, or to see if a crime has occurred, or both. There is also a somewhat broader 'assessment interview' with the child, and thirdly the 'therapeutic interview' which occurs at a later stage. In practice, the situation is less simple, as most interviews have various sub-goals. For example, an assessment interview will often have these objectives; determining whether abuse has occurred, assessing the child's psychological condition or mental state, and initiating the process of healing or repair.

The nature and purpose of interviews inter-relates with the question of the number of sessions. In the past, often the unstated assumption has been that there should be a single evaluation interview. Many authors now are moving away from that idea, if they ever held it, towards the need for flexibility. White *et al.*, (1987) recommends two. The present writer favours between one and three interviews and rarely more than six, depending upon the clinical situation (Jones, 1988). The length of the sessions is also relevant. It is recommended in the literature that the first interview should last no longer than half-an-hour. However, currently the best advice is that it needs to be developmentally appropriate to the child. The problem is that all these issues are inter-related and the question of number and length of sessions cannot be divorced from the issue of general style. For example, one short but extremely driven, coercive interview could be expected to create considerable harm and error, while six sessions with an open, unbiased style could be without harm.

Interview structure

The question of whether to use a pre-determined interview structure has caused controversy. A minority of authors suggests an extremely rigid pre-set interview protocol whereas, particularly in this country, most believe that this is contrary to all that is known about the benefits of child-led and child-centred interviews. However, an overall or skeletal structure might be useful in training and in planning the content of certain parts of the interview and may be especially helpful to new interviewers. As a minimum, a check list of *additional* questions can be usefully drawn upon if a child describes having been abused. These questions can help to direct the interviewer towards particular areas of enquiry, such as whether anyone took photographs.

Boat and Everson (1988a) provide an example of an interview framework, using the concept of escalation. Starting with a body-part evaluation and naming of body-function, using automatically correct dolls, they move to four different levels of what they perceive as increasing escalation. They talk first about events which may have occurred, and then move on to talk about suspect people. In the absence of a response to these questions, they progress to direct enquiry of the child and then to direct enquiry about specific individuals. However, it may be unnecessary to open each case with the body-part evaluation since that in itself may be unwarranted escalation.

Another structure is summarised in Figure 1 (Jones and McQuiston, 1988; Jones, in press). Initially, the interviewer establishes rapport with the child and explains the reason for the meeting. This rapport-gaining stage also may provide leads into the main areas of enquiry, including the child's expressed concerns, any suspicions about specific persons, and physical or behaviour changes in the child.

Children do not appear for interview without a reason. They come because some alarm has been raised, which can be useful in starting to talk with children. In our study (Goodman *et al.*, 1989), the majority of children came to the attention of child protection services because they talked to a peer or a friend or to some other adult who passed information to the professionals. The initiation of the referral can tell us how to start talking to the child. For example, the child might be asked to talk about any worries that have been shared with a parent. Similarly, if there is suspicion about a place or a person, it might be possible, after building rapport, to open with some general questions about that particular person or place — not whether that person has actually done something directly abusive but simply exploring the child's positive and negative perceptions. In this way one is logically following up on the child's expressed concerns — as opposed to the interviewer's structure (Jones, in press).

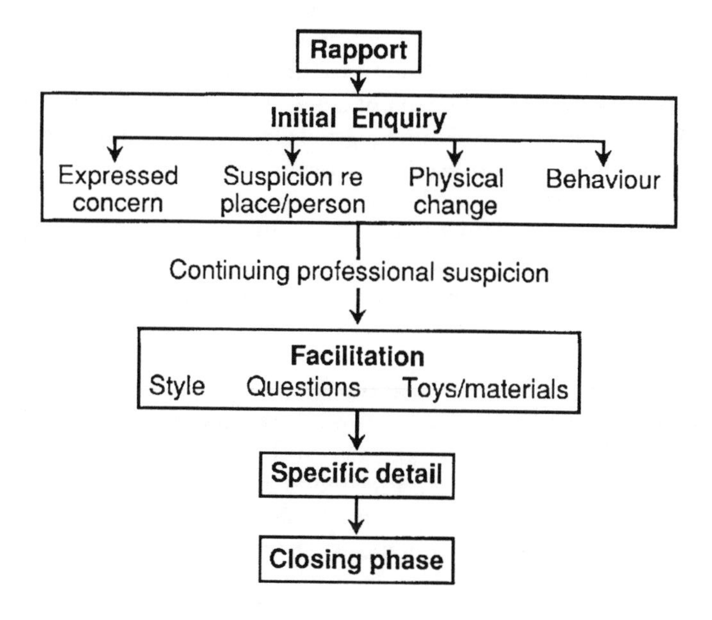

Figure 1: Interview format

With respect to physical change, as in disease or illness, naming the body-part, either on a drawing or on a doll, can provide a basis for talking to the child. For example, questions such as 'How can this part of you get sore?' would be appropriate for a child who is presenting with recurrent vulvo-vaginitis. Similarly, 'Has anyone ever played games with you down there that you didn't like?' might be asked within the context of a paediatric examination (Jones and McQuiston, 1988). If the child's behaviour has aroused suspicion, there is scope for talking to the child about the behaviour which has led to the referral.

If these initial enquiries result in continuing or elevated professional suspicion, the interview can become more facilitating in order to assist the child to unlock both feelings and information (without prejudice as to *what* may be revealed). There are at least three related issues that need to be considered with regard to this stage: style, the questions asked, and the use of toys and other materials while interviewing.

Interviewing style

Most authors agree that a child-centred and relaxed yet purposive style is required. Additionally, care must be taken to control the display of disgust and shock that may be felt by the interviewer. There is also a risk that the interviewer becomes vicariously interested in the sexual content of the child's story. Both occur, and those who talk to children, therefore, should know how their own feelings are resonated by the things that children tell them. It is important to remember that the children themselves may be so consumed with guilt and remorse that they find it extremely difficult to tolerate the direct gaze fixation of an interviewer.

Although the aim should be to put children as far as possible at ease, to reward their answers with 'well done', 'good girl', 'you're doing very well' is probably both clinically and legally inappropriate. There is an enormous difference between, on the one hand, creating a context within which the child is aware of the empathy towards his or her plight and, on the other hand, adopting a 'driven' style where the interviewer's agenda is clearly the more prominent. Since the research literature confirms that a driven style of interview is one of the most important correlates of error production it has to be carefully avoided.

An important issue which few authors have discussed is touch. Because touch may have very different connotations in a child who has been sexually abused, it should be used with extreme caution. A touch on the head or shoulders, which people do when they feel sorry for others, can transmit a sense of empathy. However, to a sexually abused child, touch may have significantly more ominous connotations. There is a danger also that touching is used to lead interviews. For example, in one case an investigator working for a defence attorney was determined to show that the child had not been genitally abused and thereby prevent his client being convicted. The investigator, with his hand on the inside of his own thigh, asked, 'Did he touch you here?', then moving his hand to his crotch asked, 'Did he touch you here?'. Before the investigator could finish the boy hastily said, 'No'. This indicates the extent to which touch can be leading. However, although touching is an inappropriate method of transmitting empathy, the ever-present prospect of court appearance can make the interviewer cold and distant. The existing general work on interviewing and talking to children clarifies that the qualities of warmth and especially empathy are associated with the most accurate responses and the best results in terms of enabling children to talk (Cox and Rutter, 1985).

Interview questions

The second major issue after style is the questions themselves. Various kinds of questions can be posed. There are open enquiry questions and also open permission-giving questions such as, 'Well, you know sometimes grown up people play games with children and sometimes the kids don't like that very much; has that kind of thing ever happened to you?' Questions may also contain elements of circularity as well as various aspects of style which help to reduce the child's anxiety. In contrast, objective questions are more like, 'Did "x" happen to you?' inviting 'yes' or 'no', true or false answers. Similarly, multiple choice questions are either, 'Did "x" or "y" happen?', or sometimes, 'Did "x", "y" or "z" happen to you?' Some questions can be hypothetical, such as, 'If "x" had happened to you, who could you tell?' or 'If "x" had happened to you how might that have felt?' However, parallel issues of style are important to consider. For example, any particular type of question can be delivered in an anxiety-reducing way, but could also be delivered in a driven and coercive way. The research evidence reveals that coercion increases error production. The present author considers that the sequence of questions is also very important (Jones and McQuiston, 1988). A series of objective questions, for example, or a series of multiple choice questions could be expected to produce more errors than one multiple choice, one objective or a permission giving type of question followed by an open-ended enquiry such as — 'Tell me more about that'.

Open-ended questions raise concerns when posed to the mentally handicapped or the very young (Cox & Rutter, 1985). These may be more prone to error than the more specific questions which focus on the field, as a mentally handicapped child may have great difficulty in absorbing the whole scope of an open-ended enquiry as opposed to a more direct enquiry. It is not only the type of question but also content, in the sense of what does the question *presume* about its answers. For example, a hypothetical question such as, 'If "x" happened to you, who could you tell?' must be different from, 'If "x" happened to you, how far would it go in?' Once again, research findings lend support to the clinical impression that the content may be at least as important as type of question. (See Cole and Loftus, 1987, for a review of this and related issues.)

Use of toys and play materials to assist interviewing

Apart from style, and the types of questions, there is also the choice of materials and the use of toys. Play is not a direct replica of reality; it is an indirect replica or it has an indirect relationship to reality and remembered events. It is not direct and may not mean what one thinks it means. One good example is provided by the use of anatomically correct (or incorrect) dolls in an interview situation. If children are allowed to lead they will often change the identity of the doll throughout the session. Since the identity may not remain constant, it is essential to check this regularly. Omitting to do this could cause error if dolls were introduced to the child by the interviewer saying, 'Let this be daddy'.

Another important issue is the question of 'grounding' which brings back imaginary play to whether it is something that the child had actually remembered from the past, whether or not it is grounded in reality or whether it is some elaborated fear or even an elaboration of experienced events. A good example is shown in Kee MacFarlane's video (1988) where the child's use of talking puppets is brought down to real, remembered events. A form of questioning that is too direct as to the identity of the puppets is in danger of being leading for children.

This author argues against having the interview room resembling a toy shop, with drawings around the wall and toys available on all the shelves. The anxious child will flit from toy to toy compelling the desperate interviewer to ask more and more leading questions. A well tried and tested approach is to bring out only that which is specifically needed.

Is it helpful to have a free play session? The present author prefers to allow free play throughout children's sessions as indicated by the child rather than have a set period of free play or a block of free play as suggested by others (for example, Vizard and Tranter, 1988). Which of these is better can be answered only by further research.

Play materials are often used to assist reference to different parts of the body so that children readily can indicate where they might have been hurt or where something may have been done to them. Although most interest has been in the use of dolls, there are other potentially useful materials and techniques. For example, anatomical line drawings, such as those produced by Groth (1984) can be used. These are anatomically correct back and front drawings of children and adults of different ages and ethnic background which can be helpful in talking to children.

Figure 2 is a drawing produced by a five-year-old child during an interview. It is a very immature drawing which also reveals how unhappy the child feels. However, the usefulness of the picture is not so much in its interpretation but as a vehicle for a verbal account. During the interview the child talked about her drawing. She started talking about the top of the picture and then moved down to talk about her belly button. When the interviewer refrained from responding in any untoward way she continued by talking about her vulval area, drawn in black.

Figure 2

Figure 3 is a clay model by a four-year-old girl. The model has three legs, the middle one being the father's large penis with which she played the 'ding dong game'. The child was able to describe her experience through modelling this figure in clay although she had previously been unable to describe it by using other toys and materials.

Figure 3

It is clear that anatomically correct dolls, though the most widely debated medium, are only one form of material that can be used to enable young children to communicate their experiences. A few of the analytically orientated analysts, particularly in the United States but also in this country, believe that anatomically detailed dolls sexualise the child (e.g. Terr, 1988). This is a possibility but it is likely to depend upon the kind of use made of the dolls. In other words, questions of style again create a link between materials used, the questions asked and the degree of pressure used within the interview. There is also the quality of the relationship between the interviewer and the child.

Observational studies of the free play of abused and non-abused children provide no real evidence that children frequently play in a sexualised manner with sexually complete dolls. Some children do play sexually but they are a distinct minority. Perhaps the real question is whether the use of anatomically complete dolls leads to erroneous *verbal* responses. The only available relevant data comes from a study by Aman and Goodman (unpublished data). When three and five-year-old children were presented with anatomically correct, anatomically neutered or no dolls, Aman and Goodman found no increase in error production with anatomically correct dolls compared with anatomically incorrect dolls. They found also that three-year-old children were occasionally susceptible to the interviewer's suggestion, and to the interviewer's use of authority. These findings suggest caution when interviewing young children, generally, but do not show anatomically correct dolls to be especially error prone even in young children. Further experiments are needed on interview style in relation to these various materials and questions.

Recently Boat and Everson (1988b) drew attention to the variation in the dolls themselves. In some dolls, the anal margin, the vaginal margin and the mouth are pink, suggesting that something is there and any self-respecting investigatory child is likely to stick a finger in them. As the dolls themselves vary enormously with regard to the parts that are attached and those not attached and whether they can be removed (some have removable hair), the responses are also likely to vary. From their study of 295 professionals, Boat and Everson (1988b) point also to the inadequacy of the training and of the guidelines on how to use such dolls (at least in North Carolina). There is no information on whether the variations in the method of presenting dolls to children have an effect on accuracy. For example, if the examiner says, 'Let this be daddy' or if the examiner first undresses the doll, does this actually affect accuracy? Finally, error production may vary in relation to whether the interviewer is seeking to get the child to demonstrate activities, or alternatively to recall memories verbally.

Key issues of interpretation

In Boat and Everson's recent study (1988b) professionals were asked how they would interpret certain kinds of children's behaviour with anatomically complete dolls. One such behaviour, which placed one doll on top of another in the missionary position, was variously considered to be normal by between six and 48 per cent of different professional groups; 52 per cent believed it was abnormal.

The features of genuine accounts have been described by clinicians in the field (Jones and McGraw, 1987). Attempts are being made to apply research methods to this elusive area, but thus far there are no absolute indices or numerical approaches to validation which are scientifically valid. In the meantime, however, the clinical approaches are useful if they are used with due caution as to their limitations. Research carried out by Conte and Jones (unpublished data) found, not surprisingly, that professionals are able to distinguish between a bad and a reasonably good videotaped interview but they also believe that the bad interview, even the outrageously bad, is typical. Furthermore, they also used the bad interviews for making child protection decisions. They made errors of commission and omission even in relation to such things as whether anal abuse had occurred, which has serious implications for the importance of interviewing and its validation.

In summary, there are in this field many areas of agreement and also many unresolved issues and dilemmas. Typically, children find themselves in a wide range of different kinds of situations and predicaments that demand professional sensitivity. It would therefore seem premature to argue for one particular type of interview but rather we have to find ways of talking to children in as flexible a way as possible. Those working in the area of child sexual abuse have done much to convince mental health, child protection and legal practitioners of the great importance of talking to children. The debate continues on the role and purpose, on technique, method, structure, use and mis-use of anatomically correct dolls and perhaps most of all on the interpretation of findings. In my view, there is insufficient concern about style, basic rapport and relationship with the child — who may be frightened, fearful, confused and often shrouded in secrecy.

These debates must be kept alive and the forensic implications should not be allowed to cause premature closure on the key issues. The proper place to resolve these matters is not in the courts but in conferences, journal articles and between clinicians in different settings. A fundamental objective of interviewing children is to enable the way to be cleared for the initiation of repair and healing in the affected children. This must be one of the key criteria through which successful interviewing practices are measured in the future.

REFERENCES

Boat, B. W. and Everson, M. D. (1988a) 'Interviewing young children with anatomical dolls: guidelines for interviewing young children in sexual abuse investigations.' *Child Welfare*, 67; 337-352.

Boat, B. W. and Everson, M. D. (1988b) 'Use of anatomical dolls among professionals in sexual abuse evaluations.' *Child Abuse and Neglect*, 12; 171-179.

Cole, C. B. and Loftus, E. G. (1987). The memory of children. In, Ceci S., Toglia, M. and Ross, D. (eds) *Children's Eyewitness Memory*. New York: Springer-Verlag.

Conte, J., Berliner, L., Shuerman, J. R. (November 1986) *The Impact of Sexual Abuse in Children: Final Technical Report*. Bethesda, MA. NIMH.

Conte, J. and Jones, D. P. H. Unpublished Data.

Cox, A. and Rutter, M. (1985). 'Diagnostic appraisal and interviewing.' In Rutter, M. and Hersov, L. (eds) *Child and Adolescent Psychiatry; Modern Approaches*. (2nd Edition) London: Blackwell.

Goodman, G. S., Pyle, L., Jones, D. P. H. England T., Port, L., Rudy, L. and Prado L. (1989) *The emotional effect of criminal court testimony on sexually abused children*. Final report submitted to U.S. National Institute of Justice. Grant No. 85-CJ-CX-0020.

Groth, A. N. (1984) *Anatomical Drawings*. Forensic Mental Health Associates: Newton Centre, MA, 02159; USA.

Jones, D. P. H. (1988) 'Some reflections on the Cleveland affair.' *Association for Child Psychology and Psychiatry Newsletter*, 11; 13-18.

Jones, D. P. H. 'Talking with Children.' (In Press) In Oates, R. K. (ed.) *Understanding and Managing Child Sexual Abuse*. Sydney, Harcourt Brace Jovanovich.

Jones, D. P. H. and McGraw, J. M. (1987) 'Reliable and fictitious accounts of sexual abuse to children.' *Journal of Interpersonal Violence*, 2, 27-45.

Jones, D. P. H. and McQuiston, M. (1988). *Interviewing the Sexually Abused Child*. (3rd Edition) Gaskell, London.

MacFarlane, K. (1985) Diagnostic Evaluations and the Use of Video Tapes in Child Sexual Abuse Cases. *University of Miami Law Review*, 40; 135-165.

MacFarlane, K. (1988) *Response: Child Sexual Abuse. Part 2: The Clinical Interview,* Video from Children's Institute International, Tavistock: London.

Terr, L. (1988) 'Anatomically correct dolls: should they be used as a basis for expert testimony.' *Journal of the American Academy of Child and Adolescent Psychiatry,* 27; 254-257.

White, S., Strom, G. A., Santilli, G. and Quinn, K. M. (1987) *Guidelines for Interviewing Pre-schoolers with Sexually Anatomically Detailed Dolls.* Available from the first author at Case Western Reserve University School of Medicine, Cleveland Metropolitan General Hospital, Cleveland, Ohio 44109.

Vizard, E. and Tranter, M. (1988) 'Helping young children to describe experiences of child sexual abuse'. In Bentovim, A. *et al.* (eds.) *Child Sexual Abuse Within the Family: Assessment and Treatment.* London: Wright.

3

INTERVIEWING FAMILIES

LUCY BERLINER

INTERVIEWING FAMILIES has received much less scrutiny and evaluation than interviewing children, although talking to a child nearly always also involves talking to a family. Appointments to be interviewed about possible sexual abuse are being sought by adults rather than by children, and in most cases the adults are family members who are calling on behalf of children.

Purpose of interviews

In the literature on child sexual abuse, the discussion is concerned largely with interviewing for the purpose of determining whether a child has been abused. Yet this comprises only one small part of interviewing children and families about child sexual abuse. It is salutory to remember that in other areas of mental health disturbance usually the focus is not on what happened, but on determining what is the problem for the child and family and how help might best be offered. In other areas of work there is also less scepticism about the patient's account of what has happened. Bulimia patients, for example, are believed when they say they force themselves to vomit. Agrophobics are believed when they say that they have not left their homes for years. The difference in assessing whether children have been sexually abused is that the consequences of the assessment are so far-reaching. Because a higher level of affirmative evidence is required from patients before a positive assessment is made, the facts of the case become a major focus of interviews with families.

Usually it is impossible to determine whether children have been sexually abused by interviewing their families. Most families do not know whether their children have been sexually abused, except when offenders are part of the family. Ultimately the offender and the child are the only people who really do know what, if anything, has happened. Unfortunately, offenders cannot be trusted to admit to the abuse. Sometimes they will admit to child sexual abuse but almost never until after the child has reported it elsewhere. Offenders very rarely come forward voluntarily and, in the absence of a report from a child, disclose sexual abuse. Ironically, such an admission would be believed by professionals as people would not normally admit to abuse unless it were true.

If offenders admit to abuse, many of the complex issues involved in interviewing children (see David Jones, this volume) become irrelevant. The way in which children are interviewed only becomes an issue when there is no other means of determining whether abuse has occurred. In a community known to the author a sophisticated network of mental health professionals work alongside a criminal justice system which offers sexual offenders who enter into a treatment programme an opportunity to avoid imprisonment. As a result, offenders frequently reveal more detailed information about the offences than the children, many of whom reveal details of what occurred only after a long period of work. In practice, unfortunately, the experience of most professionals is that accused adults deny the accusations, and it is difficult to determine whether a child was or was not a victim of abuse.

There is no known procedure or psychological test battery which can reveal whether or not an accused adult has abused a child. Sexual offenders are a heterogeneous group and there is no profile or set of psychological characteristics or history which discriminates them from other people, or from other people with psychological or behavioural problems. In a recent review of current empirical studies on incest offenders, Williams and Finkelhor (1989) found that more than a third of incest offenders had no identifiable psycho-pathology on standard measures of disturbance and that only about a quarter to a third had a measurable sexual response to children. In the absence of an admission, therefore, a good psychological assessment does not tell us whether an individual committed abuse. Occasionally, an interview by a police investigator or a clinician will yield an admission which saves the child from a considerable amount of investigative and fact finding procedures.

Although admissions by offenders are relatively rare, there is still value in interviewing and talking to the families of children who may or may not have been sexually abused. In most cases, the professional will not be the first person to hear or become concerned about sexual abuse. The great majority of children tell their parents about the abuse, or the parents discover something which arouses their suspicion. Parents can explain to the professional how sexual abuse first became an issue and what the child said or did to alert the parent to the possibility of sexual abuse. It is crucial to know how the child first communicated that there was some justification for concern.

In addition, parents may, and very likely will, have seen or heard things from their child long before the report, or the specific events that led to bringing the child to the office may corroborate or help to make sense of the child's statement. A past history of changes in behaviour, emotional reactions, interactions with possible offenders, a prior history or complaints or concerns, medical problems, or simply the child's adjustment to their surroundings and circumstances are all extremely important in evaluating and making sense of what children say to professionals during interviews.

Children are better known to their parents than to professionals. Parents are familiar with their children's personalities and possible reactions to different situations, with significant life events, and with the important experiences and traumas that have affected them. In the early stages of assessment parents can offer a rich picture of a child in the child's context, which is unavailable in a professional's office. It is unfortunate that families in cases of sexual abuse have been given a bad image. Much of the conventional and negative thinking about these families is unsupported either by the direct experience of most practitioners or by systematic investigation or research. For example, the vast majority of parents are supportive and believe their children's reports of sexual abuse. Research into how parents responded to children disclosing sexual abuse found that parents usually were supportive. The commonly held notion that parents are generally not believing and supporting may arise from the strong clinical impression left by the few particularly difficult and complicated cases where parents were not supportive. A danger of remembering these worst cases is that new families might be approached on the assumption that they will be uncaring and unsupportive of their children. Even in cases of incest, only a small percentage of cases involves an unsupportive or non-believing parent. A study at Tufts New England Medical Centre found no statistical difference between the level of support given by the parents of children abused by a non-family member and by the parents of children abused by a biological father. The study found that mothers were only less likely to be supportive where the offender was a step-father.

Further evidence comes from a prospective study on the effects of intervention on children thought to have been abused by fathers or father figures. This study estimated that in about a third of these cases there was an unsupportive parental response (Runyan *et al.*, 1988). However, it is also important to remember that general population surveys show that while incest is very prevalent in cases referred to the treatment settings, it is not the most common form of sexual assault against children. Even in cases of intra-familial abuse parents are more often than not supportive.

Families of victims

There are also stereotyped ideas about how families with children who have been sexually abused function as families. Current empirical investigations and clinical experience indicate that there is no type of family that is a 'sexually abusive family'. There is no certain family structure, certain family constellation, certain family pattern that is isomorphic with sexual abuse. There are studies which show that in some cases of father/daughter incest the families conform to a typical pattern of rigid external boundaries and diffuse internal boundaries (Saunders, *et al.*, 1988). Researchers have noted increased conflict and decreased support in families where children are sexually abused but this has been found in both incest and non-incest cases (Freidrich, *et al.*, 1987). There are also some family factors which appear to heighten the risk for children being abused, including an impaired relationship between a child and a parent, an absent or working mother, and a stepfather present in the home (Finkelhor and Baron, 1986). However, it is important to remember that the presence of family characteristics associated with incest does not mean that incest necessarily occurs. It is also important to note that at least one study was unable to differentiate the families of sexually abused children from the families of a matched comparison group of non-sexually abused girls using standardised family measures (e.g. Einbender and Freidrich, in press).

Divorce and separation

A different but similar effect of stereotyping is currently emerging in cases of separated parents. Historically, work with incest cases has focused largely on the mother. She has been accused of not listening to and being unaware of cues from her child that something was wrong, disbelieving her child when told that sexual abuse was going on, being unable to feel anger towards the offender but of feeling sorry for him and allying with him, being unwilling to protect her child from that individual. Mothers have been criticized in the medical literature also for colluding with the abusing parent.

More recently many mothers have been coming forward who are alert to and respond to the possibility of sexual abuse. They believe their children's reports of sexual abuse. They are extremely negative to the offenders and do not want the children anywhere near them. However, because they may be doing this in the context of a separation or a divorce, they are not identified as appropriate protective parents but as vindictive, hysterical and paranoid. This is an untenable position for mothers. In any other situation the mother's behaviour would be seen as admirable and appropriately protective, yet in this particular context it is seen as pathology and as evidence that they are creating the problem. The stereotype is that in an incest situation the child is more likely to have been abused if a mother neither believes nor supports the child. Conversely, the child is thought more likely not to have been abused if the mother *does* believe and support her child. Clearly, in situations of sexual abuse, it is necessary continually to pay attention to the expectations of professional staff and of society in general regarding parents, and, in particular, the mothers.

Careful evaluation of reports is necessary. There has been a series of studies examining samples of cases to try to determine what proportion of reports of sexual abuse are unreliable or do not involve sexual assault. The consistent finding of a range of studies is that reports from children are highly reliable and only a very small proportion — perhaps two to six per cent — do not involve an actual event of child sexual abuse. However, the proportion of reports which emanate from parents without a corresponding report from the child, in fact may be much more likely to be untrue cases of sexual abuse. In a study by David Jones, about two per cent of the reports from children were considered unreliable compared to nearly eight per cent of the reports from parents (Jones and McGraw, 1987). In another study at Tufts New England Medical Centre, five per cent of the reports from children and ten per cent of the reports from adults were considered unreliable (Horowitz, *et al.*, 1985). This provides some clues in terms of being more cautious and thorough in evaluating situations where there is a report or a concern from a parent and no reports from the child. But even with unreliable or false reports, where sexual abuse does not seem to be the explanation, it is not usual for a parent to deliberately and malevolently make up a report or attempt to get a child to say something that is not true. More often it is that something causes a parent to be concerned about the possibility of abuse and they then seek out professional assessment.

Of course, parents can be mistaken or have a misplaced emphasis about what has occurred to a child. For example, a child may make an ambiguous statement about being touched in the genital area and, in the context of separation and divorce which may be highly volatile and full of conflict, the child's statement may acquire an exaggerated meaning. The mother herself, for example, may have been sexually abused or she may be very angry at the suspected offender — at her ex husband. She may have experienced aggressive or sexually aggressive conduct in the marriage which caused her to be concerned that the child's statement was related to intentional sexual behaviour rather than the touching of the child's genitals in some appropriate care-taking role.

It is unfortunate that all these cases where a parent may consider or may believe sexual abuse occurred are cast in the light of malicious behaviour (usually on the part of the mother). Research evidence is sometimes cited to support this but such studies need to be interpreted with caution. For example, a commentator from Michigan (Guyer, 1988) noted that 80 per cent of cases of allegations of sexual abuse in divorce proceedings were classified as false. However, a detailed explanation of the results indicated that almost all the reports arising from children were considered to be reliable. Furthermore, the cases involving reports from parents rather than children included *any* situation where a mother raised concerns about the possibility of sexual abuse in the family. There is an enormous difference between a parent saying that she has worries or that she does not know how to interpret a situation, and a direct allegation that a person has sexually abused a child. That these issues become so confused even in the reporting of research findings again suggests that there are wider social issues impinging on the clinical situation.

Separated parents provide one of the most difficult set of circumstances in which to try to evaluate an accusation of sexual assault. More than in any other situation the professional has to decide whether abuse did or did not happen. In other cases, for example, where allegations of sexual abuse are made about a day care facility, it is still possible to protect the children by removing them from the day care, even if they do not report abuse and professionals are unable to elicit any clear history of the allegations. A parent simply would not want to return a child to a day care centre without being certain of what, if anything, happened. In the situation of separated parents, however, the person under suspicion is the person who is asserting the right to have custody or some other contact with the child. Someone has to decide whether or not abuse occurred in order to inform the access and custody decisions. If abuse did occur then the child may be at risk, and if abuse did not happen then the child deserves to have an uninterrupted relationship with that parent. This type of case has forced professionals to the nexus of all the legal and clinical dilemmas about forming an opinion about sexual assault.

There are many other issues which tend to influence the approach to these kinds of cases. One example is that there are discussions — at least in the United States — only about cases where accusations come from mothers. In fact, a national survey conducted in family courts, which deal with these cases in the United States, discovered that one third of the cases where sexual abuse was raised as a concern in a divorce came from fathers (Thoennes, 1989). However, it is only mothers who seem to be described as hysterical, paranoid or vindictive for alleging that their ex-partners are a risk to their children. Caution in interpreting case referrals is of course warranted but the evidence is that up to ten per cent at most of all accusations come from a parent without a supporting statement from a child.

The legal context

In the United States there are laws in every state which require certain professionals who work with children to report suspected or known incidents of child abuse. Criminal penalties are attached to failing to make those reports and people can be prosecuted for not reporting. The law does not require proof or certainty but simply suspicion of abuse and the laws give civil immunity to citizens who make a good faith report about suspected or known child sexual abuse to the authorities. It is not always easy to inform a child or family that an official report will be submitted on what has been learned from them in the interview, but the discomfort may be felt more by the professionals than by the children and families themselves. When professionals are comfortable with this legal duty and explain it in a matter of fact way, with support for the concept and for the law, families normally accept that the report must be made.

This becomes a moral issue for society. If there were no reporting laws, children and families would receive the message that practitioners in the health care professions know, but do not necessarily take action to prevent abuse, even when they know it is occurring. Inevitably, there are many situations where reports are made and families are subjected to interviews and investigations which subsequently do not produce any kind of confirmed abuse report. The system can be criticized for producing unnecessary investigations, but many of the unconfirmed cases involve situations where children are living in a context where there is a legitimate reason to be concerned about the children, even if this is not defined as child abuse.

The children may be living in squalor, not being cared for, or have parents who are alcoholics or drug addicts. The child abuse investigation becomes a vehicle for accessing the social services in the community. In the absence of a National Health Service or an automatic guarantee of certain services to families, something has to go wrong before people can receive help from the state.

There is no doubt that asking children, families and offenders to tell the truth about what happened and gaining their co-operation with intervention can be difficult. In countries without mandatory reporting, there is sometimes the view that such a formal process makes relations with families more difficult, but, in fact, it creates a context in which reporting is seen as positive and necessary. In the community in which the author works there is a long tradition of prosecuting cases of sexual assault of children both in and out of the family. The offender has the option to seek an evaluation and to look for treatment under the supervision of the legal system and the Court. This provides an incentive for children to talk about the abuse because they are not made to feel responsible for the consequences of the investigation and intervention.

A child victim may not want to see the offender again or live with them or spend time with them but they still might want that person to be helped. Given that an increasing and substantial proportion of sexual offenders are teenagers (almost a third of the cases that come to the author's clinic), it is not appropriate for prison to be the only available form of intervention.

If an offender tells the truth he is evaluated by a competent professional and in the vast majority of cases he will be allowed to remain in the community in a supervised treatment programme. Almost 75 per cent of convicted sex offenders against children in our community are not in prison — they are in treatment programmes in the community, supervised by the courts.

Society has to offer a range of options that can be applied depending on the specific circumstance and the appropriateness of the context. Some offenders ought to go to prison both because they deserve it and because they are too dangerous to be in the community, or because effective interventions to help them change their behaviour are not fully developed. The personal preference of children and families should not determine what is best for society, since many offenders who assault children in the family are also a danger to children in the community. However, despite the possibility that imprisonment will be the consequence of investigatory interviews, in the author's experience a strong legal framework enhances rather than impedes the process of dealing honestly and effectively with families and is not necessarily punitive.

Conclusion

At the beginning of this chapter it was stated that unless the offender is within the family, the parents will not know whether or not the child was abused, but that there were still reasons to speak to the family. It is therefore important not to approach families with the idea that what they say, what they look like, or how they are structured and interact with each other is a test that can be applied to resolve whether or not a child has been sexually abused. It is important to learn about the children and about their lives and about the things that are important to them. Both common sense and current empirical investigations of the impact of sexual abuse on children have shown that the capacity of a family to support a child who has been sexually assaulted is the most important set of variables yet identified in predicting improvement or the recovery of children from the effects of sexual abuse. Persuading families to a view that their child was in fact sexually abused, if that is the professional's view, and that abuse is harmful to children and the children need intervention and help, is the most important contribution to be made by a clinician, having made a diagnosis. It is very important to be reminded that, unlike the legal system, diagnosis is only the beginning and not the end of the work. Treatment is vitally important and the reason for making a correct diagnosis is that the treatment should come from the diagnosis. In order to engage families in this process they should not be approached as if they caused the problem. Families do not sexually assault children — offenders do. Nor can they be blamed for not fully and immediately accepting the fact of abuse or for failing to respond in a completely supportive manner. To acknowledge that your child has been sexually assaulted is often a devastating and painful recognition for families that brings with it many other consequences. To know that your child has been sexually assaulted is to acknowledge that you have been unable to provide an abuse-free childhood.

Professionals and families need to understand and communicate that they share a common goal to achieve the safety and well-being of children. As with all good clinical practice, it begins with treating people with respect and providing a setting that facilitates and guides people towards health. Families are the professionals' most important allies in achieving that goal for children.

REFERENCES

Einbender, A. and Freidrich, W. (in press). 'The psychological functioning and behaviour of sexually abused girls.' *Journal of Clinical and Consulting Psychology.*

Finkelhor, D. and Baron, L. (1986) 'High risk children', in D. Finkelhor (ed.) *Sourcebook on Child Sexual Abuse* (pp. 60-88). Beverly Hills, CA, Sage.

Freidrich, W., Beilke, R. and Urquiza, A. (1987) 'Children from sexually abusive families: A behavioural comparison.' *Journal of Interpersonal Violence*, 2, 391-402.

Guyer, M. (1988) 'Allegations of Child Sexual Abuse in Families of Divorce. Panel presentation.' The American Orthopsychiatric Association, Annual Meeting, March 28, San Fransisco, CA.

Horowitz, J., Salt, P., Gomez-Schwartz, B. and Sauzier, M. (1984) 'False accusations of child sexual abuse.' In Tufts New England Medical Centre, Division of Child Psychiatry 'Sexually Exploited Children and Service Research Project.' Final report for the Office of Juvenile Justice and Delinquency Prevention, U.S. Department of Justice, Washington, D.C.

Jones, D. and McGraw, M. (1987) 'Reliable and fictitious accounts of sexual abuse to children.' *Journal of Interpersonal Violence*, 2, 27-46.

Runyon, D., Everson, M., Edelsohn, G., Hunter, W. and Coulter, M. (1988). 'Impact of legal intervention on sexually abused children.' *Journal of Paediatrics*, 113, 647-653.

Saunders, B., McClure, S. and Murphy, S. (1987) 'Structure, function and symptoms in father-child sexual abuse families; a multi-level, multi-respondent empirical assessment.' Presented at Family Violence Research Conference, Durham, NH, available from the first author, Crime Victims Center, Medical University of South Carolina, Charleston, SC 29425.

Thoennes, N. (1988) 'Allegations of sexual abuse in custody and visitation cases: An empirical study of 189 cases from 12 states.' The Association of Family and Conciliation Courts, Research Unit, 1720 Emerson Street, Denver, CO 80218.

Tufts New England Medical Center, Division of Child Psychiatry (1984) 'Sexually Exploited Children; Service and research project.' Final report for the Office of Juvenile Justice and Delinquency Prevention, U.S. Department of Justice, Washington, DC.

Williams, L. and Finkelhor, D. (1989). 'The characteristics of incestuous fathers: A review of recent studies', in W. Marshall, R. Laws and H. Barbaree (eds.). The Handbook of Sexual Assault; Issues, theories and treatment of the offender. N.Y., N.Y. Plenum.

4

PHYSICAL EXAMINATION

ASTRID HEGER

The physician's dilemma

PHYSICIANS RECEIVE NO rewards for making a diagnosis of sexual abuse. Even in the State of California, they rarely receive financial rewards as no fees attach to carrying out these medical examinations, and when they are required to attend court their medical evidence and professional competence may be attacked. There is an in-built sense of conflict between physicians and attorneys. Hence, in the United States physicians are largely resistant to make a diagnosis of child sexual abuse and are eager neither to appear in court nor to have dealings with attorneys. Furthermore, many will readily acknowledge that they are much more likely to under-diagnose than to over-diagnose the problem. Indeed, in the field of medicine, the role of devil's advocate is less open to attack and in many ways is easier than being the child's advocate.

However, if the consequences of making a diagnosis of sexual abuse are serious for the physician, the consequences of not making a diagnosis are even more serious for the child victim. To draw an analogy, the consequences of not making a diagnosis of meningitis are serious for the patient, as are the consequences of failing to consider the possibility of a heart attack when a patient with chest pains arrives in the hospital emergency room. Hence, a diagnosis of sexual abuse must be considered as part of the differential. As in any medical examination, it is critical that everything is taken into account, including a history, a physical examination, and appropriate laboratory evaluation.

One of the dilemmas in writing on this subject is that people generally are much more comfortable with a positive medical evaluation. Whether they are physicians, teachers, social workers, attorneys or the public at large, all give much greater weight to the medical examination than to the child's own statement. It will already be clear from other chapters in this book that people prefer to listen to doctors because their professional qualifications give them a special kind of authority.

In a sense, writing about physical examinations does a disservice to the majority of molested children who have no physical findings. The reasons for the absence of physical evidence are twofold. First, because the children do not disclose at the time of the abuse, there is rarely an opportunity to examine them physically in an acute state, when the findings might have more significance and the abuse might be more easily detected. Secondly, as children are not usually subjected to a type of abuse associated with violence, it does not leave scarring. For example, perhaps the most offensive thing a child may be asked to disclose is that he or she has been orally copulating the father. There is scarcely ever any evidence of oral copulation having taken place. Extremely young children can be caught up in types of abuse that leave neither scarring nor any physical changes. Too often, findings that are seen in the early stages rapidly resolve and the case returns to normal.

Sources of and reasons for referral

Sexually abused children come from a range of backgrounds. They may be referred by police, courts, social workers, therapists or by other physicians seeking a second opinion.

The majority of children are referred for medical examination, not because they have disclosed abuse but because of some behavioural indicator, most commonly a change in behaviour. This might include anything from sexually acting out to regressive behaviour, running away, or school failure. Other children may be referred because of medical indicators such as vaginal discharge resulting from some kind of genital injury and are evaluated to rule out sexual abuse.

Medical examination

Assessment of a child is no different from other medical assessments. It includes taking a significant past medical history in terms of injuries and other types of indicators. A careful history from adult caretakers should precede the history from the child. If the child is of an appropriate age, it is important always to take a history from the child. Ideally an evaluation will already have been completed in a multi-disciplinary setting. Those children who have not disclosed abuse but are referred because of behavioural indicators are interviewed by talking to the child about possible sexual abuse and recording the responses.

In doing a medical examination it is important not to re-rape the child. One way to try to minimise this is to let the child have a sense of control through the option of having someone of the child's own choice present during the examination. While children are rarely restrained, they are sometimes sedated but every effort is made not to abuse them again. It is terrifying to hear children say that the worst part of the whole sexual abuse experience was the physical examination, although that still is true for many children. A physician doing a medical evaluation is responsible for reassuring the child. This is a therapeutic part of the process and not just someone doing invasive types of things such as taking cultures and drawing blood. They need to understand that most children do not disclose sexual abuse and have great difficulty in talking about it. Physicians, like all medical professionals have a responsibility to do appropriate, thorough, sensitive, conservative evaluations of children that are always in the best interests of the child.

Normal examinations and the need for them

The recognition of a normal examination is the most critical factor in any medical evaluation. If a normal examination is understood, it should be possible to diagnose the absence of normal which is crucial to coming to any diagnosis. The importance of emphasising the normal has not been fully recognised. Even in suspected cases of child sexual abuse, the embarrassment of doctors in looking carefully at children causes them to be less than thorough in their examination. The doctor feels more comfortable sitting the child on a table and quickly glancing at the genitalia than asking the child to submit to more thorough examination. Very often the child's genitalia are recorded as normal when in fact they have not been visualised. For example, examination of a child who had been hospitalised for five months because of chronic vomiting, produced negative results. On being transferred to another hospital the child was re-examined and found to have old healed lacerations to the hymen. As a consequence of having had a negative examination followed by a positive finding, the second hospital was then sued for sexually abusing the child. Hence, it can be very devastating not to do an adequate examination.

Between 25 and 30 per cent of 600 children referred to a Los Angeles county hospital will have positive physical findings. Seventy-five per cent of the children who complain of painful vaginal penetration will have positive findings. But that is not the history given by most children. When the child says to the doctor, the attorney or the social work interviewer, 'My daddy humps me', it means to that individual that the adult is having sexual intercourse with that child. In fact that may not be what is happening. To the adult, sexual intercourse means penile-vaginal penetration. But often either simulated intercourse or anal intercourse is actually taking place, not vaginal penetration.

The other matter that has not been touched on is the idea of childhood sexuality and the nature of a child's normal sexual response. Adults who are preoccupied with their own sexuality may find it difficult to appreciate that a very young child has as much or greater capacity to come to orgasm/climax than an adult. Children are so often coerced into acting sexually with adults, because it feels good. Adults have difficulty accepting that children have normal sexual responses. The fact that children are afraid to tell is hardly surprising when the consequences of telling are that the police come and father may go to jail, and all the time the sexual touching feels good.

Examination techniques

Positions: The different positions used in examining children are the subject of intense debate in the United States. Some of the positions used are illustrated in Appendix A, figures 1-5. A very young child may sit on her mother's lap and the examining physician on the floor. Another helpful position is to put the child on top of the mother, have the mother cradle the child and then put the soles of the child's feet together and look at the genitalia. There is a similar position with the child alone on the table and gentle traction is applied to the labia majora, the little fat pads pulled forward. In the pre-adolescent child this gives a very good view of the hymen. Occasionally the knee-chest position is used with boys, or when additional help in visualising a redundant hymen is needed.

The colposcope: This tool has become part of the standard examination in the United States. Basically the colposcope is an instrument with magnification, a good light source and a photographic potential. Research which compares an examination with and without magnification points to the use of magnification as more likely to result in normal examinations, and as clarifying findings as normal that may have been interpreted by others as abnormal. Hence, the colposcope is a very critical device, very useful in teaching and peer review.

The debate in the United States over the use of the colposcope arose from accusations made by defence attorneys that the colposcope made it possible to see things that were not present. In fact the opposite is true. When an instrument is available that makes you look at something carefully and a light source is incorporated into it, it will guarantee that you will do a better examination. In addition to photographic potential, the colposcope will provide a permanent record for peer review and is an excellent teaching tool. However, the use of a colposcope is not essential to the diagnosis of child sexual abuse. If the physician does not possess the skill to make the diagnosis in the first place, the colposcope will not help. It is a good, expensive light source and certainly a useful tool but can be no substitute for skilled history taking from the child.

Anal dilatation test: This test may have significance depending on time since abuse and severity of abuse, but degree of dilatation and position during examination must be considered.

Medical diagnoses of vaginal child sexual abuse

The physician needs to be aware of the very wide range of normal hymens and the equally wide range of normal hymen diameters. For many years it was assumed that the hymen was annular, a doughnut shaped piece of tissue with a hole in the centre: that is not the case. In spite of the fact that most hymens are not annular, the absence of an annular hymen was considered abnormal by some examiners.

Hymenal diameters are a subject of controversy in the US. These diameters vary according to the technique that is used: whether the child is examined on their back in a supine position or in a knee chest position or prone. It also depends on the technique used. A relatively small hymenal diameter will open up considerably when some traction is applied to the labia major. Some individuals believe that an enlarged hymenal diameter greater than 0.4 to 0.5 millimetres is diagnostic of sexual abuse or most consistent with it and would report on that basis. These kinds of measurements might be utilised by that individual specifically in their practice but should not be generalised to other clinics.

Another problem in looking at hymens is that one can look distorted until the child is flipped over into a prone position. When under the pull of gravity the hymen will fall down to reveal a normal translucent posterior edge.

Hymens change their appearance rapidly as children develop and physicians need to be aware of what they look like at different stages. There is a wide range of normal (see Plates 1 and 2).

The majority of young pre-adolescent girls will have cresentric or annular hymens. A small percentage will present with a septated or cribriform hymen (Figures 6 and 7, Appendix A). In addition there are developmental changes that occur as the child matures. The newborn, under the influence of maternal estrogens, will have a thickened, redundant hymen, which will gradually change into the 'scanty' hymen (see Plates 1 and 2) of the pre-adolescent. Some girls will continue to have a fimbriated or 'sleeve-like' hymen throughout childhood (see Plate 3).

The majority of children who appear for medical examination are within the normal range. Even children who describe painful manipulation and digital penetration can have a normal examination. Simulated or vulva intercourse also can result in normal examination.

Acute vaginal penetration: These are among the easier cases to diagnose, especially when there has been ejaculation. Again the history is critical. An adult normally assumes that if a child describes vaginal intercourse or penetration then ejaculation will have occurred intra-vaginally. But that is not necessarily the case. Ejaculation may occur on the chest, on the legs, on the bed or on whatever surface the child was abused. Hence, a history must be taken before the absence of forensic evidence can lead to the conclusion that the rape did not occur.

It is very clear to all those experienced in looking at children with acute vaginal lacerations that they heal quickly and often leave no trace of trauma. This is particularly true of single episode penetration. Even in many acute cases the victim will remain free of any findings.

Chronic vaginal penetration: In most clinical presentations the complaint is old or ongoing penetration. Certain features are highly significant. Obviously healed lacerations and scars are significant findings. Another is an attenuation — the fact that the hymen has been pushed to the side and essentially has disappeared. The medical community may disagree about a number of things but there is agreement on the

PLATES

PHYSICAL FINDINGS

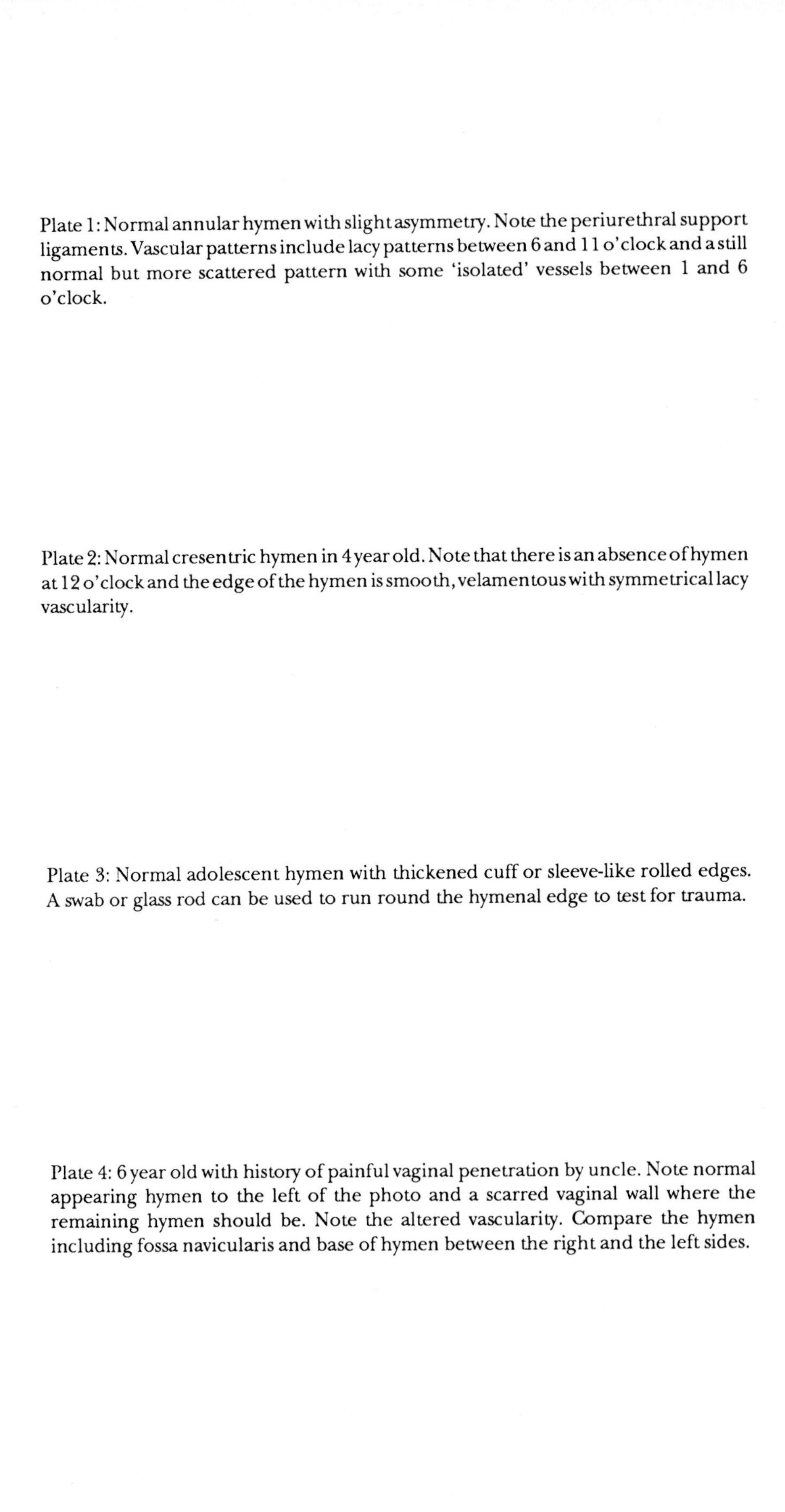

Plate 1: Normal annular hymen with slight asymmetry. Note the periurethral support ligaments. Vascular patterns include lacy patterns between 6 and 11 o'clock and a still normal but more scattered pattern with some 'isolated' vessels between 1 and 6 o'clock.

Plate 2: Normal cresentric hymen in 4 year old. Note that there is an absence of hymen at 12 o'clock and the edge of the hymen is smooth, velamentous with symmetrical lacy vascularity.

Plate 3: Normal adolescent hymen with thickened cuff or sleeve-like rolled edges. A swab or glass rod can be used to run round the hymenal edge to test for trauma.

Plate 4: 6 year old with history of painful vaginal penetration by uncle. Note normal appearing hymen to the left of the photo and a scarred vaginal wall where the remaining hymen should be. Note the altered vascularity. Compare the hymen including fossa navicularis and base of hymen between the right and the left sides.

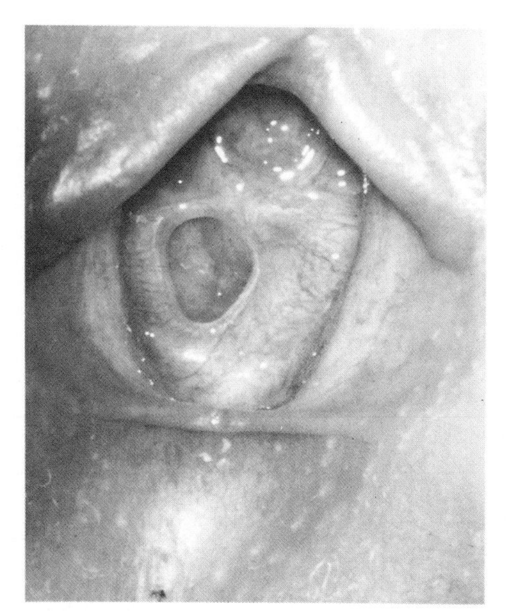
Plate 1.

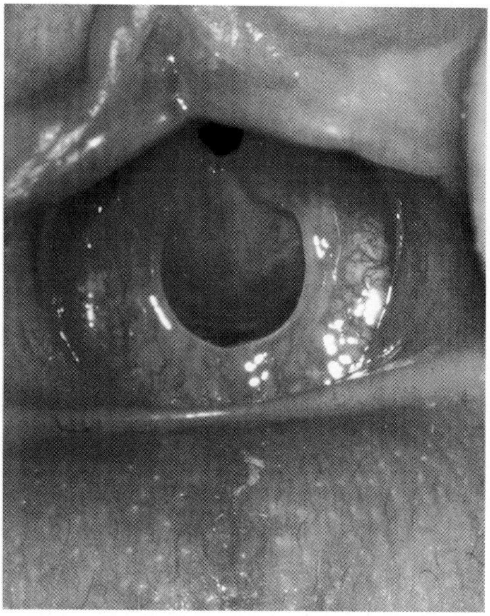

Plate 2.

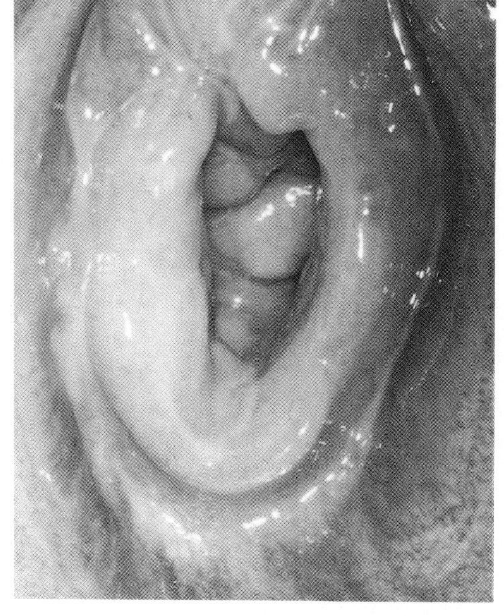
Plate 3.

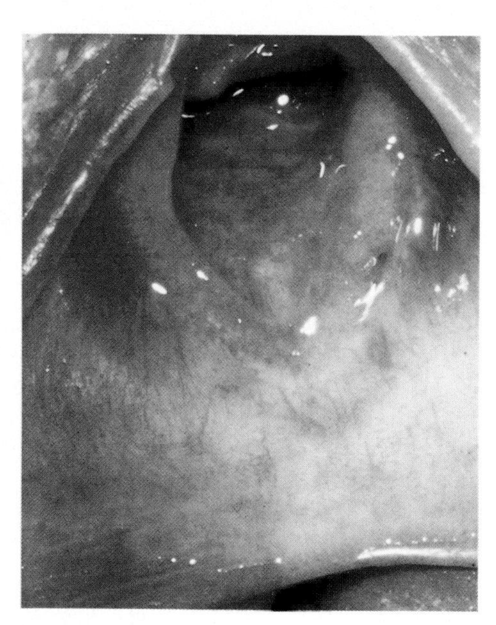
Plate 4.

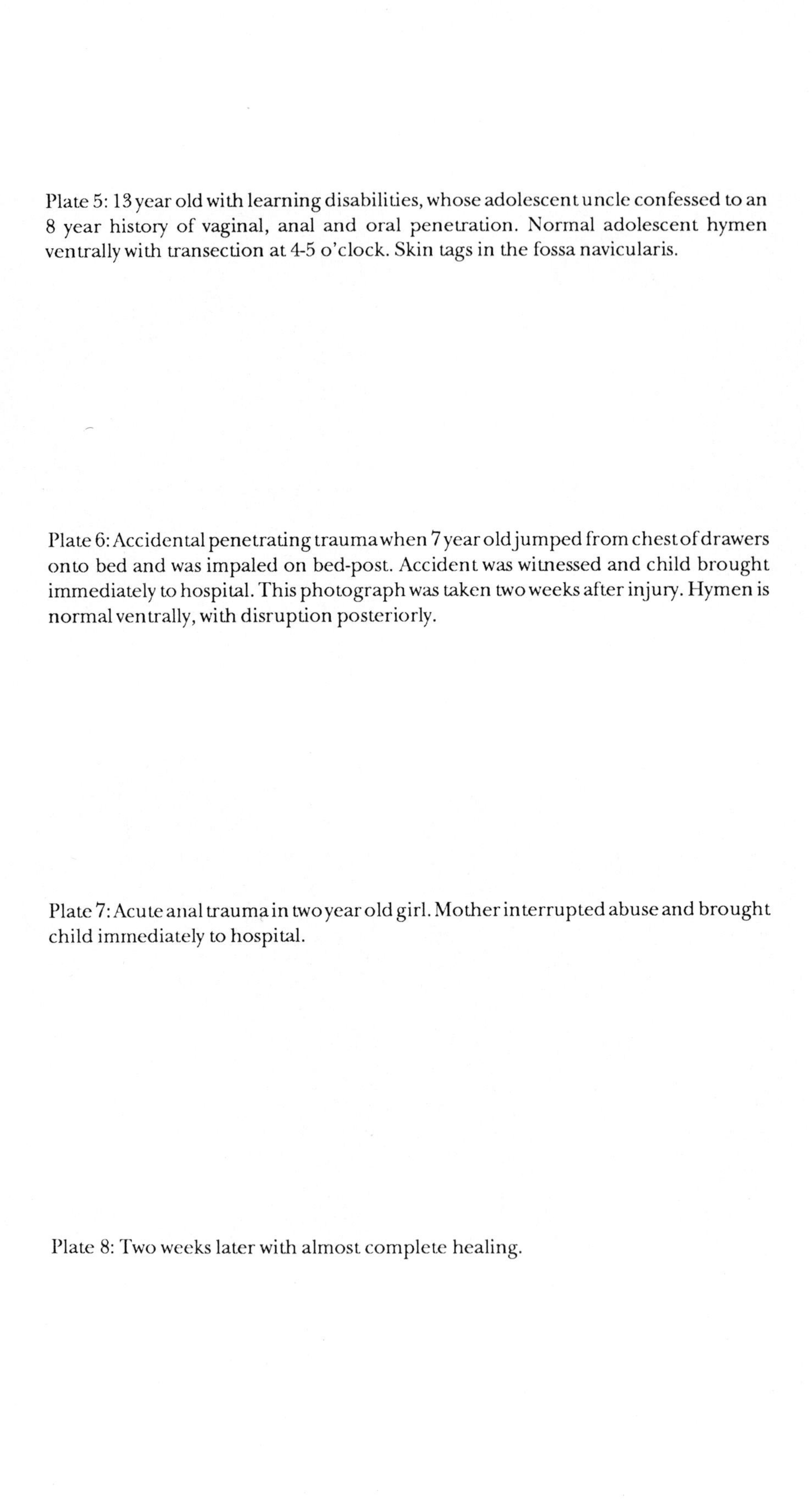

Plate 5: 13 year old with learning disabilities, whose adolescent uncle confessed to an 8 year history of vaginal, anal and oral penetration. Normal adolescent hymen ventrally with transection at 4-5 o'clock. Skin tags in the fossa navicularis.

Plate 6: Accidental penetrating trauma when 7 year old jumped from chest of drawers onto bed and was impaled on bed-post. Accident was witnessed and child brought immediately to hospital. This photograph was taken two weeks after injury. Hymen is normal ventrally, with disruption posteriorly.

Plate 7: Acute anal trauma in two year old girl. Mother interrupted abuse and brought child immediately to hospital.

Plate 8: Two weeks later with almost complete healing.

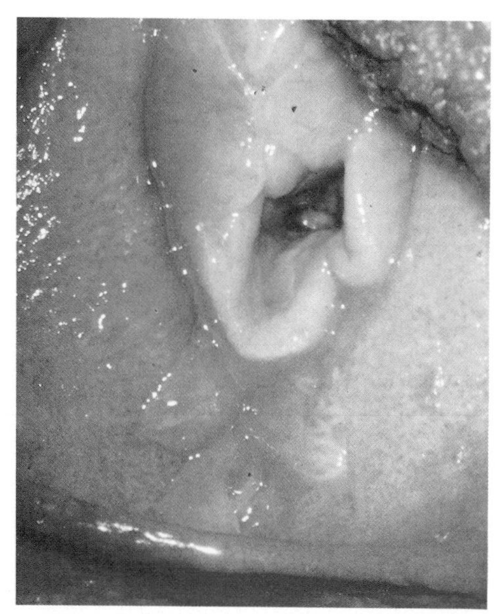

Plate 5.

Plate 6.

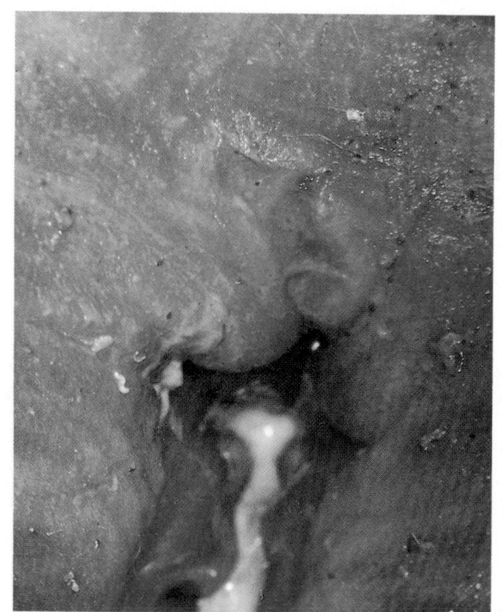

Plate 7.

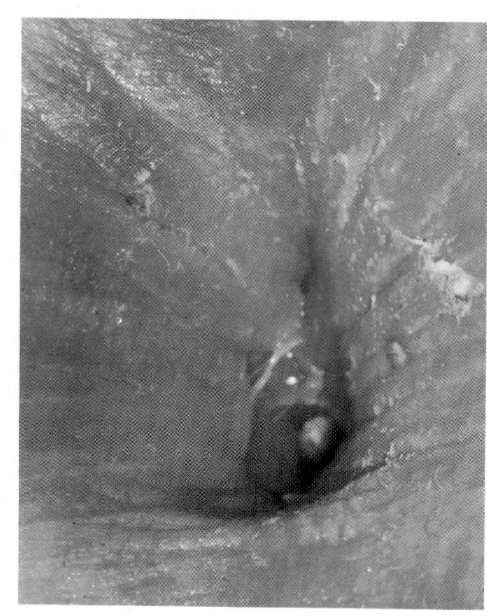

Plate 8.

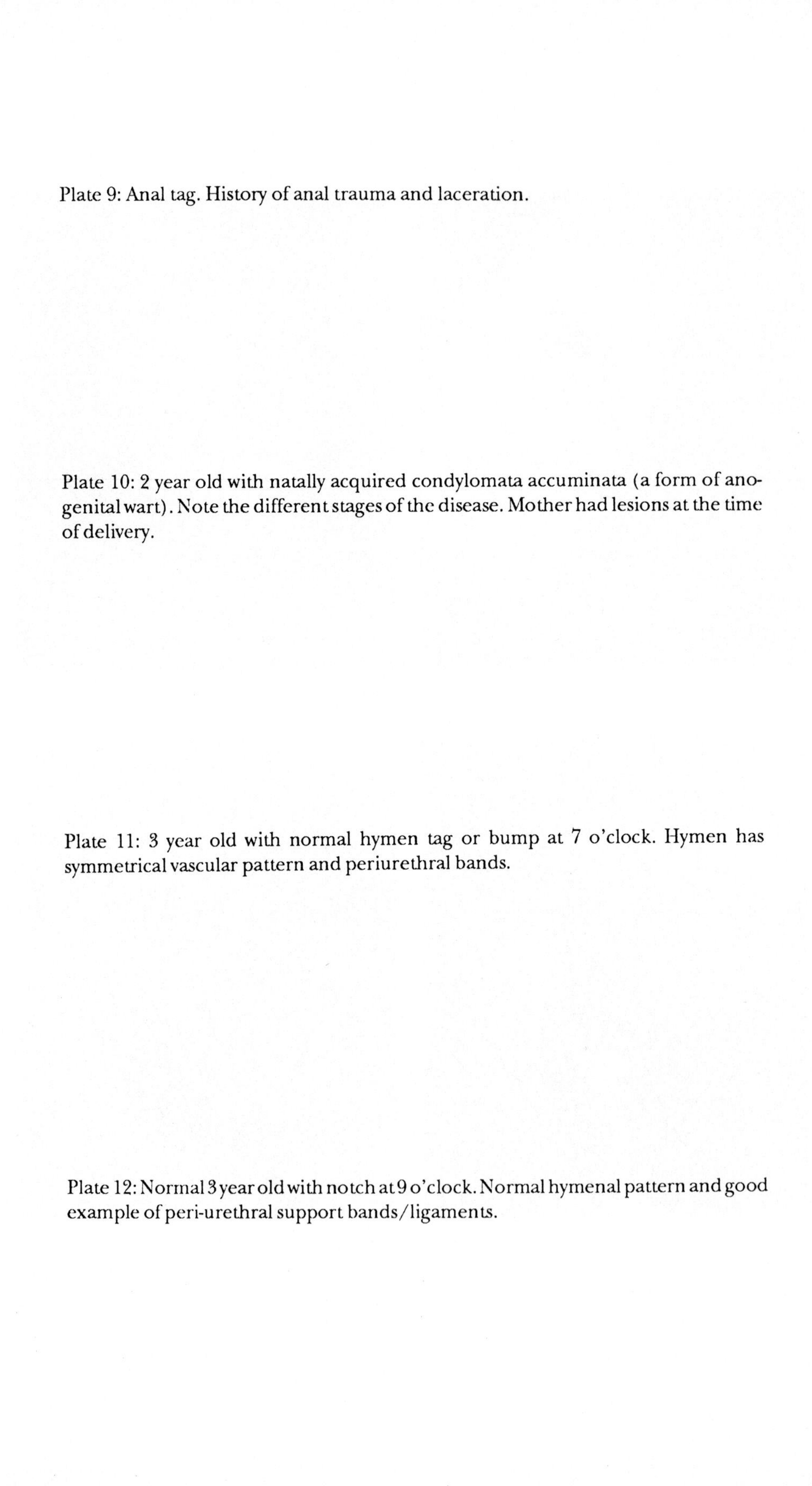

Plate 9: Anal tag. History of anal trauma and laceration.

Plate 10: 2 year old with natally acquired condylomata accuminata (a form of ano-genital wart). Note the different stages of the disease. Mother had lesions at the time of delivery.

Plate 11: 3 year old with normal hymen tag or bump at 7 o'clock. Hymen has symmetrical vascular pattern and periurethral bands.

Plate 12: Normal 3 year old with notch at 9 o'clock. Normal hymenal pattern and good example of peri-urethral support bands/ligaments.

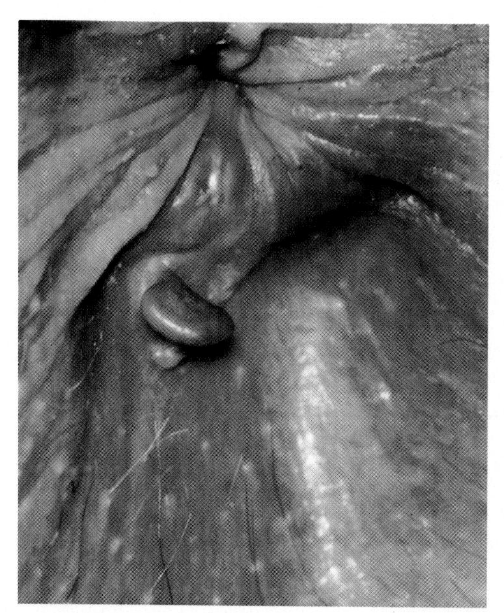

Plate 9.

Plate 10.

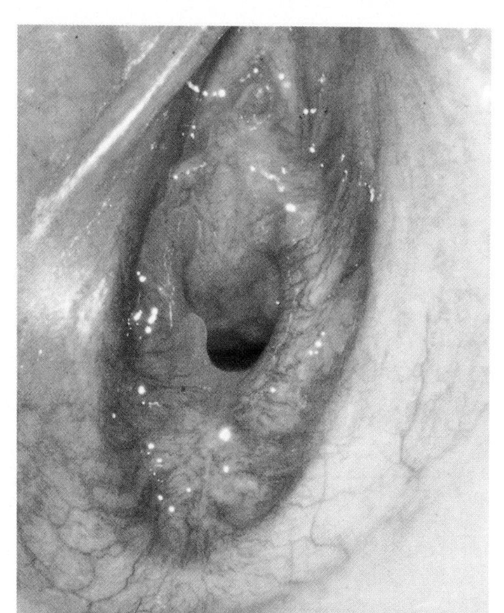

Plate 11.

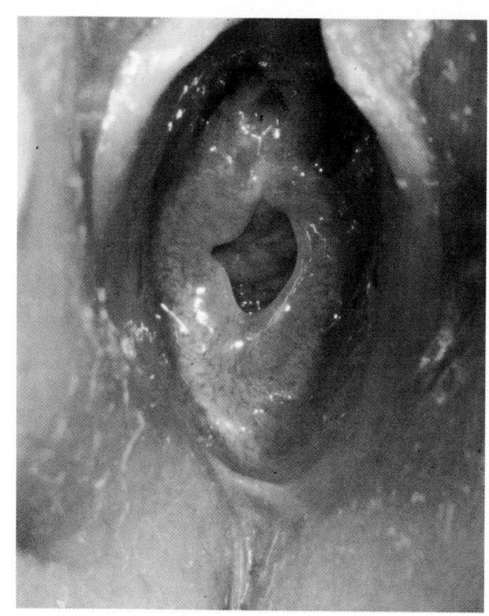

Plate 12.

significance of these points (see Plates 4 and 5).

Accidental trauma is frequently investigated. A fall on a bicycle or open cupboard door or any kind of straddle injury results in damage towards the front of the body. But the hymen is an internal structure and must be damaged through penetrating trauma of some kind. Straddle injuries usually cause trauma externally to the mons pubis, clitoris, laterally to the labia minora and majora and finally to the peri-urethral tissues (see Plate 6).

Anal examination

The evaluation of children who describe anal penetration, even when there is a confession of on-going sodomy, will rarely provide positive findings. Furthermore, whatever the physical effect— tone, scarring or changes in the rugai — they all return to normal very rapidly, usually within two weeks. Although certain physical findings can arouse suspicion that something has happened to the child, there is great danger in focusing on only one small part of the whole evaluation process. The absence of physical findings does not mean that the child is not abused.

Acute anal penetration: Most children will remain free of any medical finding. However, some children will present with abrasions, lacerations and bruising. The degree of trauma will depend on force and lubrication.

Chronic anal penetration: In the majority of cases the examination is normal. Positive findings should not be expected in either the acute or chronic case. Even in a case where there exists videotaped documentation of repeated sodomy or buggery the examination was normal. Acute trauma heals quickly, and within days may be free of all evidence of past trauma (see Plates 7 and 8).

It is important to clarify the terms that we use to describe changes in the soft tissues as well as physiological responses. An anal skin fold is a congenital finding of redundant issue at the 12 o' clock (supine) position. A skin tag is a pedunculated piece of tissue which usually forms after a fissure or laceration (see Plate 9).

Sexually Transmitted Disease

Children as well as adults can contract sexually transmitted diseases but they can only do so as a result of sexual contact, or via the birth process (see Plate 10). A list of diseases that may indicate that children have experienced sexual contact is presented in Appendix C.

It is interesting to note that in the United Kingdom it has been standard practice for sexually transmitted disease clinics to report the statistics nationally. Each year the statistics included a certain number of children. Unfortunately this group of clinicians have identified a disease without understanding or recognising what these statistics really mean.

Diagnostic problems

It is important to understand that hymens change their appearance and size of openings depending on position and examination techniques. Normal anatomical variations like bumps, notches and tags may be misinterpreted as post-traumatic by the inexperienced examiner. With proper positioning of the child it is possible to visualise intravaginal structure like rugae and ridges, which may extend to the rim or edge of the hymen. Symmetrical bands of tissue are frequently found lateral to the urethra and have been termed 'periurethral support ligaments'. These bands are found in most girls, and may be continued symmetrically around the base of the hymen (see Plates 11 and 12).

By placing the girl in the supine, frog-legged position and then applying gentle traction on the labia major, by grasping gently between the thumb and fingers and pulling towards the examiner, it is possible to gain the best view of the hymenal edge. This will also significantly increase the hymenal opening diameter.

Peer review

Physical examiners' peer review groups are ideal means of learning about child sexual abuse. Clinical experiences can be exchanged, individual cases shared and discussed, photographs scrutinised. Like most of medicine it also creates a consensus of opinion as to the interpretation of signs and promotes a scientific, conservative and appropriate evaluation of the abused child.

APPENDIX A

SCHEMATIC DRAWINGS

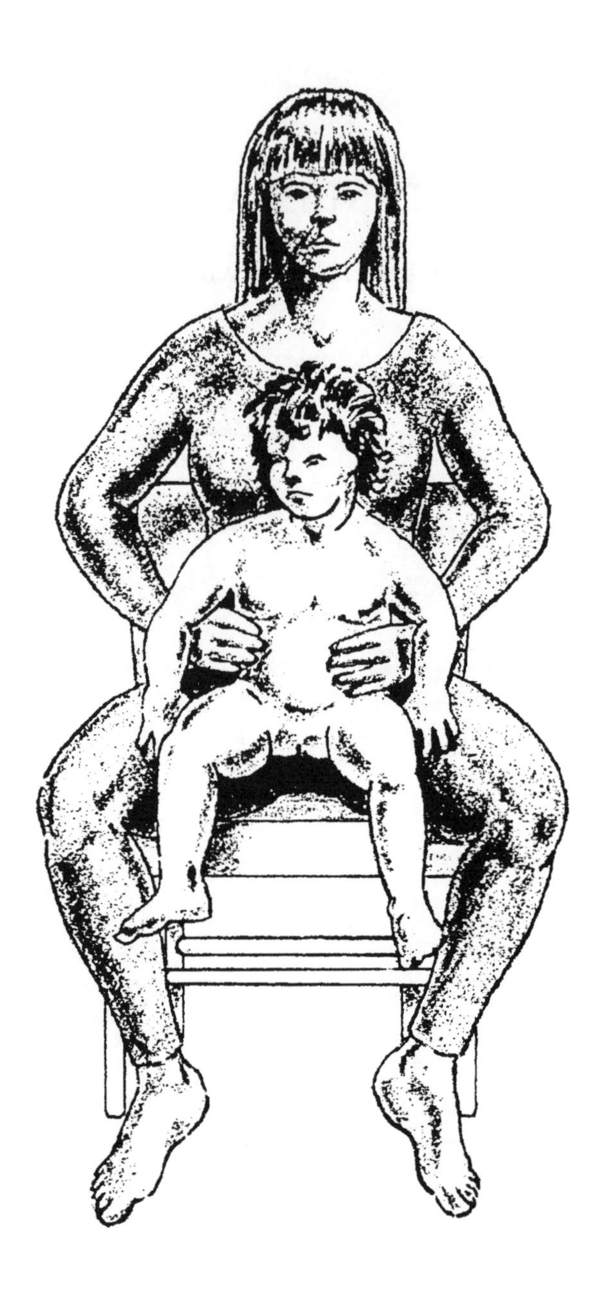

FIGURE 1
Young and frightened children can be examined while sitting on the parent's lap or being held in their arms.

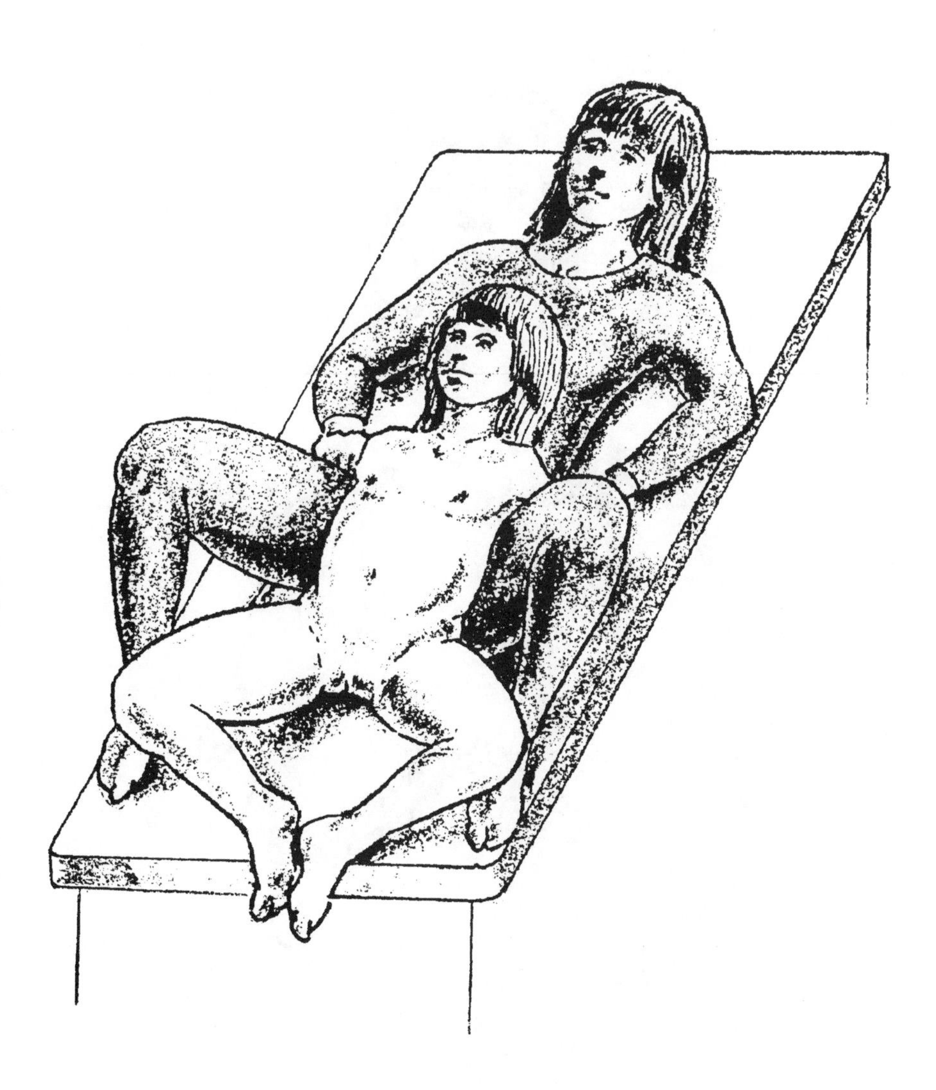

FIGURE 2
Placing the child on top of the mother/father can be comforting and allow for a better examination. (Note: by placing the child's legs on the outside of the parent's legs the genitalia is easily evaluated).

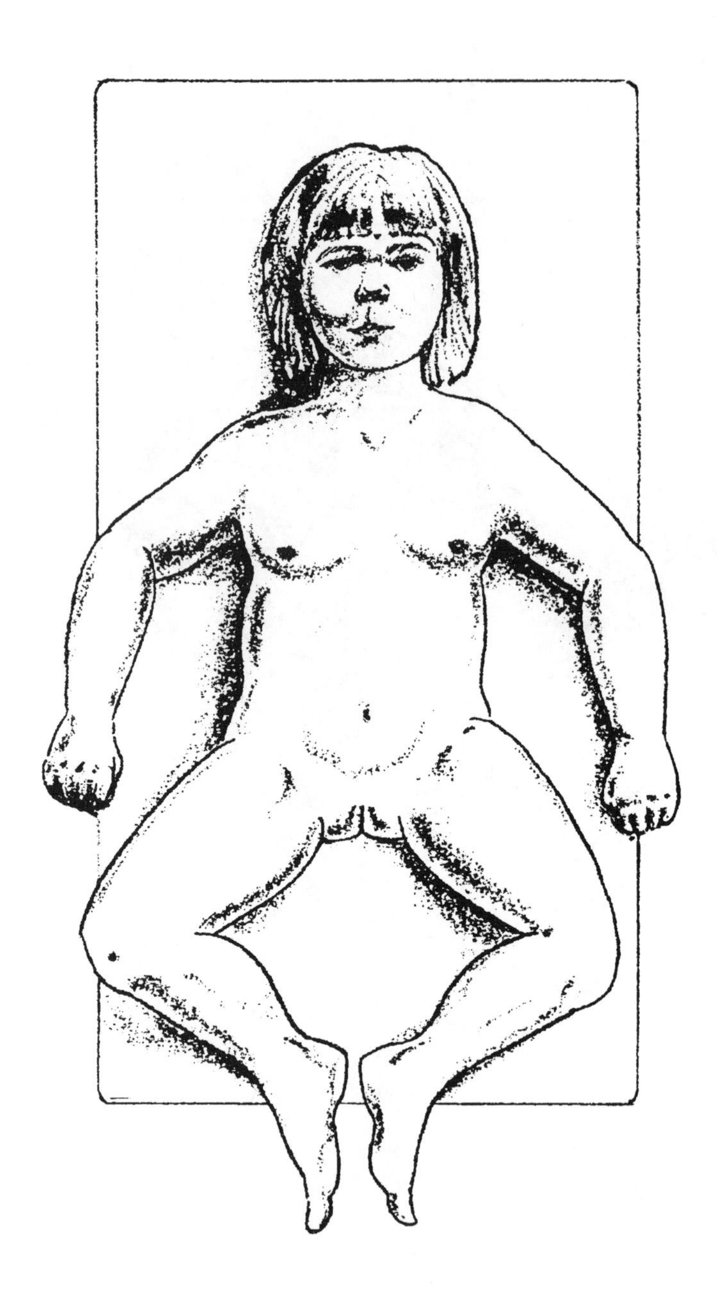

FIGURE 3
Child in a frog-legged position.

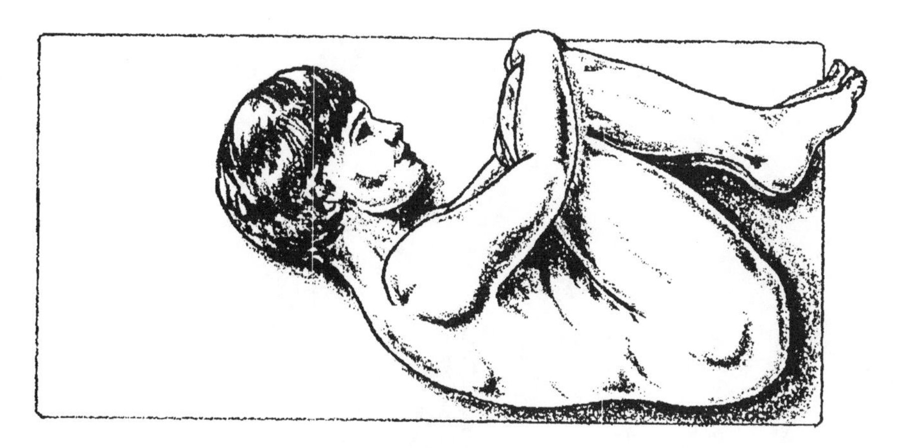

FIGURE 4
Evaluating boys in the left-lateral position is less traumatic than the knee-elbow prone position.

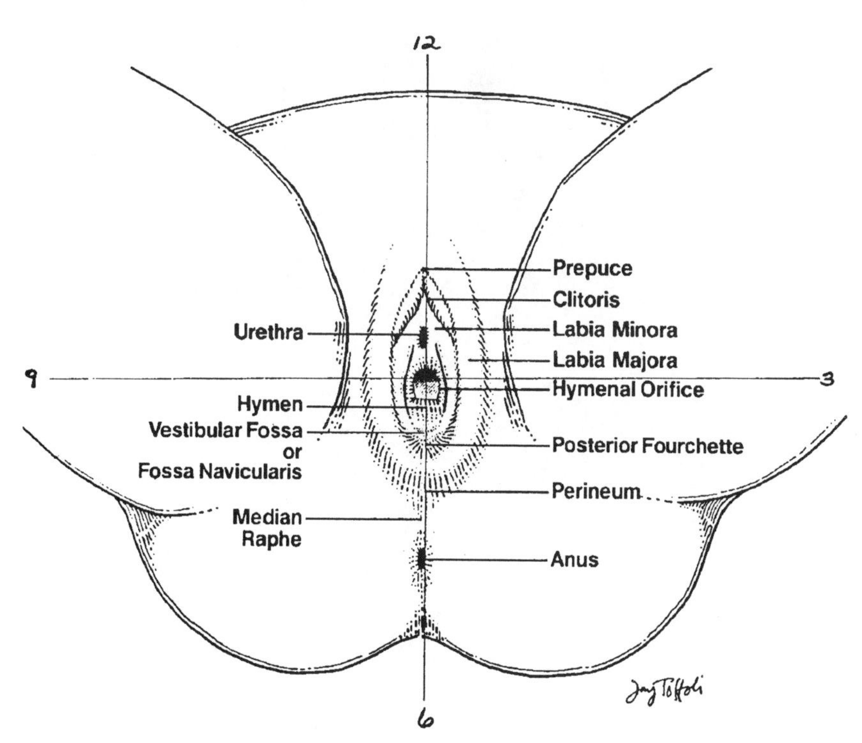

FIGURE 5
Major anatomy

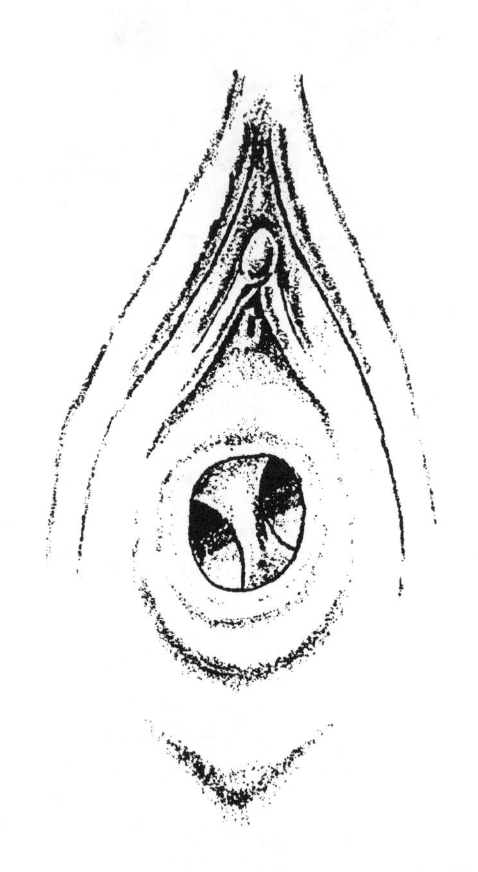

FIGURE 6
Septated hymen

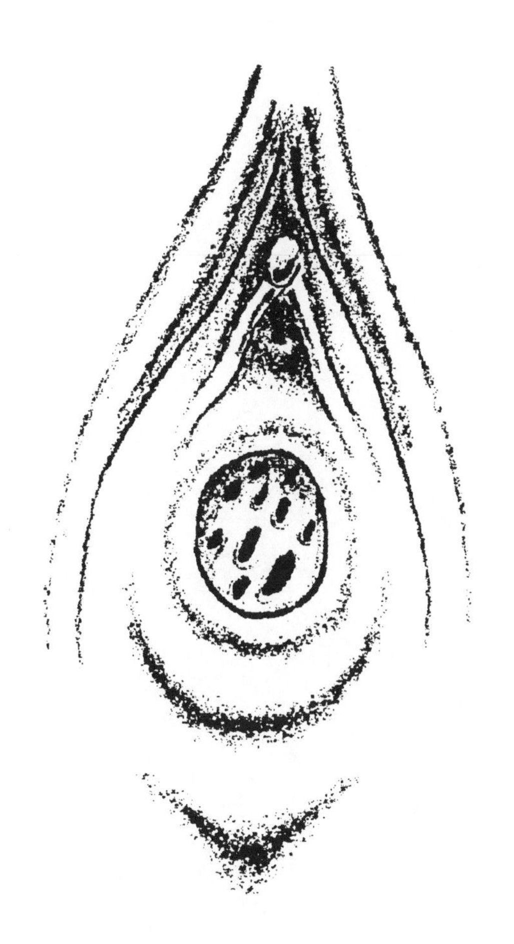

FIGURE 7
Cribriform hymen

APPENDIX B

GLOSSARY OF TERMS

MAJOR ANATOMY

Vagina	Tubular structure with normal folds and rugae between hymen and cervix.
Labia Majora	Outer lips to vagina. Covered by pubic hair after puberty.
Labia Minora	Inner lips to vagina.
Clitoris	Erectile tissue located above urethra.
Urethra	Opening to the bladder.
Hymen	A fine membrane which separates the external genitalia from the vagina.
Posterior Fourchette	External tissue extending from the hymen toward the anus, but contained within the labia.
Fossa Navicularis	Concavity in posterior fourchette at the base of the hymen.
Anus	Opening to the rectum.

ANATOMICAL VARIATIONS

Clefts	Division, notch, or split of edge of the hymen.
Bumps	Elevation of tissue.
Longitudinal intravaginal ridges	Congenital vaginal folds or ridges.
Tags	Flap of tissue

Fold	Normal crease or redundancy
Periurethral bands or ligaments	Symmetrical bands of tissue lateral to urethra extending to vestibular wall. These same bands may be located at other points around the base of the hymen.

HYMEN VARIATIONS

Annular	Circumferential: a hymen that covers the vaginal opening to 360 degrees.
Crescentric	Posterior rim of hymen with attachments at 11 o'clock and 1 o'clock.
Fimbriated	Redundant and folded with a ruffled and/or fringed edge.
Septated	Two hymenal openings with band of tissue between.
Cribiform	Multiple openings.
Imperforate	No hymenal opening.

PATHOLOGY

Abrasion	Abraded injury through the basal layer of skin.
Laceration	Transection through the skin.
Ecchymosis	Bruise.
Contusion	Tender injury either with or without bruise.
Erythema	Redness.
Transection	Cut or tear through tissue.
Synechiae	Band of tissue/adhesion.
Petechiae	Small hemorrhages about pinhead size.

Vaginitis	Vaginal infection.
Vulvitis	Inflammation of the labia.
Urethritis	Infection of the urethra.
Pelvic Inflammatory Disease (PID)	Infection of the fallopian tubes or ovaries

APPENDIX C

SEXUALLY TRANSMITTED DISEASE AS EVIDENCE OF SEXUAL CONTACT IN CHILDREN

Condition	*Incubation*	*Indicative of Sexual Contact*
GONORRHOEA — in children under two years the cause could be perinatally acquired	3-4 days	almost certain
CHLAMYDIA — in children under three years could be perinatally acquired; need to exclude asymptomatic maternal infection	7-14 days	almost certain
HERPES GENITALIS — requires close personal mucosal contact	2-20 days	probable
GENITAL WARTS — cause could be perinatal infection and appearance may be delayed up to two years — exclude possible innocent infection e.g. from warts on child's or parents' hands	months	probable
GARDNERELLA VAGINALIS — uncommon in non-abused non sexually active healthy girls (less than 5%)		possible/probable
TRICHOMONAS VAGINALIS — perinatal may persist six weeks	1-4 weeks	almost certain
HUMAN IMMUNODEFICIENCY VIRUS (HIV) (preferable to test at time of assault and at three months) — exclude maternal transmission, I.V. drug abuse, treatment with blood products	usually 6 weeks to 3 months	probable

SYPHILIS; exclude transplacental infections (EARLYINFECTIOUS) — rare	3-4 weeks (up to 13 weeks)	almost certain

The presence of the same infection in the alleged perpetrator, or the presence in the child of more than one STD, makes the diagnosis of abuse almost certain.

* Adapted by Dr Betty Priestley, Consultant Paediatrician, Sheffield Health Authority from a table produced by Dr Angela Robinson, Consultant in Genito Urinary Medicine, University College Hospital, London.

APPENDIX D

MEDICAL BIBLIOGRAPHY

* denotes referencer on sexually transmitted diseases.

*Alexander, E. R. (1984) 'Maternal and infant sexually transmitted diseases,' *Urology Clinic North America,* 11.

AMA (1985) Diagnostic and Treatment Guidelines Concerning Child Abuse and Neglect, *Journal of American Medical Association,* 254.

Berkowitz, C. D. (1987) 'A simulated "acquired" imperforate hymen following the genital trauma of sexual abuse,' *Clinical Pediatrics,* 26.

Berkowitz, C. D. (1987) 'Sexual abuse of children and adolescents,' *Advances in Pediatrics,* 34.

*Bump, R. C., Sacks, L. A., Buesching WJIII (1986) 'Sexually transmissible infectious agents in sexually active and virginal asymptomatic adolescent girls,' *Pediatrics,* 77.

Cantwell, H. (1983) 'Vaginal inspection as it relates to child sexual abuse in girls under 13,' *Child Abuse and Neglect,* 7.

Cantwell, H. (2987) 'Update on vaginal inspection as it relates to child sexual abuse in girls under 13,' *Child Abuse and Neglect,* 11.

Cowell, Carol (1981) 'The gynecologic examination of infants, children and young adolescents,' *Pediatric Clinics of North America,* 28 (2).

Ellerstein, N. S. (1980) 'Sexual abuse of boys,' *American Journal of Diseases of Children,* 134.

Emans, S. J. (1982) *Pediatric and Adolescent Gynecology.* Boston: Little and Brown.

*Emans, S. J. (1986) 'Vulvovaginitis in the child and adolescent,' *Pediatrics Review,* 8 (11-19).

Emans, S. J. (1987) 'Genital findings in sexually abused, symptomatic and asymptomatic girls,' *Pediatrics,* 79 (5).

Enos, W. F., Conrath, T. B., Byer, J.C. (1986) 'Forensic evaluation of the sexually abused child,' *Pediatrics,* 78 (3).

Finkel, Martin (1989) 'Anogenital trauma in sexually abused children' *Pediatrics,* 84 (2).

*Frau, L. M., Alexander, E. R. (1985) 'Public health implications of sexually transmitted diseases in pediatric practice,' *Journal of Pediatric Infectious Disease,* 4.

Frith, Kathleen (1970) 'Rape, divorce and nullity,' *British Journal of Hospital Medicine,* 4 (6).

Frith, Kathleen (1976) 'Sexual offenses, divorce and nullity,' The late Francis E. Camps (ed.), in *Gradwohl's Legal Medicine*, 3rd Ed., Bristol: John Wright.

*Glaser, J. B., Hammerschlag, M. R., and McCormack, W. M. (1986) 'Sexually transmitted diseases in victims of sexual assault,' *New England Journal of Medicine*, 315.

*Hammerschlag, M. R., Alpert, S., Rosner, I. *et al.* (1978) 'Microbiology of the vagina in children: normal and potentially pathogenic organisms,' *Pediatrics*, 62.

Heger, A. H. (1985) *Response: Child Sexual Abuse. A Medical View.* Los Angeles: United Way, Inc.

Heger, A. H. with Michael Durfee and Bruce Woodling (1986) 'Medical evaluation,' in Kee McFarlane and Jill Waterman *et al. Sexual Abuse of Young Children*, New York: The Guilford Press.

Heger, A. H. and Emans, S. J. (1990) 'Introital diameter as criterion for sexual abuse,' *Pediatrics*, 85 (2).

Herjanic, B. (1978) 'Sexual abuse of children,' *Journal of American Medical Association*, 239 (4).

Herman-Giddens, M. E. (1987) 'Prepubertal female genitalia: Examination for evidence of sexual abuse,' *Pediatrics*, 80 (2).

Herman-Giddens, M. E. (1989) 'Harmful genital care practices in children,' *Journal of American Medical Association*, 261 (4).

Hobbs, C. and Wynne, J. M. (1986) 'Child abuse: Buggery in childhood — a common syndrome of child abuse,' *Lancet* V 2.

Hobbs, C. J. and Wynne, J. M. (1989) 'Sexual abuse of English boys and girls: the importance of anal examination,' *Child Abuse and Neglect*, 13 (2).

Horowitz, D. A. (1987) 'Physical examination of sexually abused children and adolescents,' *Pediatrics Review*, 9 (1).

Huffman, John (1981) *The Gynecology of Childhood and Adolescence.* Philadelphia: Saunders.

Jenny, Carole (1987) 'Hymens in newborn female infants,' *Pediatrics*, 80 (3).

Jones, J. G. (1982) 'Sexual abuse of children,' *American Journal of Children*, 1136.

Josephson, G. W. (1979) 'The male rape victim: Evaluation and treatment,' *Journal of the American College of Emergency Physicians*, 8 (1).

Kramer, D. G., Jason, J. (1982) 'Sexually abused children and sexually transmitted diseases,' *Review of Infectious Diseases*, 4 (supp.).

Krugman, R. (1986) 'Recognition of sexual abuse in children,' *Pediatrics Review*, 8 (1).

Ladson, S., Johnson, C. F. and Doty, R. E. (1987) 'Do physicians recognise sexual abuse?' *American Journal of Diseases of Children*, 141.

Levitt, C. J. (1986) 'Sexual abuse in children: A compassionate yet thorough approach to evaluation,' *Post Graduate Medicine*, 80 (2).

McCann, J., Voris, J., Simon, M. and Wells, R. (1989) 'Perianal findings in prepubertal children selected for non-abuse: a descriptive study,' *Child Abuse and Neglect*, 13 (2).

McCann, J., Voris, J., Simon, S. M., and Wells, R. (1990) 'Comparison of genital examination techniques in prepubertal children,' *Pediatrics*, 85 (2).

McCauley, J. (1986) 'Toludine blue in the detection of perineal lacerations in pediatric and adolescent sexual abuse victims,' *Pediatrics*, 78 (6).

Muram, David (1986) 'Genital tract injuries in the prepubertal child,' *Pediatric Annals*, 15 (8).

Muram, David (1989) 'Child sexual abuse — genital tract findings in prepubertal girls. The unaided medical examination,' *American Journal of Obstetrics and Gynecology*, 160 (2).

Muram, David, and Elias, S. (1989) 'Child sexual abuse — genital tract findings in prepubertal girls, II Comparison of colposcopic and unaided examinations,' *American Journal of Obstetrics and Gynecology*, 160 (2).

*Neinstein, L. A., Goldenring, J., Carpenter, S. (1984) 'Nonsexual transmission of sexually transmitted diseases: an infrequent occurrence,' *Pediatrics*, 74.

Norvell, M. (1984) 'Investigation of microtrauma after intercourse,' *Journal of Reproductive Medicine*, 29 (4).

Orr, D. P. (1979) 'Emergency management of sexually abused children,' *American Journal of Diseases of Children*, 133 (6).

*Paradise, J. E., Campos, J. M., Friedman, H. M. *et al* (1982) 'Vulvovaginitis in premenarcheal girls: Clinical features and diagnostic evaluation', *Pediatrics*, 70.

Paradise, J. E. (1985) 'Probability of vaginal foreign body in girls with genital complaints,' *American Journal of Diseases of Children*, 139.

Paradise, J. E. (1989) 'Predictive accuracy and the diagnosis of sexual abuse: a big issue about a little tissue,' *Child Abuse and Neglect* (13) (2).

Paul, D. M. (1975) 'The medical examination in sexual offenses,' *Medicine, Science and the Law*, V 15 (3).

Paul, D. M. (1977) 'The medical examination in sexual offenses against children,' *Medicine, Science and the Law*, V 17 (4).

Pokorney, S. F. (1987) 'Configuration of the prepubertal hymen,' *American Journal of Obstetric Gynecology*, October.

*Shafer, M. A., Sweet, R. L., Ohm-Smith, M. J. *et al* (1985) 'Microbiology of the lower genital tract in postmenarcheal adolescent girls: Differences by sexual activity, contraception and presence of non-specific vaginitis,' *Journal of Pediatrics*, 107.

Spencer, M. J. and Dunklee, P. (1986) 'A study of sexual abuse in boys,' *Pediatrics*, 78 (1).

Teixeira, R. G. (1981) 'Hymenal colposcopic examination in sexual offenses,' *American Journal of Forensic Medicine and Pathology*, 2 (3).

Tilelli, J. (1980) 'Sexual abuse of children,' *New England Journal of Medicine*, Vol. 302 (6).

Tipton, A. C. (1989) 'Child sexual abuse: physical examination techniques and interpretation of findings,' *Adolescent Pediatric Gynecology*, 2.

Underhill, R. A. and Dewhurt, J. (1978) 'The doctor cannot always tell: Medical examination of the "Intact" hymen,' *Lancet*, Feb. 18.

White, S. T. (1987) 'Vaginal introital diameter: A diagnostic aid to child sexual abuse,' Abstracts, *American Journal of Diseases of Children*, 141.

White, S. T. and Ingram, D. J. (1989) Vaginal introital diameter in the evaluation of sexual abuse,' *Child Abuse and Neglect*, 13 (2).

White, S. T., Loda, F. A., Ingram, D. L. *et al.* (1983) 'Sexually transmitted diseases in sexually abused children,' *Pediatrics*, 72.

Woodling, B. and Heger, A. (1986) 'The use of the colposcope in the diagnosis of sexual abuse in the pediatric age group, *Child Abuse and Neglect* Vol. 10.

Woodling, B. A. (1986) 'Sexual abuse and the child,' *Emergency Medical Services* 15 (3).

Woodling, B. and Kossoris, P. (1981) 'Sexual misuse: rape, molestation and incest,' *Pediatric Clinics of North America*, 28 (2).

Wynne, J. M. (1980) 'Injuries to the genitalia in female children,' *South African Medical Journal*, 57.

5

GATHERING LEGAL EVIDENCE

PATRICIA A. TOTH AND HARRY ELIAS

DISTRICT ATTORNEYS, Prosecuting Attorneys, Commonwealth's Attorneys and State's Attorneys are some of the different names given to prosecutors in each of the American states. The 1950s radio show, 'Mr District Attorney' portrayed prosecutors as the 'good guys', champions of the people, and defenders of truth. Since then, the title 'Public Defender' has come to be used by state-compensated defence attorneys. In the child abuse field, prosecutors have more recently been included in the group of 'bad guys'. They are often considered to be either inept or unscrupulous, ambitious, politically motivated and tough on child abuse cases only to advance their own careers. In fact, some prosecutors well known to the public at large are those whose careers have been tarnished because they have taken a strong stance on child abuse. In addition, prosecutors are frequently perceived to be uncaring about victims and concerned only with punishment of the offender, despite many indications to the contrary.

Along with other child abuse professionals, prosecutors have been the target of intense public scrutiny and criticism. This criticism comes from both sides and can create dilemmas. When prosecutors decide not to prosecute a case where others believe abuse occurred, it is alleged that they do not care about children. On the other hand, prosecutors who aggressively prosecute child abuse come under fire from those who claim there is a witch hunt which creates abuse in the minds of children when it does not really exist.

As a result of dramatic increases in the number of reports of suspected child abuse and neglect in the United States in the past decade, many professionals have been called on to respond. Interdisciplinary teams have begun to work together to improve investigations, with a shared goal of maximizing protection of children. In the summer of 1988, a similar situation emerged in the United Kingdom. Social workers had been severely criticised for failing to act promptly and positively to secure the protection of children. They responded by determining in Cleveland and elsewhere that whenever children appeared to be at risk, effective steps should be taken to intervene.

In the United States, the National Center for Prosecution of Child Abuse was created to provide training and help to the thousands of state and local prosecutors responsible for criminal child abuse cases. The Center's services are available to all prosecutor's offices throughout the country, from those such as Los Angeles with hundreds of assistant prosecutors to the smallest single lawyer offices. The Center was created as the result of prosecutors' desire to improve their level of knowledge and standard of skillful investigation and prosecution of child abuse cases. Underlying this concern is the strong belief that effective practice requires a more determined effort to co-ordinate and communicate with all other professionals working with cases in this field. This requires a fundamentally different approach for prosecutors who, historically, have not had to consult with other professionals. In more traditional criminal cases such as burglary, robbery or drug abuse, the police are likely to play the most direct role. Child abuse involves many other agencies and parts of the system. The only effective way to handle these cases is to work jointly with other professionals and make efforts to understand the roles of each.

A further rationale for this co-operative effort is the emerging 'backlash' against professionals fighting against child abuse. In his book *The Battle and the Backlash* (1988), David Hechler describes this phenomenon which finds the media and the public increasingly questioning the legitimacy and actual extent of child abuse cases. They appear to be doing likewise in the United Kingdom. Without doubt, false accusations can have a powerful negative impact on those involved. Media coverage demonstrates the tension between the need to intervene to protect children and the danger of false reports. Newspaper and television stories about individual cases may stress one or the other interest, but are generally critical. Professionals find themselves vulnerable if children are left in situations of manifest danger, while at the same time accused of intrusiveness, excessive zeal and disregard for human rights of parents when they do intervene.

In 1984, following the notorious Jordan Minnesota case (Humphrey, 1985), a group called 'VOCAL' (Victims of Child Abuse Laws) was formed in the United States. Its members are largely people who claim to have been falsely accused of abuse. There are now chapters in almost every state which attempt to influence public opinion, legislators and judges. VOCAL holds an annual conference and offers advice and assistance to those defending against allegations of child abuse. For example, in an early VOCAL newsletter, an advertisement appeared for a group called the 'A-Team', an abbreviation for 'Annihilation Team' which they claimed was designed to help 'annihilate false accusations of abuse' by providing expert legal, medical and psychological consultation. Books such as *The Child Abuse Industry* (Pride, 1986) and *The Politics of Child Abuse* (Eberle, 1986) — not to be confused with Nigel Parton's book bearing the same title published in the UK — make claims that in America, police and social workers rip children away from their families without just cause, that the fight against child abuse is actually a witch hunt similar to that which occurred in Salem, Massachusetts, that true child abuse is being perpetrated by the professionals responsible for intervention, and that the actual extent of child abuse is in fact quite low. Paul and Shirley

Eberle, who describe themselves as objective, impartial investigative journalists, appeared on many popular US talk shows following publication of their book and received a good deal of attention in their criticism of the child protection system. However, it is interesting to note some of the other journalistic endeavours of these authors, which include the 'LA Star' and 'Finger' magazine. the 'LA Star' is an adult soft-core pornographic tabloid published in the Los Angeles area. 'Finger' was published in the 1970s and was a hard-core pornographic magazine, containing not only offensive adult pornography but letters, pictures, photographs and articles regarding sexual activity with children. The Eberles are listed as editors of and contributors to both publications, and in fact appeared naked and involved in sexual acts themselves in issues of 'Finger'.

The prosecutor's role

It is against this highly charged background that agencies have had to develop and maintain their response to child sexual abuse. The central focus of case investigation is determination of the truth. Indeed, it should be the aim of all evaluating professionals to do a fair, thorough and prompt job of ascertaining the truth.

The topic *Gathering Legal Evidence* raises for consideration the central question whether 'legal' evidence is special or different from evidence gathered by other professionals during the disclosure process, 'Legal' evidence suggests that which is admissible in court to prove whether a crime occurred, requiring that it be both relevant and reliable. However, prosecutors can and should consider all available evidence, whether ultimately admissible in court or not. In deciding whether to pursue a criminal child abuse case, the prosecutor must consider three key questions: (1) Did the crime actually occur, and if so, precisely what happened? (2) Is there a reasonable likelihood of proving the abuse in court and obtaining a conviction? (3) Assuming there is a reasonable likelihood of conviction, are there other reasons the case should not be pursued?

All evidence which is obtained should be presented to the prosecutor so that fair and intelligent decisions can be made. It is vitally important that all those who gather evidence communicate and co-operate with each other. Despite often strained relations between doctors and lawyers, and lawyers and social workers, effective handling of child abuse cases requires them to interact. Disagreements are still bound to occur, but better communication and understanding will allow professionals to continue to work together and respect one another. Multidisciplinary approaches involving therapists, police, prosecutors, and physicians are being pursued in many jurisdictions across the United States in attempts to improve the quality of investigations. Professionals involved in such efforts must first define and understand their respective roles, as well as procedures currently in use. They must exchange views regarding problems in the system and their ideas for change. The role and responsibility of prosecutors, while specific and separate, is nevertheless linked to others in the system.

Gathering legal evidence

Each one of the fifty American states has its own set of laws defining child abuse crimes and court procedures and these can vary widely from state to state. Even within individual states, procedures regarding case-handling may be completely different from county to county and community to community. For example, the Center for Child Protection in San Diego is an adjunct of the Children's Hospital where a group of seven paediatricians conduct medical examinations and more than fifteen mental health workers, some of whom are licensed clinical social workers, carry out forensic interviews as part of the process of gathering evidence. In each suspected child abuse case investigated by a law enforcement agency, there will usually be some disclosure that causes the child's transfer to the hospital setting where the social work interview takes place. This interview is almost always videotaped. The medical examination takes place under the auspices of both Child Protective Services and law enforcement, and police officers generally act as operators of the video camera during the interview.

Videotape has also been used in San Diego to record suspects as they view the videotape of the child's disclosure of abuse. While being photographed the suspect is often asked to explain the child's story. These videotapes become part of the package presented by the investigating police agency to the prosecutor, which also includes the statements of other witnesses and any physical or other evidence that has been gathered. The case is then assigned to a Deputy District Attorney who is responsible for all subsequent steps in the prosecution process, a practice termed 'vertical prosecution'. With the same prosecutor handling the case from beginning to end, a familiar face is established on whom the child and family can rely.

The San Diego Center for Child Protection has been in existence for a number of years. Other communities have systems for responding to child abuse cases which are often quite different from San Diego's. Some are far less organised while others are highly organised but with their own distinctive features. Not all communities videotape child or suspect interviews. Interviews and medical examinations often occur at different sites. In some areas, a separate neutral facility has been created at which children are interviewed and counselled. Specially trained police investigators are designated to conduct child interviews in many places. While specifics vary, the characteristic shared by all successful approaches is a method by which all involved agencies and professionals get together to develop a co-ordinated system which meets their particular needs and circumstances.

While working together, each profession must recognise both common and competing goals, and realise how their actions might be relevant to other parts of the system. For instance, mental health professionals assessing the placement and safety needs of a child will routinely talk to other family members and neighbours to determine if the child can be safely placed with relatives or not. In the course of their inquiries, they may discover facts which shed light on the alleged crime and should thus be shared with law enforcement for possible use in court.

The child's disclosures are often the single most important part of the evidence gathered. Therefore, the nature and method of disclosures should be carefully examined. Information related to the circumstances surrounding statements made by the child, as well as the specific content of those statements, will be significant to determining credibility and establishing the facts of the case.

In order to pursue criminal charges, the prosecutor must be able to establish a time frame in which the alleged abuse occurred. While children are often unable to pinpoint an exact date or time, their account may refer to other significant events in their lives such as birthdays, vacations, or particular place of residence. Relevant dates associated with such events can then be determined with information from other sources.

The child's statement may also contain other details which can be used to verify or refute the accuracy of the account. For example, the child may describe sexual abuse as always occurring in a particular room with a picture on the wall, bed in the corner and a blue blanket. During the investigation, the reliability of this information can be checked by taking photographs of the room. If appropriate, the picture, blanket and bed can even be seized and retained as potential exhibits for use in court. While these items do not prove that the child was abused, if the child's description of things related to the context of the abuse is correct, you have shown that he or she is capable of being an accurate, reliable and credible historian of related events. Corroboration, while no longer a formal legal requirement in the United States, is a practical necessity often satisfied by this type of evidence.

Any statements given by the suspect are extremely important to mental health and law enforcement personnel. While many suspects deny the allegation, they may furnish information which corroborates the child's account in some respects. In cases involving intrafamilial abuse and civil dependency proceedings, the child's placement will be influenced by the content of and reasons for the denial. In criminal court proceedings, if the defendant testifies and denies that abuse occurred, the prosecutor may still be able to demonstrate that the child was credible and told the truth about many factors and details surrounding the abuse. The defendant can often be forced to acknowledge under oath that, with the sole exception of the alleged acts of abuse, the child has told the truth. The following shows the kind of questions a prosecutor might ask to make this point:

Mr Smith, isn't it true that when your stepdaughter said she was in the first grade at the elementary school she was telling the truth?
Isn't it true that her teacher is Mrs Jones?
Isn't it true that when she comes home in the afternoon at four o'clock you are the sole caretaker?

When your stepdaughter told us those things here in court, she was telling the truth wasn't she?

Leading questions such as these are deemed proper and, in fact, are standard practice during cross-examination of any witness. Some have described leading questions as 'the most effective engine in the determination of truth'. Ironically, mental health professionals who seek leading questions during interviews of children are generally accused of programming them with suggestive questions and eliciting unreliable evidence. Yet, they may be necessary to help children overcome their fears and to deal with their conceptual immaturity. This issue illustrates some of the difficulties inherent in balancing the needs and practices of different disciplines in trying to achieve a sensible co-operative system for child abuse intervention. Most importantly, getting at the truth requires skill, care and objectivity.

All professionals involved in child abuse can benefit from special training. Lawyers in particular need specialised training to understand the types of evidence available in child abuse cases, and to be able to make effective presentations in court. Attendance at multidisciplinary conferences is increasing throughout the United States and is a valuable way of improving levels of skill. Ongoing contact with peers and colleagues, and experience in individual cases also leads to greater skill and sensitivity. Judges can be educated simply by being exposed to expert and lay testimony in court, especially when presented by a knowledgeable prosecutor. Everyone involved in the legal process must continue to learn.

Determining the truth

How does one determine if a child is telling the truth about an allegation of abuse? Recent studies have consistently shown that deliberately false reports of sexual abuse, especially from children, are rare. Yet we must still be concerned with the possibility that an account could be false. Unfortunately, this is not an easy task. A skillful, thorough, prompt and sensitive investigation is the best way.

Still, there are some who claim to have developed special methods of more easily evaluating the reliability of a child's statement. Two methods for assessing validity discussed with increased frequency in the United States recently are 'statement validity analysis' or 'statement reality analysis' and the 'sex abuse legitimacy scale'. 'Statement validity analysis' is a system which apparently originated in Germany and is now promoted by professionals in Canada and the United States. This method analyses features of the content of the child's statement. An early description of it appeared in the article 'Assessing Credibility,' by Farr and Yuille in the publication *Preventing Sexual Abuse* (1988). The 'Sex Abuse Legitimacy Scale' is described by Richard Gardner in his book, *The Parental Alienation Syndrome and the Differentiation Between Fabricated and Genuine Child Sex Abuse* (1987). Gardner and others promote this scale as a way of differentiating between fabricated and genuine child sex abuse. It utilises a series of 'yes' or 'no' questions, with points given for every 'yes' answer. The points are totalled and the resulting score is supposed to indicate whether or not it is likely abuse occurred. While all professionals involved in child abuse investigation naturally welcome improved techniques which promise to reduce the difficulty and complexity of child abuse cases, these systems should be viewed with careful skepticism. Not only are they new to America and its court system, they are not (to the knowledge of these authors) empirically based or validated. They are, however, becoming more popular with defence attorneys representing those accused of abuse, and thus prosecutors must become familiar with their weaknesses.

The initial interview

In some parts of the United States, prosecutors are directly involved in the initial investigative interview with the child. Such is the case in Seattle in Washington State where the assigned police investigator and social worker from Children's Protective Services meet with the child in a special interview room in the prosecutor's office. Together with the prosecutor assigned to the case, they decide who among them would be best to talk to the child. As in San Diego, cases are vertically prosecuted and this prosecutor will continue to handle all aspects of the case. During the interview, the interviewer attempts to elicit the information all three need. The others view the interview behind a one-way mirror and, before concluding, consult with the interviewer about the need for any additional queries. Thereafter, they discuss with one another the next steps in the investigation. This system has been in use in Seattle for a number of years and works quite well for them, with the rate of criminal prosecution relatively high.

Other approaches in which the prosecutor is not directly involved in the initial investigative interview are probably more common in other jurisdictions. Still, the prosecutor can be and often is consulted beforehand by those who will be conducting the interview to discuss the kind of information that will be helpful in court. In addition, the interviewer needs to be aware of the ways in which interview techniques can be challenged by the defence on the witness stand. A procedure for initial investigative interviews which is developed with input from the prosecutor is more likely to withstand attack.

Since most children do not reveal the full extent of abuse in a single interview, the investigative procedure should allow for the possibility of talking to the child more than once. If at all possible, the same person should interview the child each time. Any other statements about the abuse made by the child should be ascertained and documented. Usually a case will be brought to the attention of the authorities as the result of a disclosure to someone, such as a parent or trusted friend. The specific facts revealed by the child to other people may not always be admissible at trial, but more often than not, there are ways of presenting before the jury at least some of the specifics of the content or circumstances of these revelations, which can prove to be extremely important.

The child's statement

The child's statement is generally the starting point for any investigation and one of the most crucial pieces of evidence in the case. Information in the child's statement must be carefully evaluated since it will often serve as the primary basis for making initial decisions about the risk of further harm and the kind of protection needed for the child, about whether or not a suspect should be arrested and incarcerated, about whether other potential victims should be interviewed, about whether or not there are other potential offenders, and about what kind of physical, medical or other evidence should be sought. It will also suggest other potential witnesses and ways to approach and obtain statements from suspects. Prosecutors will also rely on the child's statement to determine whether to file a criminal case, and what, if any, plea offer to make. It will also influence the kind of sentence the prosecutor is willing to recommend and the likelihood of obtaining a conviction. Thus, input from prosecutors can and should be sought in determining how investigative interviews of children will be conducted.

Corroborating the child's statement

Corroboration refers to evidence which supports a witness's testimony. Since child sexual abuse is a crime of secrecy, eye witnesses are rare and there is unlikely to be direct corroboration of the molestation itself. Despite recent advances in scientific knowledge, medical examinations will rarely detect definite evidence of sexual abuse. Hence, the victim's account will generally provide the most direct evidence of abuse.

Information is gathered by doctors for the purpose of providing diagnosis and treatment, by social workers for the purpose of securing protection and appropriate placement of the child, and by law enforcement officers for the purpose of determining whether the crime occurred. Some of this information will be evidence admissible in a court of law which will assist the fact finder in deciding what happened and determining the child's credibility. Therefore, it can be useful to begin an interview by building rapport with the child and asking about family history. Information provided by the child can be verified and then used in court to demonstrate that the child is an accurate historian regarding siblings, parents and place of residence, for example. It can then be argued that children who accurately report this kind of information should be considered equally accurate when describing the abuse experience.

Other information gathered during the interview can lead to corroborative evidence. Legally, corroboration is not required in order to prosecute any criminal case in the United States, including child abuse. This is in contrast to the law in Scotland, where corroboration is required for every crime. Corroboration is, however, viewed as a practical necessity by American prosecutors who are unlikely to present any criminal child sexual abuse case without calling other witnesses in addition to the child. Generally, such witnesses do not offer testimony which proves that a child was abused, but testify about matters which indirectly corroborate portions of the child's statement.

A good investigation will often turn up other sources of corroborative evidence. If written communications have passed between the offender and child, they should be obtained since they may become important items of evidence which corroborate a child's account. Some child molesters take photographs of their victims or collect photographs of other children. These photographs may show children with clothes, without clothes or possibly involved in sexual activity. Offenders may also possess other types of pornography or sexually explicit material which indicate their sexual orientation, or were used to encourage children to participate in sexual activity. These are just a few examples of potential types of additional evidence and illustrate the importance of conducting timely searches for physical evidence and of thoroughly investigating the alleged perpetrator. Such evidence will assist the prosecutor in determining whether or not abuse occurred and often will also be admissible at trial to help the judge and jury.

Preparing the child for court

Following interviews with the child and the gathering of other relevant evidence, the prosecutor will determine whether criminal charges should be pursued. A majority of the filed cases result in guilty pleas without being tried. Hence, relatively few children are actually required to testify in criminal trials. However, predicting which cases will plead can be difficult and the prosecutor must always be prepared for the possibility of a trial. Defendants are more likely to plead guilty when they know the prosecutor is well prepared and thus more likely to present a strong cases.

Previously collected evidence must be presented as completely and understandably as possible to the trier of fact. It is not enough to have interviewed the child to ascertain details of the abuse; in most trials the child must be able effectively to communicate the facts in court. This does not happen by simply bringing the child to the courthouse on the day of trial and expecting convincing testimony. A great deal of work and attention are required of the prosecutor and other professionals specifically to prepare the child.

The goal in preparing children for court is to decrease unnecessary anxiety and thus increase the accuracy and completeness of their testimony. The familiar is far less frightening than the unknown and the more a child knows about what to expect in court, the more comfortable he or she will be. Children can be familiarized with the court process in a number of ways. In some areas, 'court schools' have been instituted where small groups of children are taught about court. A variety of techniques is employed, including the use of model courtrooms, role playing, and discussion of court procedures. Actual testimony is not rehearsed and specific information about the alleged abuse of the children involved is not shared. The point is to make the child more aware of and comfortable with the courtroom environment. Parents attend some sessions separately to discuss their concerns and become educated about the court process as well.

'Court schools' are a recent innovation in the United States but are possible only where adequate numbers of pending cases exist. Individual preparation of children is always possible and should always be done. Courtroom visits ought to be part of this process. Before trial, a child can be taken to a courtroom where another case is being heard to see what is going on and realize that actual trials are not as dramatic as appears on the television or in movies. In addition, arrangements can be made with court staff to take a child into an empty courtroom where he or she can sit in the witness chair, and practise answering some preliminary questions similar to those which are likely to be asked at the beginning of actual testimony. The child can see where participants will be located in the courtroom, and the prosecutor can assess how best to assure that the child will be comfortable and able to be heard during trial. To the extent possible, the child should be prepared for cross-examination and potentially confusing courtroom behaviour. For example, the process by which objections are raised and ruled on should be explained in a way children can understand. They should be told that sometimes attorneys will argue with each other and the judge will decide what to do, and that this does not mean the child is in trouble or has done something wrong. It should be emphasized that the most important thing for the child to remember is to tell the truth. Some prosecutors provide children with simple written 'rules of court' which can even be carried into the courtroom — 1. Be polite. 2. Answer the questions. 3. Tell the truth.

Judges have a great deal of discretion regarding the conduct of proceedings in the courtroom. Prosecutors should not hesitate to ask judges to allow reasonable modifications of the courtroom setting to make children more comfortable. For instance, the prosecutor might request that a child be allowed to sit down rather than stand in the witness box. This would not violate any right of the defendant but might be resisted because it goes against tradition. However, tradition should not stand in the way of minor concessions to increase a child's comfort. Other measures can put children at ease, such as more frequent breaks to allow them to go to the bathroom or fetch a drink of water. Their testimony can be scheduled at a time of day that avoids regular nap and meal times. These and other options should be considered and brought to the attention of judges. Because of natural reluctance to change traditional practices, there may not be immediate change, but experience in the United States has shown that change begins when one judge accommodates a child in the courtroom in a way which is still fair to the defendant, and other judges follow. Experienced and successful prosecutors constantly look for innovative ways to improve the truth seeking process. By sharing information about what works to help children, the court system can be a place where they experience justice.

The role of the mental health professional

Mental health professionals have two distinct roles in child sexual abuse cases. The first is diagnostic: they can assist those with less experience, such as judges and lawyers, in recognising features of the child's behaviour which may indicate whether the child was in fact molested. But to the prosecutor, perhaps an even more important role is that of reminding adults that children are indeed children. Despite the experience of many jurors, judges and lawyers as parents, a child walking into the pristine courtroom environment is all too often expected to act like an adult and answer questions like an adult. Mental health experts can be used to explain developmental levels and cognitive skills of children at various ages. Judges and juries are then better able to evaluate a child's understanding of and answers to complicated or confusing questions. Reminding participants of the child's relative immaturity and different cognitive skills helps them more accurately to judge the child's credibility, accuracy and reliability.

The concepts of establishing responsibility and imposing punishment are two distinct though inter-related functions of the criminal justice response to child abuse cases. Maximizing protection of children in the community is the most important responsibility of the prosecutor and requires sensitivity to the potential negative impact of the court system on children. The need for punishment must be balanced together with the child's best interest. Professionals must work together to seek a resolution which acknowledges what happened to the child, protects the child from further abuse, and minimizes trauma experienced in the intervention process.

REFERENCES

Eberle, P. and Eberle, S. (1986) *The Politics of Child Abuse.* Secaucus, N.J.: Lyle Stuart.

Farr, V. L. and Yuille, J. C. (1988) 'Assessing Credibility', *Preventing Sexual Abuse,* Vol. 1, No. 1, Winter.

Gardner, R. (1987) 'Sex Abuse Legitimacy Scale', in *The Parental Alienation Syndrome and the Differentiation between Fabricated and Genuine Child Sex Abuse.* Creative Therapeutics.

Hechler, D. (1988) *The Battle and the Backlash: The Child Sexual Abuse War.* Lexington, Mass.: Lexington Books.

Humphrey, H. H. (1985) *Report on Scott County Investigation.* Minnesota Attorney General, 111, Feb. 12.

Pride, Mary (1986) *The Child Abuse Industry.* West Chester, Illinois: Crossway Books.

6

THE ENGLISH LEGAL SYSTEM

JOHN R. SPENCER

THE FIRST PART of this chapter will briefly describe the different procedures the English legal system provides for dealing with suspected cases of child sexual abuse, and the courts in which they operate. The second part will address the matter of evidence: when an allegation of sexual abuse is disputed how do the various courts go about deciding whether or not it happened? Do they listen to what the child has to say about it, and if so, what weight do they place on the child's account?

COURTS AND COURT PROCEEDINGS

In England, as elsewhere, there is a major division between civil and criminal proceedings. Criminal proceedings — prosecutions — are brought with the main object of punishing the offender. Civil proceedings are brought to determine who is to have custody of the child, who may visit him or her, and related matters. In theory, civil and criminal proceedings are brought by different people and are independent of one another. Thus difficult problems can arise when both are taking place at the same time. For example, where a father is being prosecuted for abusing his daughter, whom the local authority are also trying to remove from his custody by means of care proceedings, can he have the care proceedings stayed pending the outcome of the prosecution? (No, according to *R.* v. *Inner London Juvenile Court ex pte G* [1988] FCR 316.) In practice the authorities usually co-operate with one another and such conflicts are generally avoided.

In criminal proceedings an allegation that a child has been abused must be proved beyond reasonable doubt. In civil proceedings there was some uncertainty about the standard of proof required, but this was resolved earlier this year when the Court of Appeal ruled that abuse was proved for the purpose of civil proceedings where it was shown 'on the balance of probabilities': that is, where the court is convinced that the child was more probably abused than not (*H.* v. *H.; K.* v. *K.* [1989] 3 WLR 933). The lower standard of proof in civil cases, plus the fact that a failure of a civil court to act on a well-founded allegation of child abuse may involve particular risks for the child, mean that civil courts can and do pronounce people guilty of child abuse whom the criminal courts have earlier acquitted. This is logical enough, although it is obviously a source of bitterness to those who discover their acquittal does not mean that they have been 'cleared', as they are inclined to believe; as in *re G.* [1988] FCR 440, where a stepfather who had been acquitted of injuring his 8-year-old stepdaughter was found to have committed the injury in subsequent wardship proceedings.

In England, prosecutions used to be conducted by the police. In 1986 this was changed, and the position is now that the police begin a prosecution, and then hand over the job of conducting it to an independent body called the Crown Prosecution Service. This is an organisation which is modelled, but only very loosely, on the Scottish system of procurators fiscal. A striking feature of the English criminal justice system, which was retained when the Crown Prosecution Service was set up, is the right of any private person to start a prosecution. Although the vast majority of prosecutions for sexual offences against children are begun by the police, there are indeed some private prosecutions — usually in cases where the police or the Crown Prosecution Service have refused to act. In 1986-87 there was a much-publicised case where the public authorities refused to prosecute a doctor for raping a girl of eight, and her mother then brought a private prosecution, financed by the *Sun.* (The prosecution was unsuccessful, and the final result was that the newspaper was punished for contempt of court for publishing matter calculated to influence the outcome of the case: see *A.-G.* v. *News Group Newspapers* [1989] QB 110.)

As far as civil proceedings are concerned the picture is a complex one, because nearly everything is about to change. Following an avalanche of official reports — the DHSS Review of Child Care Law in 1985, the Government White Paper on the Law on Child Care and Family Services in 1987, the Report of the Cleveland Inquiry in 1987, and the Law Commission's Review of Child Law, Guardianship and Custody in 1988 — Parliament has now recast and codified this area of the law in the Children Act 1989 (1989 ch. 41; see White Carr and Lowe 1990). Although this Act received the Royal Assent on 16 November 1989, it will be many months before it comes fully into force — and much longer before it is possible to say how the changes are working. For the moment, we must look at both the old law and the new.

Before examining the rules in detail, two major aims of the Children Act 1989 should be noted. The first is to make the law simpler and more consistent. In the past, new procedures have been created for new problems with little consideration of how they would fit into the general picture. The result was an unwieldly tangle of different remedies, with the added complication of some being available in one type of court but unavailable in another. The Children Act 1989 introduces a regime under which the number of different procedures is reduced, the scope of each is widened, and there are fewer restrictive rules about which court can do what. A second major aim is to make all the available procedures subject to the same set of overriding principles. Section 1 (1) of the 1989 Act says:

> 'When a court determines any question with respect to —
> (a) the upbringing of a child; or
> (b) the administration of a child's property or the application of any income arising from it,
> the child's welfare shall be the court's paramount consideration.'

The rest of the section elaborates this principle, itemising the matters which the court must always consider, and stressing that 'any delay in determining the matter is likely to prejudice the welfare of the child'.

In principle, a child sexual abuse case can result in any or all of four different types of civil proceedings.

Emergency protection

To protect a child in cases of emergency there are procedures for removing the child quickly from a setting where he or she is in immediate and serious danger. For many years the machinery in England has been the 'place of safety order' (or 'PSO'), under which a magistrate can make an order compulsorily removing a child to a 'place of safety'.

The PSO had (and while it lasts, still has) a number of serious defects. First, there is its duration. PSOs are granted *ex parte*, which means that the parents need not be notified of the proceedings or given the chance to oppose them. This is sensible enough, but the legislation gives the court power to make a PSO for a period of up to 28 days — a fearful length of time if the order can be made when the parents have no opportunity to oppose it. Secondly, there is the question of when one can be made. Although the idea is that they are for use in emergencies only, the legislation fails to make this plain, and they can and occasionally have been granted in less than urgent cases. Thirdly, the legislation is very vague as to what the legal effects of a PSO are. When one is made, can the child be lawfully subjected to a medical examination? Or a psychiatric examination? Can the parents be lawfully denied access to their child? Fourthly, there is the question of who is entitled to apply for one. Any person may apply for a PSO (although in practice the usual applicant is a social worker), and in England there is no official like the reporter to the children's panel in Scotland whose job it is to oversee the making of orders, and to make sure they are not applied for in unsuitable cases.

Part V of the Children Act 1989 answers the first three of these criticisms. The 'place of safety order' becomes an 'emergency protection order' — hereafter called an 'EPO', and its maximum period is eight days only — although it may be extended, once only, for a further seven days. The new order is available only when 'there is reasonable cause to believe that the child is likely to suffer significant harm' unless the order is made. Some of the doubts about the effect of orders are clarified; the court which makes the EPO is given the power to make orders about the child's contact with parents and others, and about medical or psychiatric examinations. However, the Act does not really deal with the fourth problem — or perceived problem; that of applications being made in unsuitable cases by over-zealous people. At one stage the Lord Chancellor's Department floated the idea of creating a 'Child Protection Officer' to scrutinise applications, but there was little support for this, and doubt about whether enough people of the right calibre could be recruited. In the end this idea was dropped.

In the past, problems have arisen where social workers suspected that a child had been abused, and would have liked to have him or her medically or psychiatrically examined to see if their fears were correct, but the parents refused to allow this. It cannot be done without obtaining a place of safety order, taking the child into care, or making the child a ward of court — and the evidence necessary for these proceedings cannot be obtained unless there is an examination. With the conditions for emergency protection being tightened up considerably, and access to wardship reduced (see below), it was thought that this problem would recur more frequently in future. To meet the problem, the Children Act 1989 creates a new kind of measure called the 'child assessment order', under which those who have care of the child can be required to allow the child to be assessed or examined. By section 43 (1), this order may be made where

> '(a) the applicant has reasonable cause to suspect that the child is suffering, or is likely to suffer, significant harm;
>
> (b) an assessment of the state of the child's health or development, or of the way in which he has been treated, is required to enable that applicant to determine whether or not the child is suffering, or is likely to suffer, significant harm;
>
> (c) it is unlikely that such an assessment will be made, or be satisfactory, in the absence of an order under this section.'

As a supplement to the place of safety order, the police have long had a statutory power to remove a child to a place of safety in emergency. Under the Children Act 1989 this power is retained: but the period for which a child may be detained under this procedure is reduced from eight days to 72 hours.

Care proceedings

Care proceedings are civil proceedings brought by the public authorities in order to remove a child from the parents' custody and to place the child in local authority care. At present, the grounds upon which the court can make a care order are set out in the Child and Young Persons Act 1969 s. 1 (2). They are long and complicated, but still contrive to leave a number of well-known loopholes — mainly concerning children who are not in danger at present but are likely to become so. Under the Children Act 1989 the grounds for making care orders are made much simpler and more comprehensive. By section 31 (2)

> 'A court may only make a care . . . order if it is satisfied —
>
> (a) that the child concerned is suffering, or is likely to suffer, significant harm; and
>
> (b) that harm, or the likelihood of harm, is attributable to (i) the care given to the child, or likely to be given to him if the order were not made, not being what it would be reasonable to expect a parent to give to him; or (ii) the child's being beyond parental control.'

Custody proceedings

This is the name usually given to the various types of civil proceedings which may be brought to determine disputes between parents and others about who shall have custody of children or access to them. As the law stands, custody disputes in England may come before the courts under any one of four different sets of statutory procedures, depending on whether the dispute arises following a divorce or a separation, and who is disputing for custody with whom. In addition there is a further set of statutory provisions to contend with if someone wishes not merely to have custody of the child, but to adopt.

Part II of the Children Act 1989 effects a drastic and much-needed simplification. A distinct set of rules is retained for adoption, but apart from this a standard procedure is created for dealing with such questions irrespective of the context or court in which the custody dispute arose. Even more radically, the Act changes the concepts with which the courts must work. Heretofore there has existed a concept of 'custody', which is a composite collection of rights over a child, which the court awards to one parent or the other as a bunch, and 'access', which is the right to see the child from time to time. In the new Act these terms are abandoned. Under the Act, there is a new concept of 'parental responsibility', which section 3 (1) defines as 'all the rights, duties, powers, responsibilities and authority which by law a parent of a child has in relation to the child and his property'. This every parent has, and will usually retain, whatever the outcome of the dispute. But the operation of 'parental responsibility' may be limited by the court making any of the orders contained in section 8: 'contact orders' (determining who shall and shall not have contact with the child), 'prohibited steps orders' (prohibiting certain things being done without the consent of the court), 'residence orders' (determining who the child shall live with), and 'specific issue orders' (giving directions about any other specific question arising in connection with parental responsibility).

Wardship

It is possible for any person to apply to the High Court to have a child made a 'ward of court', and where the child is made a ward, custody of the child then vests in the High Court, with the consequence that a High Court Judge must then supervise and authorise every major step that is taken in the child's life. Wardship is a very ancient institution. It began life as a remedy concerned with the property of rich orphans, and changed its function over the years so that it is now a protective measure for children generally. Wardship jurisdiction is open-ended: there are no limits on the types of case where a child may be made a ward, and few if any limits on the judge's powers when a child has been made one. Thus until recently wardship has been widely resorted to when, for technical reasons, care proceedings were not available. And as the powers of the judge in wardship trump those of the lower courts in care proceedings and custody disputes, wardship is often used as a means of challenging decisions in custody or care proceedings where there is no right of appeal as such, or where there is a regular right of appeal but an appeal is unlikely to succeed. (Although the scope of using wardship as a means of appealing against the outcome of care proceedings was much cut down by the House of Lords decision in *A.* v. *Liverpool City Council* [1982] AC 363, which held that the wardship was not generally available to parents as a means of challenging care proceedings in which their children had been taken away from them.)

The judges of the High Court Family Division are able and experienced people, and wardship has long provided a useful method for handling the really difficult civil cases which would tax the powers of the lower courts. On the other hand, like all High Court proceedings it is expensive, and its ever-widening use in recent years has not pleased the Treasury which must find the funds for legal aid; nor has it pleased the Lord Chancellor's Department, because the High Court, where wardships are dealt with, is considerably overworked. When the Children Bill was drawn up, a high-level policy decision was therefore taken to make wardship less readily available. This has been achieved by section 100 of the Children Act, which limits the use of wardship by local authorities. The Government justified this by saying that as the deficiencies in care proceedings would be cured by earlier sections of the Act, local authorities would no longer need to use wardship. Time will tell if this argument was correct.

The court system

If the civil procedures are simple to explain, the same is not true of the court system in which they operate. In principle the pattern of first-instance courts in England is simple enough. There are two levels of first-instance criminal court: magistrates' courts for the less important work and the Crown Court for the weighty cases. And there are two levels of first-instance civil court: the County Court for the less important civil cases, and the High Court (with its specialist Family Division) for the bigger and more important matters. What makes matters complicated is the surprising fact that a range of civil matters affecting children are handled by the magistrates' courts, although these are primarily courts for criminal cases. The origin of this is historical. The office of justice of the peace (alias magistrate) is ancient and dates from before the County Courts were created. In the old days the justices of the peace were seen as a useful dumping ground for civil law matters too trivial for the High Court, and part of this civil jurisdiction still remains. Thus in addition to trying minor criminal cases the magistrates issue licences for alehouses, order the destruction of dangerous dogs, and order verminous persons to be compulsorily deloused. Their residual civil jurisdiction includes a number of matters relating to children. Hence it is the magistrates who make place of safety orders, and, as an off-shoot of their jurisdiction to try juvenile crime, it is the magistrates who deal with care proceedings. As a development of their ancient power to make deserting husbands support their families the magistrates also acquired power to decide certain custody and access disputes arising from separation rather than divorce. A map of the courts that have jurisdiction over the various types of civil and criminal proceedings that can arise in a case of child abuse is therefore very complicated and it gets even more complicated when we look at the rights of appeal (figure 1).

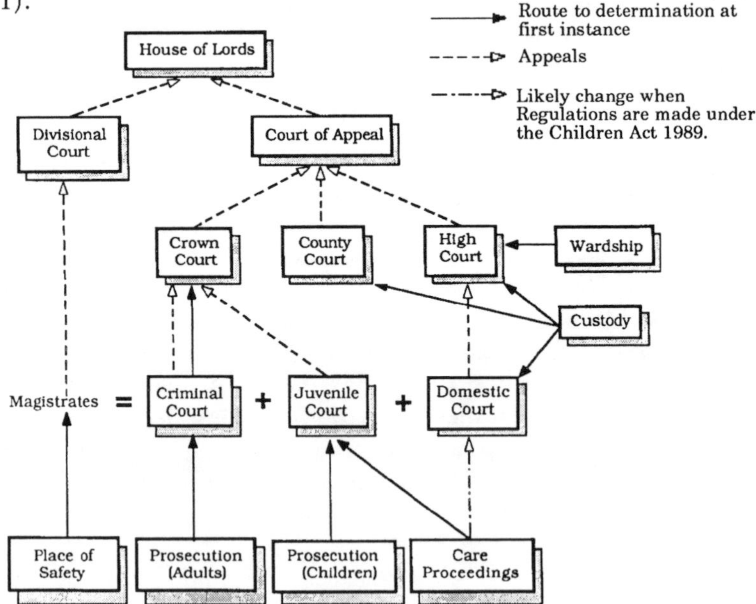

Figure 1: Courts having jurisdiction over various types of civil and criminal proceedings

This chaotic non-system has some serious drawbacks. One is that the same child abuse case can easily result in proceedings in several courts at once — not only where there is a prosecution as well as civil proceedings, but even where all the proceedings are civil. This causes needless confusion, delay and expense. Professor Brenda Hoggett gives a hypothetical example involving five different types of court, and including three separate juvenile courts, the High court (twice), the Crown Court, and three separate county courts (Hoggett, 1986). Another problem is inadequate expertise. Instead of all matters concerning the care and custody of children being handled by one set of courts which are able to acquire specialist knowledge, they are distributed in little bits among a range of courts, some of which are mainly concerned with other matters. Particular difficulties occur in the magistrates' courts, where the judges are laymen whose experience of all legal matters is limited. Although magistrates courts must now use panels of justices with special training to deal with custody and care proceedings, it is still the case that any one of our 24,000 magistrates can make a place of safety order, and such orders are sometimes made by magistrates who have never made one before and who are never likely to make one again. The range of courts involved in family cases also causes needless complications over the rules of evidence. England once had a single unified law of evidence for both civil and criminal proceedings, but in 1968 the Civil Evidence Act was passed, which reformed the law of evidence in civil proceedings, and as a result we have in England two sets of legal rules, one for civil and one for criminal evidence. This raises the question: which set applies when the criminal courts are hearing civil proceedings involving children? Surprisingly, the Civil Evidence Act 1968 does not apply to magistrates' courts, and in principle the magistrates courts operate under the rules of criminal evidence, even when engaged on civil proceedings. But in practice they bend the rules of criminal evidence in civil cases, with a certain amount of encouragement from the appeal courts above them. So we have not two but three sets of rules of evidence: civil evidence, criminal evidence, and a mongrel version for the use of the magistrates' courts when handling civil proceedings.

This messy structure is quite indefensible, and most people agree that there ought to be a single unified family court to deal with civil cases. In 1974 the idea was put forward by the Finer Committee on One Parent Families. Since then a pressure group called the Family Courts Campaign has been formed to fight for it, and all the political parties seem to have been converted to the idea. There are some people who would go even further and also give the new family court jurisdiction over criminal proceedings involving children (either as defendant or as victim). But this is a minority view. Most people feel that it would be politically impossible to remove prosecutions for child sexual abuse from the ordinary criminal courts, where the defendant has the protection (or perceived protection) of a right to jury trial and a rigid system of evidence. And one of the criticisms of the present system is that civil proceedings in the magistrates' courts carry an unpleasant stigma, because magistrates are associated in the public mind with criminals and crime.

Obviously this criticism could not be met by a Family Court that was criminal as well as civil.

If the case for a unified Family Court is so strong, why have we not got one already? In the past successive Governments resisted the idea on grounds of cost. More recently the Government has realised that a Family Court does not necessarily require a whole new set of courtrooms and judges, which would be very expensive, but could be achieved by restructuring what we have already, which would be comparatively cheap. On these terms, both Lord Mackay, the Lord Chancellor, and his predecessor, Lord Hailsham, have expressed sympathy for the idea. The line the Lord Chancellor has taken, however, is that the first step is to reform the law. When we have decided what the most suitable procedures are, and made a uniform set of them available to all the existing courts that handle family matters, the time will have come to alter the structure of the courts. With the Children Act 1989 the first step has been taken, and the second step now seems likely to follow.

In England, unlike the USA, there is no legal requirement on anyone to report a suspected case of child abuse. The DHSS Review of Child Care Law examined the idea in 1985 and came out against it. But section 47 of the Children Act — building on a duty that already exists under the Children and Young Persons Act 1969 — imposes on local authorities the duty to make enquiries wherever they have 'reasonable ground to suspect that a child who lives, or is found, in their area is suffering, or is likely to suffer, significant harm'. This is only one of a number of duties which are imposed upon local authorities by the Act; and the question that those who work for local authorities are now asking is whether they will be given any extra funds to enable them to carry these duties out.

THE EVIDENCE OF CHILDREN

The law governing children's evidence has been the subject of much recent criticism in England. As a result, a number of important changes have already been made by statute, and further changes seem likely to follow the report of the Home Office Advisory Group on Video Evidence — otherwise known as the Pigot Committee — which was published in December 1989.

There is no doubt that changes are needed. A child who has been beaten or sexually abused knows better than anyone else who did it and what it was they did, and one would expect any court dealing with a child abuse case to listen to the child's version of events. Yet in their traditional form several English rules of evidence usually combine to make sure that the child's account is kept from the court, or if it is heard, that no notice is taken of it. The usual result of this is that for want of evidence guilty persons go wrongly free. But it can also cause the conviction of the innocent. In the leading case of *Sparks* v. *R.* [1964] AC 964 a white man was prosecuted for indecently assaulting a little girl of three, and the courts ruled that he could not call evidence that after the attack she had described her attacker as black!

The traditional restrictive rules have now been modified in civil proceedings; but in criminal proceedings they are still largely in force. This section of the chapter will be concerned mainly with the rules of criminal evidence, but it will also aim to explain how the rules in civil proceedings now differ.

The competency requirement

At one time the courts seem to have been willing to listen to child witnesses of any age in sexual abuse cases, and also to accept hearsay accounts from others who had heard the child's account. In the late seventeenth century, Chief Justice Sir Matthew Hale wrote this in his *Pleas of the Crown.*

> 'But if it be an infant of such tender years, that in point of discretion the court sees it unfit to swear her, yet I think she ought to be heard without oath to give the court information, tho singly of itself it ought not to move the jury to convict the offender, nor is it in itself a sufficient testimony, because not upon oath, without concurrence of other proofs, that may render the thing probable; and my reasons are, (i) The nature of the offense, which is most times secret, and no other testimony can be had of the very doing of the fact, but the party upon whom it is committed, tho there may be other concurrent proofs of the fact when it is done. (ii) Because if the child complain presently of the wrong done to her to the mother or other relations, their evidence upon oath shall be taken, yet it is but a narrative of what the child told them without oath, and there is much more reason for the court to hear the relation of the child herself, than to receive it at second-hand from those, that swear they heard, or otherwise represented at the second-hand, than when it was first delivered.'

But in the late eighteenth century this changed. In *Brasier* (1779) 1 Leach 199, East P.C. 441, it was held, first, that no child may give evidence unless he or she has sufficient understanding to swear an oath, and secondly, that no one may give any evidence of what he or she said about the incident except the child herself or himself when giving sworn evidence. To give sworn evidence the child had to 'understand the nature of an oath', which in those days meant that the child had to believe he or she would go to Hell for ever if he or she failed to tell the truth in court. This rule was fearfully restrictive in child abuse cases—despite the practice which then grew up of adjourning the proceedings for a crash-course in religious instruction, something which gave the hapless child an eternity in Hell to occupy his mind, in addition to the trauma of abuse and having to give evidence about it. In 1885, after a big public agitation led by what is now the NSPCC, *Brasier* was partially reversed by a statute, still in force as section 38 of the Children and Young Persons Act 1933, permitting a child to give unsworn evidence in criminal proceedings 'if, in the opinion of the court, he is possessed of sufficient intelligence to justify the reception of the evidence, and he understands the duty of speaking the truth'.

Since then, two developments have taken place. First, in *Wallwork* (1958) 42 CrApR 153 the courts glossed this section by ruling that no child should be called as a witness when aged 5 or under. 'The court deprecates the calling of a child of this age as a witness,' said Lord Goddard CJ, '. . . A jury could not attach any value to the evidence of a child of five; it is ridiculous to suppose they could.' Secondly, in *Hayes* [1977] 1 WLR 234 the Court of Appeal lowered the threshold of knowledge required for a child to give evidence on oath. Under this decision a child may give sworn evidence if he or she appreciates the solemnity of the occasion and the extra importance of telling the truth in a court of law: the child need no longer believe in Hell, or even have heard of God. The result is that there is now little real difference between the requirements for a child to give sworn and unsworn testimony.

The requirement that a child witness should have an understanding of 'duty' and 'truth' before his or her word is acceptable as evidence undoubtedly deprives the court of a lot of useful information. The combined effect of the 'understands the duty to tell the truth' requirement in section 38 and the decision in *Wallwork* is that in England one may scarcely ever call a child as a witness under the age of 6, and rarely call one much under the age of 8. (This is in sharp contrast with the position in Scotland, where despite the existence of a competency requirement the courts are nevertheless willing to listen to children down to the age of 3 or 4.) Of course, if the child cannot give evidence in court, the hearsay rule prevents anyone else such as a parent, or a doctor or policeman from repeating what the child said out of court.

If a child is too immature to understand or explain the difference between truth and falsehood, common sense suggests that we should be cautious in accepting what the child says. But it does not suggest that we should simply refuse to listen to the child, particularly if he or she is alleged to be the victim of an offence and the only witness except for the offender. Common sense is reinforced by psychological research suggesting that there is little relationship between a child's understanding of the difference between truth and falsehood and the ability to give reliable answers (Goodman, Aman and Hirschman, 1987).

In England, the competency requirement is now under serious attack (Spencer and Flin 1990, chapter 4). There was an unsuccessful attempt to abolish it when what is now the Criminal Justice Act 1988 was before Parliament. In December 1989, its abolition was recommended by the Pigot Committee. There are also signs that the courts are losing patience with it: *Wallwork* was restrictively interpreted in the recent case of *B* (*The Times*, 1 March 1990).

Section 38 of the Children and Young Persons Act 1933 applies only to criminal proceedings. For many years this had the strange result that if a child was to give evidence in civil proceedings he or she had to satisfy the theoretically more stringent competency requirement for giving evidence on oath. In practice, the problems to which this might have given rise were usually circumvented by the civil courts being willing to bend the hearsay rule (see below) and to allow adults to repeat to the court what the child had told them. In 1989 the Court of Appeal criticised this anomaly in *H.* v. *H.*; *K.* v. *K.* [1989] 3 WLR 933, and the Government responded by moving a last-minute amendment to the Children Bill. By what rapidly became section 96 (1) and (2) of the Children Act 1989, civil courts will be able to receive the unsworn evidence of children on the same basis as it is received in criminal proceedings. These provisions will come into force when the Lord Chancellor makes an order, which he is expected to do shortly.

Open court — 'live video link', alias closed-circuit television

The second thing that prevents the court listening to child witnesses is the rule that in a criminal case the child, like an adult, is required to testify in open court. (In civil cases things are different. If a child gives evidence in care proceedings, the magistrates have power to remove any person whose presence is likely to upset him.) Experience shows that one of the things which an assaulted child fears most about giving evidence is being confronted with the person who attacked or abused the child. The worse the incident the greater the reluctance of the child to face the attacker, and the worse the child is likely to perform in court.

In an attempt to meet this problem, the Government caused Parliament to pass section 32 of the Criminal Justice Act 1988, which makes it possible for children under the age of 14 to give evidence to the court from an adjoining room by means of a live closed-circuit television link — a scheme which is used in a number of jurisdictions in the U.S.A. This provision is now in force, and for over a year live video links have been in experimental use in a number of Crown Courts in England (Mackay 1990). When this provision was enacted, and since, many different views have been expressed about the value of the video-link (Spencer and Flin, 1990). How it works in practice time will shortly tell. Even at this stage, however, it is possible to point to several structural defects in the scheme contained in section 32 of the Criminal Justice Act.

The first is that the provision is limited to trials for offences of sex and violence. What sensible reason could there possibly be for restricting the live-link to trials for certain defined offences? Surely it should be available in any case, sex, violence or otherwise, where a young child may be able to give useful evidence, but may be afraid to do so in open court; a trial of an estranged parent for attempting to burn down the family home, for example, or of a Fagin-esque adult who has organised a group of children to steal.

A second and bigger objection is that it only applies to trials on indictment. Thus it is not available in the magistrates' courts. The magistrates' courts are not only the place where the less serious offences are tried: they are also the point at which Crown Court cases enter the system. Even the most serious child sexual abuse cases start off with 'committal proceedings', which are a preliminary hearing in the magistrates' courts, where the magistrates examine the prosecution evidence and decide whether the case is worth sending to the Crown Court for trial. They usually do this by looking at written statements from the witnesses, but the defendant may insist on the prosecution producing their witnesses so that he or she can cross-examine them at that stage of the proceedings. It is said that defendants in child abuse cases sometimes do this, or threaten to do it, simply to put pressure on prosecutors to drop the case in the interests of the child. Because the 'live link' proposal is not available in the magistrates' courts, the defendant still has the right in all cases to subject the child to a cross-examination in open court.

A third drawback is that the proposal does not allow for the possibility of a young child being questioned at the trial through some intermediate person other than the lawyers in the case. In the case of an older child it may be very right and proper that all questions should be put by the lawyers direct. In the case of a very young child, however, this procedure will often be out of the question. A tiny child will often be very shy of talking to a strange adult, particularly about an unpleasant experience, although he or she may be able and willing to talk to someone known and trusted. At present, the insistence on courtroom questioning by strange adults in the shape of lawyers is one of several matters which combine to make it impossible to put a tiny child's account of an incident before the court at all. If the child's story is to be put before the court by the child as a live witness then the prosecution must be given the option of putting questions through a person who has already gained the child's confidence.

When this idea was proposed the Government rejected it because it said it would interfere with the defendant's right to cross-examine prosecution witnesses through counsel of his or her choice. But how could giving the *prosecution* the option of putting their questions through a 'child examiner' possibly infringe the defendant's right to cross-examine through counsel of his choice? If the prosecution have this option, the defence would clearly have to be given the option too. But to give the defence the right to use the child-examiner if it wants to is not to prevent it cross-examining through counsel of its choice if it prefers to take this course. When this was pointed out the Government still opposed it. If the prosecution used someone other than their lawyer, the Minister told the House of Lords, the defendant might feel under moral pressure to do the same, and so this would undermine the defence right to examine using counsel of its choice (Hansard, 1987) House of Lords, vol. 489 co. 267). When faced with arguments like this it is difficult to see how reason can ever prevail. What the Minister was saying was that the prosecution must be forced to use an inept procedure to make sure that the defendant has no inhibitions about using an equally inept procedure. The idea that a court needs to know the truth, and that the purpose of examining a witness is to enable the court to discover it, does not seem to have crossed anybody's mind.

Shortly before the live-link was introduced, trial judges were beginning to allow child witnesses to shelter from the defendant's gaze behind various types of temporary screen. In one case this was challenged on appeal as infringing the defendant's basic rights, but on 30 October 1989 the Court of

Appeal affirmed the conviction and gave its official approval to the practice (*R.* v. *X., Y and Z, The Times* 3 November 1989).

Screens, live television links, and every other change to make it easier for children to give evidence on the day of trial have the same inevitable drawback. They do nothing to relieve the child of stress of having to wait many weeks or even months before the case comes on for trial. To eliminate this, some method must be devised that will enable the child to give evidence in advance.

Corroboration

Until recently, if the child is competent as a witness and could be persuaded to talk, the rules about corroboration made sure the court took little or no notice of what he or she had to say.

The first branch of the corroboration requirement was that there can be no conviction on the unsworn evidence of a child witness unless there is corroboration. This was laid down by section 38 of the Children and Young Persons' Act 1933 — the provision that enables young children to give unsworn evidence. As interpreted by the judges, 'corroboration' in this context meant something other than more unsworn evidence of other children. This had disastrous consequences for justice. For example, it meant that if a defendant assaults two small children in identical circumstances — or one in the presence of another — the case was bound to fail unless there was some other evidence. This was so no matter how credible each child's account, and even if there were not two small children but twenty. In 1987, the Home Office commissioned a review of the psychological evidence (Hedderman 1987), on the strength of which it threw its weight behind a proposal to change the law. By section 34 of the Criminal Justice Act 1988 it is now possible to convict on the unsworn evidence of a child — even, in theory, of a single child — without corroboration. This is a major and significant change in the law.

The second branch of the rule, which was judge-made, was that in any case involving a child — even one who gave evidence on oath — the judge had to direct the jury that it is 'dangerous' to convict on uncorroborated testimony. This may have been sensible where the prosecution case consisted of the child's evidence and nothing else: but the judge still had to give the warning, and include in it the vital word 'dangerous', even where the case was knee-deep in corroboration. Where this was so, such a warning disparaged the child's evidence unnecessarily; and it probably also confused the jury, who were likely to take it as a hint from the judge that they had better acquit. This branch of the corroboration rule was also abolished by section 34 of the Criminal Justice Act 1988. As far as judicial warnings are concerned, the judge now has a power to warn of the danger of convicting on the child's evidence where the judge thinks a conviction would be dangerous, but there is no obligation to give a warning in those cases where the judge thinks a conviction would be safe.

Unfortunately this is not quite as good as it sounds, because there is an independent rule about corroboration in sexual cases which still remains in force. This says that the judge always has a mandatory duty to warn the jury of convicting on the uncorroborated evidence of the complainant in a sexual offence. Although this duty has been attenuated by some recent pronouncements of the Court of Appeal, such a warning must still be given in any case where the sexual complainant is a child (*Chance* (1988) 87 CrApR 398). Thus as far as warnings are concerned, the change in section 34 of the Criminal Justice Act 1988 does not amount to much. Further change seems likely, however, because in December 1989 the duty to warn of the danger of convicting on the evidence of a sexual complainant received a powerful blast of criticism from the Pigot Committee.

Unlike the courts in Scotland, the English courts have never insisted on a corroboration requirement in civil proceedings. Thus in the civil courts corroboration of a child's evidence has never been an issue.

The rule against hearsay

The fourth rule which prevents the criminal courts from hearing the child's version of events is the 'rule against hearsay'. In principle, the English law of evidence does not permit a party to prove something happened by calling A, who did not see it, to testify that he heard B, who did see it, describe it. The rule equally prevents A from reading to the court a letter which B wrote to him describing the event, and — less sensibly — it also stops him playing an audio or videotape of B describing it. There are important exceptions to the rule, the best known of which is where the person accused has confessed to committing the offence. A policeman or anyone else may report his confession to the court, or play a tape-recording of it. But there is no exception, generally speaking, for statements by the victim of the offence. In a child abuse case the hearsay rule usually means that no parent, doctor, policeman or social worker may tell the court the child's initial statement; nor may the court see it if it is preserved on videotape.

Major exceptions are made to the hearsay rule in civil cases. In wardship proceedings the House of Lords has held that the hearsay rule is inapplicable (*re K.*, [1965] AC 201). In consequence, videotape evidence is often received in wardship. Here the child will often have been interviewed by a child psychiatrist or a social worker, who may refer to what the child has said if this is part of the basis of the diagnosis, and where the interview has been recorded on videotape the court is usually prepared to view it. The same practice began to spread to civil proceedings other than wardships, and when the Court of Appeal pointed out that this was technically improper (*H* v. *H.*; *K.* v. *K.* [1989] 3 WLR), Parliament promptly intervened with section 96 (3) of the Children Act 1989, which gives the Lord Chancellor power to make regulations overriding the hearsay rule in all kinds of civil proceedings concerned with the welfare of children. An Order (S. I. 1990 No. 143) has now been made which makes videotapes admissible in most civil disputes arising out of allegations of child abuse.

In criminal cases, however, the rule is still in full force. Where the child gives evidence in person to a criminal court, the prosecution may put in evidence the child's earlier statement if it amounts to a 'recent complaint': but this is not possible unless the statement was a complaint, spontaneously made, and made at the first possible opportunity. Where the child gives evidence, the defence may use earlier statements to attack the child's credibility if the earlier account differs from what is now said. But earlier statements are never more than secondary to what the child says in court. And if the child is too young, or too frightened to give evidence, the court never hears what he or she told anyone about the offence. The usual result is an acquittal for want of evidence.

The police invariably interview the child after the offence and take a statement, just as they invariably interview the suspect. They will always make notes of what the child said, and it is increasingly common for them to record the interview on videotape (Bexley Report 1987). If the court is willing to listen to a tape of the interview with the suspect, why should it not be possible to see and hear a videotape of an interview with the child? When the Criminal Justice Bill was first introduced in 1986 complete with the 'live video link' proposal, a public debate began about the desirability of admitting videotapes of earlier interviews with the child.

At first, two serious objections were made to the idea.

The first was that the evidence might be unfair, because the child might have been questioned in such a way as to put words into her mouth. Where a child is able and willing to talk spontaneously about what happened there is no problem, but where the child is unable or unwilling to talk, psychiatrists sometimes resort to suggestive leading questions. Where tapes of psychiatric interviews have been shown in wardship cases, judges have sometimes had strong things to say about the interview techniques. A number of critical judgments were reported in a Special Number of the Family Law Reports, [1987] 1 FLR 269-346. Since then, the psychiatrists involved have refined their interview techniques, and in *C.* v. *C.* [1988] FCR 458 they were praised by Mr Justice Latey. Nevertheless, some lawyers still fear that admitting videotapes would bring tendentious and unreliable evidence into criminal trials. But there is no reason why it should. If videotapes are admissible in principle, it does not follow that all videotapes have to be admitted. In a criminal case the judge has a discretion to reject evidence which he considers to be more prejudicial than probative, and a discretion to reject evidence which would render the trial unfair. In the case of police interviews with defendants, the judge has a discretion to exclude evidence of the interview if it was unfairly conducted, and the Home Office has drawn up a Code of Practice to encourage fair interviewing practices when dealing with defendants. It would be easy enough to do the same for police interviews with children. That it is possible to conduct a bad video-interview with a child is no reason for a rule which requires us to reject a good one.

The second objection was that it would deprive the defendant of the right to test the evidence of the accuser by cross-examination. It is my view, however, that we place too much stress on the value of cross-examination. There are already a number of exceptions where statements are admitted for what they are worth, although it is impossible to cross-examine on them. A further exception might be made for child witnesses, at least where they are very young. I find the idea of the defence cross-examining a child of four or five revolting, and equally revolting the idea that if the defence cannot administer a traditional Old Bailey-style in-court cross-examination, the court must not listen to what the child has to say. What is more, I think that lawyers are strangely inconsistent in objecting to videotapes on the ground that the questioner may have put words into the child's mouth, and then insisting on the value of cross-examining children. What is a cross-examination but the use of leading questions in an attempt to put words into the mouth of the person who is being cross-examined? Where possible, the defence must of course be given some opportunity to put their side of the story to the child, but a number of other legal systems manage to achieve this without cross-examining small children in court.

The cross-examination objection could be adequately overcome by grafting on to the use of videotapes the right of the defendant to conduct a cross-examination. One possible method which was proposed by Professor Glanville Williams is a version of what the Americans call a 'video deposition' (Williams 1987). The child is questioned in private at a preliminary hearing by an appointed examiner, through whom the defence are also permitted to put their questions to the child. The interview is recorded on videotape, and the tape made admissible as evidence at the trial. A precedent for this exists in section 42 of the Children and Young Persons Act 1933, which allows a magistrate to conduct such an interview with a child who is sick or injured. A written transcript of this is then admissible at the trial if there is medical evidence that a court appearance would involve serious danger to the child's life or health, and provided the defence had the opportunity to put their questions at the time the interview took place. Another and slightly less radical method is proposed by the Pigot Committee (see below).

The third argument deployed against the videotape proposal was the surprising one that allowing videotapes in evidence would cause child witnesses to suffer *increased* stress at the trial. It was said that if the tape of an earlier interview was admitted, the child would be subjected to a gruelling cross-examination by defence counsel in order to bring out the discrepancies between what he or she said when giving evidence, and what was earlier said on tape. But this is a wrong-headed argument. The cross-examination problem is something which is with us already, because the existing rules of evidence already permit the defence to use any previous inconsistent statement a child has made in order to trip her up in cross-examination. There have already been a number of cases in which the defence have cross-examined child witnesses about their previous video statements in this way, and harrowing scenes have been the result. In one recent case it caused a young witness to have hysterics, as a result of which the trial had to be adjourned (see the *Chatham News*, 23 October 1987). In my view, this can happen precisely because the prosecution *cannot* use the video statement as part of the prosecution case. At present the child must repeat in court the story originally told to the police months earlier, from memory and without any help. In the process, of course, the child probably forgets some parts and muddles others; and then the defence can take the story apart on the discrepancies between that and the original video statement. If the prosecution could use the original statement to help the child tell the story, there would only be one story before the court, and we would often avoid this particular abomination. The change proposed is actually needed to prevent the very abuse which it is said to be likely to cause.

In any case, to make the whole issue of videotape or otherwise turn on the protection of the child is surely to miss the point. As Lord Denning said in a House of Lords debate, '. . . in all criminal cases and in other cases the search is for truth and justice' (Hansard, House of Lords, vol. 490 col. 158). The courts are not concerned with protecting witnesses, or defendants, or anyone, except as something secondary to this main purpose. The real reason why we need to be able to put videotapes of early interviews in evidence is that they are capable of giving the court what is likely to be a fuller and more reliable account of what happened than it is otherwise able to hear. In our criminal justice system the interval between the trial and the incident first coming to light is likely to be several months at least, and often many months. If we know two things about human memory, one is that it fades with time, and the other is that stress impairs recall. For justice to be done — to the innocent as well as to the guilty — it is essential that the court should have before it the most accurate account possible of what the child said about the incident at the earliest moment, before time wiped certain details out of its mind and questioning by adults implanted others. This account is likely to be an interview preserved on videotape.

In June 1988, when the Criminal Justice Bill was at the Report Stage in the House of Commons, there was a lengthy debate on videotaped evidence and the Government found itself under pressure from both sides of the House. It successfully resisted this pressure, but agreed to set up a special Advisory Group to examine the question of videotaped evidence under the chairmanship of His Honour Judge Thomas Pigot QC, the Common Serjeant — a senior Old Bailey judge. In December 1989 its report was published by the Home Office, and its recommendations are radical indeed.

In outline, the Pigot Committee proposes a scheme under which a child who may be needed to give evidence in a case of sex or violence likely to be tried in the Crown Court should be examined as soon as possible after the incident in question, the examination being recorded on videotape. The examination should be done by a trained person, and there should be a Code of Practice to govern how it is done. As soon as possible thereafter, the defence should be shown the videotape. If they wish to put their questions to the child, there should be a preliminary hearing before a judge, sitting in private, where the questions are put by the defence lawyer in the presence of the prosecuting lawyer, and some suitable adult to give the child comfort and support. This session should also be videotaped. At the eventual trial, the first videotape would replace the child's live examination in-chief, and the second videotape the child's live cross-examination. Children would have the option of giving evidence in the traditional way instead — but the choice would be the child's, not the defendant's.

For good measure, the Pigot Committee also proposes the abolition of the competency requirement, of what remains of the corroboration rules, and of committal proceedings in cases involving children. Pre-empting the argument that if all this is done for child witnesses it would lead to pressure for the same treatment for other vulnerable witnesses as well, the Pigot Committee replies that similar changes should be made for their benefit too.

Unfortunately the Pigot scheme proved unacceptable to the Government. In November 1990, it introduced a Criminal Justice Bill with clauses designed to abolish the competency requirement, and to make videotapes admissible — but only where the child attends court for a live cross-examination. We shall see if Parliament enacts these clauses as they stand, or with additions or subtractions.

REFERENCES

Department of Health and Social Security (1985). *Review of Child Care Law.* Consultative Document. London: HMSO.

Department of Health and Social Security (1987). *The Law on Child Care and Family Services.* Cm 62, London: HMSO.

Goodman, G. S., Aman, C. and Hirschman, J. (1987). Child Sexual and Physical Abuse: Children's Testimony, in S. J. Ceci, M. P. Toglia, and D. F. Ross, eds., *Children's Eyewitness Memory,* 16-18. New York: Springer-Verlag.

Hale, Sir M. (1736). *History of the Pleas of the Crown.* S. Emlyn edition, London: Nutt & Gosling.

Hedderman, C. (1987). *Children's Evidence: The Need for Corroboration.* Home Office Research and Planning Unit Paper 41. London: Home Office.

Hoggett, B. M. (1986). Family Courts or Family Law Reform — Which Should Come First? *Legal Studies,* 6, 1.

Law Commission (1988). Review of child Law — Guardianship and Custody, Report No. 172.

Mackay, Lord James of Clashfern (1990). Introduction, in: J. R. Spencer, C. G. B. Nicholson, R. H. Flin and R. Bull, eds., *Children's Evidence in Legal Proceedings, An International Perspective.* Law Faculty, Cambridge University.

Metropolitan Police and Bexley London Borough (1987). *Child Sexual Abuse Joint Investigative Project: Final Report.* London: HMSO.

Report of the Inquiry into Child Abuse in Cleveland 1987. Chair: Lord Justice Butler-Sloss. Cm 412, London: HMSO.

Report of the Committee on One-Parent Families (1974). Chair: The Hon. Mr Justice Finer. Cmnd. 5629. London: HMSO.

Report of the Advisory Group on Video Evidence (1989). Chair: His Hon. Judge T. Pigot. London: Home Office.

Spencer, J. R. and Flin, R. H. (1990). *The Evidence of Children: the Law and the Psychology* Blackstone.

White, R., Carr, P., and Lowe, N., (1990). *A Guide to the Children Act 1989.* Butterworths.

Williams, G. (1987), Child Witnesses, in P. Smith ed., *Essays in Honour of J. C. Smith,* 188-203. Butterworths.

7

EVIDENCE WITHIN THE SCOTTISH LEGAL FRAMEWORK

GORDON NICHOLSON Q.C.

ALTHOUGH SCOTLAND IS an integral part of the United Kingdom its legal system is quite distinct from that in England and Wales. In criminal and civil matters the judicial and legal systems are entirely self-contained save only that in civil proceedings there is, as in England and Wales, a final right of appeal to the House of Lords. There are differences in substantive law as well as in procedure. Furthermore, in a number of areas, legislation for Scotland must be separately enacted; these areas include education, health services, criminal justice and the personal social services.

When child abuse is alleged there are, within the framework of the Scottish justice system, broadly two legal paths along which that child may be required to travel. One is designed to protect the child from further abuse and to cater for his or her future needs in terms of care and support. The other is designed to bring to justice and, where appropriate, to punish the person who has inflicted the abuse in the first place. This chapter will first describe each of these paths, and then will discuss the changes that are under consideration in relation to the way evidence is given by children and other vulnerable witnesses.

CHILD PROTECTION

In the 1960s a committee under the chairmanship of Lord Kilbrandon was set up in Scotland to consider how best to deal with children who, for whatever reason, are at risk. This included not only children who are the actual or potential victims of physical or sexual abuse but also those who truant from school and those who commit crimes or offences. The Kilbrandon Committee concluded that any distinction between children who commit offences and children who are neglected is ultimately fortuitous: they are essentially the same children. For whatever reason, their parents had failed or had been unable to provide a normal upbringing, and whether in due course they present as delinquent or as in need of care and protection is very much a matter of chance. They are equally likely to be in need of care and should therefore be dealt with under the same legislation and through the same agencies. The Report also attached considerable importance to the rights and duties of parenthood. Intervention in families is only justified when parents cannot deal with the situation, and then it should be done with the aim of rendering them capable of doing so in the future. Although a number of significant changes were made to the original Kilbrandon proposals between publication of the Report in 1964 and the passage through Parliament of the Social Work (Scotland) Bill four years later, these basic tenets remained a constant feature.

The relevant sections of the Social Work (Scotland) Act 1968, which were implemented in April 1971, define a system that differs radically from the juvenile justice arrangements in force in other parts of the United Kingdom. Central to the operation of the Scottish system are the activities of the 2.000 members of 'Children's Panels'. The panels are bodies of laymen recruited in each local government region of Scotland. Members of the community are invited to volunteer for this form of unpaid public service, and are selected on the basis of procedures intended to identify such desirable personal attributes as open-mindedness, ability to communicate, and freedom from extreme degrees of permissiveness or punitiveness. Efforts are made to ensure a reasonably balanced representation of age-groups, sexes, and broad socio-economic categories. Three members of a children's panel (provided that both sexes are represented) constitute a children's hearing, and are responsible for making decisions concerning children who in earlier times would have been dealt with by juvenile courts or similar bodies (as is still the case in many other jurisdictions). They differ from such forums however, not merely in name but in a number of extremely significant respects.

The decision to refer a child to a children's hearing is made by a regional official known as the reporter to the children's panel. The reporter—whose background is normally either in law or social work—is notified by the police, by an education authority, or indeed by any statutory or voluntary body, or by any private individual, of any child who is thought likely to be 'in need of compulsory measures of care'. A 'child' includes persons under sixteen years, and additionally persons between sixteen and eighteen years who are already under the supervision of a children's hearing. The reporter has complete freedom to decide whether to bring a referred child before a hearing, to make some informal arrangement with the social work department, or to take no action at all. In trying to determine an appropriate course of action on the basis of information that others have gathered, the reporter is not guided by any centrally established formal rules or criteria for decision-making. In their absence he is likely to be influenced by his personal conviction, however founded; by informal group norms, evolved from the shared experience of colleagues; and by such rule-of-thumb principles as may have been incorporated into departmental practice. Children in the 'at risk' category are much more likely to be referred to a hearing than alleged offenders: some 65 per cent of 'at risk' cases compared with 36 per cent of offence referrals proceeded to hearings in 1988 (Social Work Services Group, 1989).

The hearing members, on referral of a case, are not empowered to debate guilt or innocence. The grounds of referral must be put to the child and his or her accompanying parents. If the grounds are not accepted by a parent or by the child, and also where the child is too young to understand the grounds of referral, the hearing has, at that stage, no further jurisdiction. Before it can take any further steps, the matter must be referred to a sheriff for proof—that is, for a judicial decision as to whether the grounds of referral are valid. (In Scotland, a sheriff is a professional judge holding judicial office under the Crown.) If the grounds are upheld, the case must be referred back to the hearing for disposal; if not, the sheriff must dismiss the referral. Disposal means, in effect, a decision whether a period of supervision by a social worker is desirable, whether the child should be required to enter a residential home or school, or whether the referral should be discharged. A supervision order, with or without a residential requirement, must be reviewed within a year and may be reviewed at any time if requested by the social worker, and any time after three months if requested by the child or the parents. In reaching its decision, the hearing is required to take into account not only the events specified in the statement of grounds but also all relevant aspects of the child's circumstances. To that end the panel members have available social work and school reports and, on occasions, reports from more specialised agencies. Before reaching a decision they are expected to involve child and parents as fully as possible in discussion of the child's problems and of the most appropriate outcome. Above all, they are required to make a disposal that is 'in the best interests of the child'.

If the hearing members feel that even with more substantial and more relevant information they are still not in a position to determine how the child's interests can best be served, there may be a possibility of seeking an independent opinion. Section 34A of the 1968 Act as amended allows for the appointment of a safeguarder in circumstances where the hearing chairman believes that there may be a conflict of interest between child and parents.

The child or parents may appeal to the sheriff against the decision of a hearing and, from the sheriff, on a point of law or irregularity, to the Court of Session. Legal aid is available for families appearing in court but not for the hearing itself.

These procedures have to be completed within fairly strict time limits. Moreover, a child cannot as a rule be compulsorily removed from his or her parents, other than for a short period, without them having, if they wish it, a full and speedy judicial review of the allegations which are said to justify that removal.

CRIMINAL PROCEEDINGS

The hearings system has now been in operation for close on twenty years and in that time it has acquired a reputation for being the most civilized procedure yet evolved for dealing with children in trouble. It is all the more curious therefore that until comparatively recently law and practice in criminal proceedings have paid little regard to the special needs of children who may be required to take part in such proceedings as witnesses.

There has of course been some attempt to treat child witnesses differently from adult witnesses, but these attempts have in the past been rather superficial and unregulated, and as a consequence have been largely unpredictable. For example, some judges direct that counsel should remove wigs and gowns while examining a child in court, but this has never been a universal practice. Likewise, some judges clear a court of spectators while a child is giving evidence, but again this has never been standard procedure. Another important trend over recent years is a growing recognition among prosecutors of the advantage of taking a child on a pre-trial visit to the courtroom, but it is only very recently that that has become a regular practice.

It is now of course well established that an appearance in court can, for many children, be at the very least an alarming and distressing experience, and in some cases a positively harmful one. With such considerations in mind the Home Secretary, in 1988, introduced, for England and Wales, statutory provisions to enable a child's evidence to be given by a live closed-circuit television link (Home Office, 1987). In Scotland, the Lord Advocate decided to have the whole matter thoroughly examined by the Scottish Law Commission before reaching any conclusion about possible new measures. The Scottish Law Commission is a statutory body which has the task of keeping the whole law of Scotland under constant review, and of promoting reform where that appears to be necessary and desirable. A Discussion Paper (1988) prepared by the Commission was circulated for comment to several hundred interested individuals and organisations, and reviews a comprehensive range of measures which might be introduced to alleviate the position of children who are required to give evidence in criminal proceedings. The Commission's final report, containing its recommendations for reform, was published in Feburary 1990 (Scottish Law Commission, 1990).

PROPOSALS FOR REFORM

Preliminary

In formulating its recommendations for reform, the Scottish Law Commission had in mind several general considerations which, in its view, were bound to influence the shape of any new practices or rules of evidence. First, the Commission considered it absolutely essential that any reforms which were designed to alleviate the position of child witnesses should not have the effect of prejudicing an accused person's right to a fair trial. In this connection the Commission was particularly mindful of Article 6 of the European Convention on Human Rights which, as interpreted by the European Court of Human Rights, makes it clear that a person cannot be convicted on the strength of evidence coming from a witness whom he has no opportunity to cross-examine. Consequently, the Commission concluded, any technique for introducing a child's evidence at second hand, and without an opportunity to cross-examine the child, would be likely to contravene Article 6; and accordingly any new measures to protect or assist a child must preserve that right.

More generally, the Commission reached the conclusion, on the basis of the evidence which they had accumulated, that in very many instances there would be no need for special measures to enable children to give their evidence to a court. The weight of the evidence put before the Commission was to the effect that many children would be able to give evidence by conventional means without undue distress or trauma provided that they were carefully prepared in advance for that experience and provided that they were treated in a sensitive way within the courthouse. Accordingly, much of the Commission's report addresses ways in which that can be achieved.

A third preliminary topic concerns the scope of the Commission's recommendations. In many jurisdictions special measures to assist the giving of evidence by children are restricted to very young children, or to children who are the alleged victims of particularly unpleasant crimes, such as forms of sexual abuse. The Commission, by contrast, took the view that its recommendations should apply to all children under the age of sixteen, and regardless of the nature of the crime about which they are required to give evidence. A child of sixteen who is required to give evidence about a domestic murder involving the death of a close relative may find that experience just as traumatic as would a child of ten who was required to give evidence as the alleged victim of physical or sexual abuse.

Improvements in practice

As noted above, it is not uncommon for judges in Scotland to require counsel to remove their wigs and gowns while a child is giving evidence, or to clear a court of spectators who are not directly involved in a trial. It is also becoming increasingly common for prosecutors to take the trouble to prepare children for the experience of giving evidence in court. However, such practices are by no means standard. The Scottish Law Commission accordingly considered the possibility of creating new rules which would require judges and others to follow such practices in all cases. At the end of the day, however, it became clear that if, as also noted above, any special procedures and rules in respect of children were to be capable of applying to all children in all kinds of cases, fixed rules would be likely to be quite inappropriate in some instances. Consequently, the Commission has accepted that practices such as those mentioned above should remain discretionary. However, the Commission recognised the need for greater uniformity of approach in dealing with children in court, and accordingly it has recommended that the Lord Justice General (who is the most senior Scottish judge) should issue guidance to judges on such matters.

More generally, the Commission has recommended several improvements in the physical arrangements for children attending court as witnesses. It is suggested that trials involving children as witnesses should, whenever possible, be held in courtrooms which are unthreatening and which have adequate acoustics or sound amplification systems so that children can be heard without having to be asked to speak up. It is also suggested that arrangements should be made for waiting rooms to be set aside for children and their families, and that such rooms should be furnished with suitable furniture, and with a supply of books and games to keep children occupied while waiting to go into court. The Commission takes the view that practical measures such as the foregoing, coupled with a generally sensitive and caring approach to children in court, will enable many children to give evidence by conventional means without undue distress.

Competency of children as witnesses

In some jurisdictions children below a certain age (sometimes around seven) are simply not permitted to give evidence in a criminal trial. In other words such children are legally incompetent as witnesses. In other jurisdictions such children are presumed to be legally incompetent, but it may be possible to establish their competency by means of some kind of pre-trial competency hearing. In Scotland there has never been any total prohibition against very young children giving evidence, but until recently there has been some uncertainty about how courts should regard the giving of evidence by those who are very young. In that situation, the Scottish Law Commission at one stage considered the possibility of a statutory provision to declare that a child of any age is *prima facie* a competent witness. However, while the Commission's final report was in preparation, a decision by the High Court in Scotland (Rees v. Lowe, 1989) laid down the approved procedure for dealing with very young witnesses and, in so doing, made it clear that in Scotland there is no bar in principle to a child of any age giving evidence in a criminal trial. In view of that decision, the Commission has made no recommendation on this matter.

Corroboration

In several jurisdictions, such as England and Wales, rules which require that a young child's evidence must be corroborated have recently been swept away. This brought some calls for a similar relaxation of the rules in Scotland. However, the position in Scotland is very different from that in many other jurisdictions in that, in Scotland, there is a general requirement in criminal cases that all evidence, from any source, must be corroborated. Consequently, the removal of such a requirement in relation to child witnesses would not involve the removal of an exception to the general rule, but instead would involve the creation of a major exception to the general rule. In those circumstances the Scottish Law Commission, with the approval of almost all those whom it consulted, has recommended that there should be no change in the present rule.

New techniques and procedures

Notwithstanding its view that, with sensitive preparation and handling, many children will be able to give evidence in court by conventional means, the Scottish Law Commission nonetheless recognised that there is a need to make provision for some special techniques and procedures to cater for those children for whom a normal appearance in court is likely to be particularly distressing or even positively harmful. Despite some earlier misgivings, the Commission concluded that provision should be made for the use of live closed-circuit television links, and for the use of screens to shield a child from the sight of an accused person. The Commission also decided that there should be provision to take a child's evidence in advance of a trial by a procedure similar to that which is known in the United States as a pre-trial deposition. Under that procedure a child would be examined and cross-examined in a conventional manner, but that examination would take place in informal and non-threatening surroundings where the child would be less likely to be distressed or alarmed than might be the case in court. Those proceedings would be video-recorded, and the video-recording should be used in court in place of a live appearance by the child.

The Commission considered whether it should recommend special eligibility rules for each of the above procedures, but came to the conclusion that such an approach would be inflexible and likely to lead to inappropriate results. Instead, the Commission has recommended a general eligibility rule based on likely harm to the child, or inability to testify, if required to give evidence in open court. Once that test has been satisfied, the court will then select the particular procedure which seems most likely to be beneficial in a particular case.

Prior statements and video-recorded interviews

Much of the discussion which has taken place in recent years in relation to children as witnesses has centred on the question whether, by some means or another, it should be possible to introduce as evidence at a criminal trial a prior statement made by a child, and in particular a video-recording of an interview with the child made at some earlier stage in the proceedings. The particular attention given to video-recordings has, of course, arisen because of the increasing practice of video-recording interviews with children, particularly in sexual abuse cases, as an aid for doctors, social workers, and others.

The rule against hearsay evidence has recently been abolished in civil proceedings (Civil Evidence (Scotland) Act 1988). However, in criminal proceedings, the Scottish Law Commission took the view from an early stage that it would not be acceptable to allow video-recorded interviews and other prior statements by a child to be used at a trial in place of any evidence at that time by the child himself or herself. Such a course would deny an accused person any opportunity for cross-examination and, as such, would be contrary to Article 6 of the European Convention on Human Rights, mentioned above. However, the preliminary thinking of the Commission was that it might be possible to allow any prior statement, in whatever form, to be used at a trial provided only that the child was available as a witness to be cross-examined as to its contents. Most of those whom the Commission consulted agreed with the general approach which had been suggested. However, several consultees expressed considerable reservations about allowing *any* prior statement to be used as admissible evidence. They pointed out that in some instances a prior statement might be distorted in the re-telling. They also pointed out that, from time to time, a witness might either deny having said what he or she was alleged to have said on the previous occasion, or might at least challenge the accuracy of what he was alleged to have said. Having reconsidered the matter, the Scottish Law Commission came to the conclusion that an acceptable reform would be to admit as evidence any prior statement made by a witness provided, first, that the statement was put before the court in a form where its accuracy and genuineness could be guaranteed, and second, that the witness accepted that the contents of the statement were true.

The foregoing recommendation was made by the Scottish Law Commission as a general one, applying to all witnesses of any age. However, its effect in relation to child witnesses is that, if the recommendation is accepted, a child who is giving evidence by any means (in court, through the medium of live closed-circuit television, or at a pre-trial deposition) will be able to have his or her evidence supplemented or confirmed by any reliable prior statement, whether in the form of a video-recorded interview or otherwise. The Commission believes that such a reform would greatly assist the giving of evidence by many children.

Other recommended reforms

Although the Scottish Law Commission's primary concern was with the giving of evidence by children in criminal proceedings, their Report also deals with certain other matters. For example, it is recommended that the new rules and facilities for children giving evidence should also be available when children are required to give evidence in civil proceedings or in referrals to the sheriff from a children's hearing (see above). It is also recommended that new facilities such as live closed-circuit television and pre-trial depositions should be available, on cause shown, for adult witnesses who are particularly vulnerable and who are likely to be significantly harmed if required to give evidence by conventional means.

The Commission rejected the suggestion that special officials should be appointed to represent the interests of a child who is called to be a witness in a criminal trial. However, the Commission has expressed the hope that social workers and others involved in child welfare work may devise practices to ensure that such children and, as appropriate, their families, are given as much guidance and support as possible.

Conclusion

The recommendations which have been made by the Scottish Law Commission are not as dramatic or far-reaching as some people might have wished. Nonetheless, they represent a considerable innovation on existing rules and procedures, but at the same time, in the view of the Commission, they preserve the right of an accused person to receive a fair trial. So far as children are concerned, the Commission takes the view that its recommendations, if implemented, will make the experience of being a witness much less distressing and traumatic than may be the case at present. Only time will tell if those hopes are realised.

Postscript

In July 1990, the Lord Justice General of Scotland issued a memorandum of guidance on the use of discretionary measures in cases where children are witnesses, based on the recommendations contained in the Law Commission's report. These include the removal of wigs and gown by judges, counsel and solicitors; seating the child at a table in the well of the court along with judge and lawyers rather than in the witness box; allowing a relative or other supporting adult to sit beside the child while he or she gives evidence; clearing the courtroom of all people who are not directly involved in the proceedings.

Under the Law Reform (Miscellaneous Provisions) (Scotland) Act 1990 which received Royal Assent on 1 November 1990, application made for children to give evidence in Scottish courts by means of a live television link (sections 56-60). The Act allows the sheriff to transfer such a case to another court in the same sheriffdom where the necessary accommodation and equipment are available. Where a child gives evidence through a live video link, the Act allows the accused to be identified by reference to a prior identification made by the child rather than identification in open court.

REFERENCES

Home Office (1987) 'The Use of Video Technology at Trials of Alleged Child Abusers', Consultation Paper; Criminal Justice Act 1988, s. 32.

Kilbrandon (1964) *Report of the Committee on Children and Young Persons (Scotland).* Cmnd. 2306, HMSO.

Rees v. Lowe, 7 November 1989, unreported.

Scottish Law Commission (1988) *The Evidence of Children and Other Potentially Vulnerable Witnesses.* Discussion Paper No. 75.

Scottish Law Commission (1990) *Report on the Evidence of Children and Other Potentially Vulnerable witnesses.* No. 125, Edinburgh, HMSO.

Social Work Services Group (1989) *Statistical Bulletin.* CH13, Scottish Education Department.

8

EXPERT TESTIMONY IN CHILD SEXUAL ABUSE LITIGATION

the American experience

JOHN E. B. MYERS

CHILD SEXUAL ABUSE is a ubiquitous socio-legal problem calling for collaboration among a broad spectrum of professionals. Few issues require the degree of inter-disciplinary co-operation demanded by sexual abuse. This is nowhere more true than in the courtroom. Medical and mental health professionals play an important role in the legal effort to protect abused children and punish wrongdoing. The goal of this chapter is to describe the ongoing American effort to utilise the expertise of medical and mental health professionals in child sexual abuse litigation.

Forums in which child sexual abuse is litigated

The great bulk of child sexual abuse litigation occurs in state court in seven types of proceedings. First, there are criminal proceedings. During the past decade, as a result of increased efforts by prosecutors, the number of prosecutions has skyrocketed. Litigation in criminal court is likely to continue to play an important role in deterring abuse and punishing perpetrators.

Second, there are juvenile delinquency cases where minors are accused of committing acts which would be crimes if committed by adults. These cases are dealt with by juvenile or children's courts. The trials are similar to adult criminal prosecutions, except that punishment is only one of a number of factors considered by the judge, and special emphasis is placed on rehabilitation and therapy.

Third, juvenile courts are responsible for protecting abused and neglected children. The goal of civil protective proceedings is to safeguard children from harm, to support and reunite families, and provide appropriate services and treatment. While parents and caretakers can be compelled to attend, and to obey court orders, the stigma of criminal conviction does not exist. Furthermore, protective proceedings are less adversarial and formal than criminal and delinquency proceedings, with more room for therapeutic approaches to problem solving.

Fourth, every state provides a judicial procedure to terminate the parent-child relationship. The juvenile court protective proceedings described above are designed to be temporary methods of protecting children and helping abusive parents to function more effectively. In some cases, however, it becomes necessary to terminate the parent-child relationship so that the child can be freed for adoption by suitable adults.

Fifth, is child custody litigation incident to divorce. The custody arrangements agreed upon by most divorcing parents are approved by the divorce court. In a minority of cases, however, where parents cannot agree on custody, the court decides the matter. After a trial, the judge determines the custodial and visitation arrangement that is in the children's best interest. In a small but increasing number of contested custody cases, a parent seeking custody accuses the other parent of sexually abusing a child.

Sixth, allegations of child sexual abuse are occasionally litigated in civil lawsuits brought by victims against alleged perpetrators, for example, for assault, battery, and intentional infliction of emotional distress. Furthermore, an increasing number of victims are suing child protection agencies which fail to protect them.

Seventh, are administrative proceedings. Agencies of state government have responsibility to license and supervise certain professions and businesses, such as, physicians, psychologists, nurses, social workers and most day care centres and nursery schools. When allegations of child sexual abuse are lodged against a licensed professional or facility, the licensing agency may commence proceedings to revoke or suspend the licence. This may be at an administrative tribunal rather than a court of law, where, for the most part, the rules of evidence and procedure governing courtroom litigation also apply.

RULES GOVERNING EXPERT TESTIMONY

The uses and limitations of expert testimony are governed by the law of evidence which is basically the same in jury and non-jury trials, and in criminal and civil litigation. The states and the federal government have codified the law of evidence into rules of evidence which do not articulate all nuances of evidence law but establish a working framework. Courts play an active role in interpreting and refining the rules.

The law of evidence varies slightly across the United States, but similarity is growing under the influence of the Federal Rules of Evidence. These were adopted in 1975 to govern litigation in federal courts, and very largely have been adopted by individual states.

General rule of admissibility

Rule 702 of the Federal Rules of Evidence establishes the basic principle governing admissibility of expert testimony. The Rule states:

> If scientific, technical, or other specialized knowledge will assist the trier of fact to understand the evidence or to determine a fact in issue, a witness qualified as an expert by knowledge, skill, experience, training, or education, may testify thereto in the form of an opinion or otherwise.

The trial judge determines whether proferred testimony meets the requirements of Rule 702. In doing so, the judge is guided by the policy of the Federal Rules, which favours admission of expert testimony. In evaluating admissibility, the most important question is whether the testimony will assist the jury. As a leading commentator put it, 'On this subject can a jury receive from this person appreciable help?' (Wigmore, 1923). This is assessed by the judge on a case-by-case basis.

Qualifications of expert witnesses

Before a person may testify as an expert witness, the judge must be convinced that the person possesses sufficient 'knowledge, skill, experience, training, or education' to qualify as an expert. The party offering expert testimony carries the burden of establishing the witness's qualifications. The normal procedure is to call the witness to the stand and ask questions about the person's educational accomplishments, specialized training, and relevant experience. An expert on child sexual abuse could be asked questions in the following areas:

i educational attainments and degrees;
ii specialization in a particular area of practice;
iii specialized training in child sexual abuse;
iv extent of experience with sexually abused and non-sexually abused children;
v membership of professional societies and organizations focused on child abuse;
vi publications regarding child sexual abuse;
vii familiarity with relevant professional literature;
viii whether a person has qualified as an expert on child sexual abuse in prior court proceedings.

The party opposing expert testimony may ask questions designed to show that a witness is not qualified as an expert. Unless a witness is clearly unqualified, however, deficiencies in qualifications go to the weight accorded the witness's testimony rather than its admissibility.

In the area of child sexual abuse, professionals from several disciplines lay claim to expertise. It is important to note, however, that simply because a person holds a particular academic qualification does not mean the person is an expert on child sexual abuse. The critical factors relating to qualification as an expert in this field are:

i extensive first-hand experience with sexually abused and non-sexually abused children;

ii thorough and up-to-date knowledge of the professional literature on child sexual abuse;

iii objectivity and neutrality about individual cases.

With the foregoing principles in mind, it is clear that not all physicians, psychiatrists, psychologists, and social workers are qualified in the highly specialised field of child sexual abuse. In reality, only a small fraction of professionals in these disciplines possess sufficient knowledge and experience to qualify as experts.

Permissible bases for expert testimony

The permissible bases for expert testimony are stated in Federal Rule 703 as follows:

> The facts or data in the particular case upon which an expert bases an opinion or inference may be those perceived by or made known to the expert at or before the hearing. If of a type reasonably relied upon by experts in the particular field in forming opinions or inferences upon the subject, the facts or data need not be admissible in evidence (*Federal Rules of Evidence*).

The facts on which an expert may base an opinion come from a variety of sources. In many cases the expert has first-hand knowledge of the child as a result of personally interviewing or treating the child. For example, a child's therapist may opine that the child experienced age-inappropriate sexual contact. However, first-hand knowledge is not always required for expert testimony about a particular child. In an appropriate case, an expert who has not met a child may testify about the child. The expert opinion might then be based on study of videotape interviews of the child and reports prepared by other professionals. Finally, some forms of expert testimony do not require knowledge of a particular child; for example, when an expert limits testimony to a description of behaviours commonly observed in sexually abused children as a class.

Under the Federal Rules of Evidence, an expert may base an opinion on information that would not be independently admissible in evidence, if such information is 'of a type reasonably relied upon by experts in the particular field in forming opinions or inferences upon the subject'. Permitting experts on child sexual abuse to formulate *ad*missible opinions on the basis of *in*admissible evidence requires judges to determine what types of facts and data are 'reasonably relied upon' by experts in the field of child sexual abuse.

The potentially inadmissible evidence that is most frequently relied on is verbal and written hearsay. Documents include medical records, psychological reports, police records, and social welfare agency reports. Verbal statements by the child are critical, and verbal statements of other persons, such as parents, also play an important role. Some of the documents and verbal statements just described are barred from evidence by the hearsay rule. Yet, under the Federal Rules, experts may rely on such inadmissible information to formulate opinions about sexual abuse if other experts in the field reasonably rely on similar information.

In many cases, it is perfectly reasonable for experts on child sexual abuse, to rely on hearsay. American law has long recognized that physicians and other helping professionals rely on hearsay. Indeed, life and death decisions are often made on the basis of written and verbal hearsay statements. Thus, it is clear that experts justifiably rely on potentially inadmissible hearsay.

EXPERT TESTIMONY OFFERED TO PROVE ABUSE OCCURRED

Child sexual abuse is often exceedingly difficult to prove. Molestation occurs in secret, and the child is usually the only eyewitness. While many children are capable witnesses, some cannot take the stand. Most children find the courtroom a foreboding place, and when a child is asked to testify against a familiar person, even a parent, the experience can be overwhelming. Consequently, children's testimony is too often ineffective. The problems engendered by ineffective testimony and lack of eyewitnesses are compounded by the paucity of physical evidence common in child sexual abuse (Myers *et al.* 1989). Faced with a vacuum of evidence, attorneys seeking to prove sexual abuse increasingly turn to physicians, psychologists, and social workers for expert testimony.

Medical testimony regarding physical evidence of sexual abuse

Expert testimony regarding medical evidence of sexual abuse is generally admissible (*People* v. *Mendibles* (1988)). A physician's testimony may take several forms. First, some courts permit an expert to state that a child was sexually abused (*State* v. *Butler* (1986)). Such testimony goes directly to an ultimate factual enquiry before the court. The second form of medical testimony is similar to the first, except that in the second the physician adds the opinion that a child has a 'diagnosis' of sexual abuse or sexual contact. This enhances the expert's opinion with the aura of scientific certainty connoted to non-physicians by the word 'diagnosis'. Third, an expert may testify that a child's condition is consistent with sexual abuse. This is less certain than the first two forms of opinion, and is one step removed from the ultimate factual inquiry. Finally, a physician may testify that a child demonstrates no physical or medical evidence of sexual abuse, but that absence of such evidence does not rule out abuse. This type of testimony should not be permitted in all cases. For example, if the charged offence is fondling, the jury does not need an expert to tell it the child will not be physically injured. If, on the other hand, the charge is anal penetration, jurors may well benefit from expert testimony which informs them that anal penetration does not always cause physical injury. Such expert testimony is particularly appropriate if the defence asserts or implies that if abuse had occurred, there would be injury.

American courts permit expert medical witnesses to describe injuries and offer opinions as to their cause (*People* v. *Mendibles* (1988)). Courts generally permit physicians to respond to questions asking whether injuries could happen in a particular way (*Owens* v. *State* (1987)). Furthermore, experts may be asked whether a caretaker's explanation for injuries is reasonable (*State* v. *Tanner* (1983)). Finally, penetration may be established on the basis of expert testimony (*State* v. *Galloway* (1981)).

In some cases, the physician's opinion is based largely on the results of a physical examination of the child. In other cases, however, the opinion is based more heavily on a child's medical and social history, with secondary importance attached to the physical examination (*State* v. *Butler* (1986)). For example, the doctor may rely on the child's description of abuse or on statements by relevant adults (Myers, 1987). In addition, physicians elicit information about behavioural and emotional reactions that are indicative of sexual abuse, for example, whether the child demonstrates age-inappropriate sexual knowledge or pre-occupation, or behaviour indicative of stress.

It is apparent that in formulating diagnostic impressions, physicians often consider information that is not strictly medical in nature. The psychological and social effects of sexual abuse are frequently as important as the results of laboratory tests and physical examination. In so far as physicians consider non-medical indicators of abuse, they depart the realm reserved exclusively for physicians, and enter the arena of expertise shared with mental health professionals. When a physician has one foot in the medical camp and the other in the psychological, the resulting opinion is scrutinized from both perspectives.

Psychological testimony on whether sexual abuse occurred

Among experts on child sexual abuse, there is considerable controversy concerning whether professionals should testify that sexual abuse occurred. Some believe that professionals cannot reliably make this determination (McCord, 1986; Melton & Limber, 1989). Others believe that in some cases it is possible to determine with reasonable clinical certainty whether sexual abuse occurred. (Myers *et al.*, 1989; Sgroi, Porter & Blick, 1982) Those who believe it possible to determine whether abuse occurred acknowledge that it is not possible to 'know' whether a child was abused. After all, the expert was not present to observe the abuse. Rather, expert testimony on whether abuse occurred rests on assessment of a wide range of information leading to a clinical judgment that sexual abuse is the most likely explanation in a particular case.

The admissibility of expert testimony relating to whether a particular child was sexually abused has divided American courts. Several appellate courts approve expert testimony on whether abuse occurred (*Townsend* v. *State* (1987)). On the other hand, a number of appellate decisions reject expert testimony that a particular child was sexually abused (*People* v. *Roscoe* 1985). In one such decision (*State* v. *Heseltine* (1984)) the Court of Appeal concluded that an opinion that a child was abused is the same thing as an impermissible opinion that the child told the truth when she described sexual abuse. This conclusion seems wrong. An opinion that a child was sexually abused is not an opinion that the child was truthful when describing abuse. It is true that professionals rely heavily on the child's description of abuse. But many other factors help to shape expert evaluation of suspected sexual abuse. Thus, an expert opinion that a child was sexually abused is not the same as an opinion on the child's truthfulness or credibility.

Because of uncertainty among experts on child sexual abuse, and because of the consequences of criminal conviction, it may be appropriate in criminal jury trials to eschew psychological testimony cast in terms of an opinion that sexual abuse occurred. However, it may be proper to allow an alternative form of such testimony. For example, it may be proper to permit an expert to express an opinion that a child's symptoms and behaviours are consistent with sexual abuse. This type of testimony would add weight to other available evidence suggesting that the child has been abused. The expert might also ferret out alternative explanations for the child's symptoms and behaviours, and might identify those symptoms and behaviours where no explanation other than sexual abuse seems plausible.

In non-criminal proceedings, it is appropriate to allow a qualified expert on child sexual abuse to offer a direct opinion on whether a child was sexually abused. Such testimony is particularly suitable and necessary in juvenile court proceedings to protect children, and in child custody and visitation litigation incident to divorce. In these proceedings there is no jury, thus concern that expert testimony may overawe jurors is eliminated.

While disagreement persists, the clinical and scientific literature supports cautious optimism that qualified mental health professionals can sometimes determine whether a child's behaviour is consistent with sexual abuse. In 1985, one of the first statements of professional consensus regarding clinical evaluation of sexual abuse appeared in the literature. The Council on Scientific Affairs of the American Medical Association published guidelines on diagnosis and treatment of physical abuse, sexual abuse, and neglect (American Medical Association, 1985). In June 1988, the Council of the American Academy of Child and Adolescent Psychiatry approved guidelines for the clinical evaluation of child and adolescent sexual abuse (AACAP, 1988). These publications support the position that experts can detect symptoms and behaviours that result from sexual abuse. Not in all cases, but in some.

Recent research lends empirical support to the clinical conclusion that properly qualified professionals can determine whether a child's symptoms and behaviour are consistent with sexual abuse. A nationwide survey of professionals with expertise in evaluating suspected child sexual abuse revealed a high level of agreement that the following factors are indicative of sexual abuse: age-inappropriate sexual knowledge, sexualised play, precocious behaviour, excessive masturbation, preoccupation with genitals, indications of pressure or coercion exerted on the child, the child's story remains consistent over time, the child's report indicates an escalating progression of sexual abuse over time, the child describes idiosyncratic details of the abuse, and physical evidence of abuse (Conte *et al.*, 1988). The fact that a broad range of experts agree among themselves that certain factors are indicative of sexual abuse does not prove that clinicians are correct, but it provides support for the position that clinicians can make reliable determinations regarding sexual abuse.

Clinicians are also asked to evaluate the child's report. Faller (1988) has shown that in most cases of substantiated abuse children were able to provide information about the context of the sexual abuse, a description or demonstration of the sexual victimization, and an account of their emotional state. These were then open to assessment by clinicians as to whether children would know this information (e.g. their emotional reaction, the context of the abuse) without having had direct experience of the abuse. Faller concluded that the 'clinical criteria employed by evaluators of sexually abused children are indeed valid predictors of whether children have been sexually abused and should continue to be used'.

A particularly controversial issue in taking reports from children is the use made of anatomical dolls to determine whether sexual abuse occurred. Recent research indicates that children referred for sexual abuse display significantly more sexualised behaviour with dolls than non-referred children (White and Santilli, 1988). However, it is important to note that although dolls can be useful in evaluating suspected abuse, a diagnosis of child sexual abuse cannot be made solely on the basis of a child's play with dolls.

Psychological testimony describing behaviors commonly observed in sexually abused children

The previous subsection focused on expert testimony describing the behaviour of a particular child for the purpose of proving either that abuse occurred or that a particular child's behaviour and symptoms are consistent with sexual abuse. We turn now to a type of expert testimony which is limited to a description of the behavioural, cognitive and emotional reactions of sexually abused children as a class, and does not focus on the child in the case at hand. Indeed, the expert need have no knowledge of the particular child, as the sole purpose is to inform the fact finder of the behaviour commonly seen in abused children. The testimony of lay witnesses — usually parents or other individuals familiar with the child's behaviour — is adduced to acquaint the jury with the behaviour of the alleged victim. Given evidence that the alleged victim demonstrates behaviours commonly observed in sexually abused children, it is the responsibility of the jury to determine whether the victim was abused.

In theory, expert testimony describing behaviours commonly observed in sexually abused children serves several purposes. In some cases, it constitutes substantive evidence of abuse, that is, evidence that abuse occurred. In other cases the evidence is offered to rehabilitate children's credibility following certain types of impeachment. Expert testimony to rehabilitate is discussed in the next section.

The presence in a young child of behaviour commonly observed in sexually abused children can be probative of abuse. Evidence of the behaviours is legally relevant because it has a tendency to prove abuse. The probative value of expert testimony describing behaviours observed in young sexually abused children is highest when there is a coalescence of three types of behaviours:

i a central core of sexual behaviours which are strongly associated with sexual abuse, such as, age-inappropriate knowledge of sexual acts of anatomy, sexualisation of play and behaviour in young children, the appearance of genitalia in young children's drawings, and sexually explicit play with anatomically detailed dolls;

ii non-sexual behaviours which are commonly observed in sexually abused children, such as anxiety, regression, sleep disturbance, acting out, depression, nightmares and enuresis;

iii medical evidence of sexual abuse.

Probative value declines as sexual behaviours and medical evidence decrease in proportion to non-sexual behaviours. When the only evidence consists of a number of ambiguous, non-sexual behaviours, the probative value may be worthless or may be outweighed by the potential for unfair prejudice to the defendant or confusion of the jury. (Federal Rule 403 permits the trial judge to exclude relevant evidence that is unduly prejudicial.)

When a child demonstrates no sexual behaviours, but does evidence signs of serious anxiety or post traumatic stress disorder, expert testimony may still be relevant. In this scenario, however, testimony serves only to establish that the child may have experienced some type of traumatic event. Such testimony is not specific to sexual abuse.

Although in a substantial number of American cases, courts approve expert testimony describing behaviours observed in sexually abused children, a number of courts do not approve such testimony when it is offered as substantive evidence of abuse (*State* v. *Black* (1988)). Rather, the testimony is permitted to rehabilitate children's credibility. Confusion arises because some decisions are less than clear on whether testimony is received as evidence of abuse, or is limited to rehabilitation of credibility (*Commonwealth* v. *Baldwin* (1985)).

It may be concluded that the presence in a young child of behaviours commonly observed in sexually abused children is sometimes probative of abuse. Expert testimony explaining such behaviours can assist the jury to determine facts in issue. Such evidence should be admitted unless its probative value is substantially outweighed by the potential for unfair prejudice or confusion of the jury.

It is important to avoid the confusion sometimes engendered by reference to 'syndromes'. At the present time, experts have not reached consensus on the existence of a psychological syndrome that can detect child sexual abuse. Misuse of the word 'syndrome' has led to confusion in some courts where it has been assumed that a clear-cut syndrome exists so that the presence of symptoms means abuse occurred and absence of symptoms that abuse did not occur. Since both are wrong, the best course is to avoid any mention of syndromes.

EXPERT TESTIMONY DESIGNED TO REHABILITATE A CHILD'S IMPEACHED CREDIBILITY

In child sexual abuse litigation, the child is often the most important witness. Thus, the child's credibility is critical. Two forms of impeachment assume particular significance in sexual abuse cases. First, the accused may assert that a child should not be believed because the child did not report alleged abuse for a substantial period of time, because the child was inconsistent, or because the child retracted allegations of abuse. Such impeachment is legitimate. However, when the defence concentrates on delay, inconsistency, and recantation, the question arises whether the party seeking to prove abuse may offer expert rebuttal testimony to inform the jury that many sexually abused children delay reporting, are inconsistent, and recant.

In the second form of impeachment, the defence seeks to undermine a child's credibility by arguing that developmental differences between adults and children render children less credible than adults.

Recantation and delay in allegations of sexual abuse

The clinical and scientific literature makes clear that many sexually abused children delay reporting their abuse for weeks, months, or even years (Finkelhor, 1979; Jones and McQuiston, 1988). Once abuse is disclosed, many children recant, denying that anything happened. Sexually abused children are sometimes inconsistent in their descriptions of abuse, and in intrafamilial abuse cases, many victims are ambivalent. To the untrained eye, such behaviours may appear inconsistent with allegations of sexual abuse. In an effort to undermine the child's credibility, the defence may focus the jury's attention on delay in reporting, recantation, inconsistency, and loyalty to the alleged perpetrator. In the face of such impeachment, the party seeking to prove abuse has a need to rehabilitate the child's credibility. To this end, the party may offer expert rebuttal testimony designed to inform the jury that such behaviours are common in sexually abused children. Such expert testimony is needed to disabuse jurors of commonly held misconceptions about child sexual abuse, and to explain the emotional antecedents of abused children's seemingly self-impeaching behaviour (*State* v. *Moran* (1986)).

Rehabilitation testimony is more readily admitted when it describes sexually abused children as a class, rather than a specific child (*State* v. *Moran* (1986)). Courts surmise that avoiding discussion of a particular child is less likely to confuse the jury. Several decisions expressly hold that an expert may not describe a particular child (*People* v. *Gray* (1986)).

Expert testimony to rehabilitate a child's credibility is usually offered on rebuttal, following impeaching cross-examination of the child. Until some form of impeachment has occurred, such expert testimony constitutes improper bolstering. It is not always necessary to await cross-examination, however. In some cases, the defence makes plain as early as the opening statement that the child should not be believed. Regardless of the timing or method of the defendant's attack on credibility, and regardless of whether the attack is aimed directly or indirectly at the child, expert rehabilitation testimony is properly admitted as soon as the assault is underway.

Courts are comfortable with expert testimony to rehabilitate a child's impeached credibility. And for good reason. The defence invites such rebuttal testimony by its attack on the child's credibility. The party attempting to prove abuse has a legitimate need to inform the jury about the dynamics of child sexual abuse so that jurors can fairly and accurately evaluate the child's credibility.

Developmental differences between children and adults

Recent psychological research indicates that many adults are disposed to regard children as less credible than adults (Goodman *et al.*, 1989). However, other research indicates that children are not necessarily less reliable witnesses than adults (Myers *et al.* 1989). When the defence argues that developmental differences between adults and children render children less credible witnesses than adults, behavioural science testimony can be invoked to rehabilitate the child's credibility. This category of expert testimony does not focus on sexually abused children. Rather, the expert informs the jury about developmental characteristics shared by all children. In particular, jurors could benefit from current information relating to children's memory, inconsistency, suggestibility, ability to differentiate fact from fantasy, and understanding of time.

The defence may attempt to convince the jury that young children are so suggestible that their testimony should be regarded with skepticism. The defence may point out that the child was interviewed numerous times, and that there was ample opportunity to plant the idea of abuse in the child's malleable young mind. Jurors may accept the argument that young children are dangerously suggestible. Faced with such impeachment, the party seeking to prove abuse has a legitimate need to rehabilitate the child. The average juror is unaware of recent psychological research indicating that young children are not always more suggestible than older children and adults. To the extent the defence asserts the contrary, expert rebuttal testimony is proper.

The defence may argue that young children cannot differentiate fact from fantasy, and that the child lives in a fantasy world. Counsel might turn to the jury and say, 'Ladies and gentlemen, can you believe the testimony of this young child, who admits that she has an imaginary friend named Julius the Rabbit, and that Julius talks to her?' Fantasy plays an important part in children's lives, but the professional literature indicates that even young children can distinguish fact from fantasy in most circumstances. If counsel paints an inaccurate picture of a child's ability in this regard, expert rebuttal testimony is warranted.

There is little American case law regarding the type of rebuttal testimony discussed here (*United States* v. *Azure* (1986)). However, lack of precedent should not dissuade courts from permitting expert rebuttal testimony designed to acquaint jurors with the developmental capabilities and limits of young children.

Direct testimony on children's credibility

In contrast to the above discussion, where expert testimony may have the *indirect* effect of bolstering a child's credibility, this subsection is concerned with the expert's *direct* testimony on the credibility of a particular child, or on the credibility of sexually abused children as a class. American courts approach unanimity when it comes to expert testimony on credibility: the majority of courts reject expert testimony which comments directly on the credibility of individual children (*State* v. *Moran* (1986)) or on the credibility of sexually abused children as a class *Commonwealth* v. *Ianello* (1987)).

Courts employ several rationales to reject expert testimony on credibility. A number of decisions hold that experts cannot discuss the statistical likelihood that children tell the truth. A great many decisions state that experts may not express opinions concerning the credibility of particular children (*State* v. *Moran* (1986)). Expert testimony on credibility is also rejected by the courts on grounds that the testimony does not assist the jury (*State* v. *Lindsey* (1986)). Others believe the evidence will over-awe the jury and tempt jurors to forego independent evaluation of credibility (*United States* v. *Azure* (1986)). Some believe expert testimony invites a battle of the experts, and a trial within a trial on a collateral issue (*United States* v. *Barnard* (1973)). Others worry the testimony will waste time (*People* v. *Snook* (1987)). A number of decisions raises the possibility that the probative worth of expert testimony on credibility may be substantially outweighed by the potential of the testimony to cause unfair prejudice (*State* v. *Moran* (1986)).

At bottom, the rationale underlying rejection of expert testimony on credibility is a well-settled belief that assessment of credibility is, and must remain, the exclusive province of the jury (*State* v. *Lindsay* (1986)).

It is appropriate to prohibit expert testimony that a child told the truth on a particular occasion. There is considerable intuitive appeal to the notion that jurors defer too quickly to 'expert' assessment of credibility. Furthermore, while qualified experts possess specialized knowledge regarding certain aspects of credibility, expert capacity to detect lying and coaching is too limited to justify admission of generalized credibility testimony.

While generalized credibility testimony is properly excluded, circumstances exist where narrowly tailored expert testimony should be received to rebut certain attacks on credibility. For example, if the defence asserts or intimates strongly that children as a group lie about sexual abuse, it seems fair to permit rebuttal expert testimony. Such testimony could draw from the clinical and scientific literature for the conclusion that fabricated allegations of sexual abuse are uncommon (Jones & McGraw, 1987).

It may occasionally be proper to admit narrowly tailored expert testimony regarding credibility in juvenile court protective proceedings and in child custody and visitation cases incident to divorce. There is no jury in such litigation. Thus, concern about jury confusion is eliminated.

EXPERT TESTIMONY FOCUSED ON THE ALLEGED PERPETRATOR

Expert testimony identifying the perpetrator

Nothing in the professional literature suggests that experts on child sexual abuse possess special knowledge or expertise that allows them to identify the perpetrator of sexual abuse. In the few American cases to discuss such expert testimony, courts quite properly reject it (*Seering* v. *Department of Social Services* (1987)).

Psychological testimony describing the profile of persons who abuse children

In a small number of American decisions dealing with physical and sexual abuse, the prosecution offered to prove that the defendant matched a psychological profile of persons who abuse children. In another group of decisions, the defence sought to establish innocence through evidence that the defendant was not similar to the 'typical' child abuser. These decisions are discussed below.

(a) *Physical abuse cases*

While the focus of this chapter is on sexual abuse, it is instructive to review cases in which psychological profile evidence was offered to prove or disprove physical abuse. Psychological research discloses that a number of parents who physically abuse their children share certain character traits. In

State v. *Loebach* (1981) a child abuse expert testified that 'abusing parents frequently experience role reversal and often expect their children to care for them. . . . (T)hey often exhibit . . . characteristics such as low empathy, a short fuse, . . . strict authoritarianism, uncommunicativeness, low self-esteem, isolation and lack of trust.'

In addition to the traits described above, many physically abusive parents were physically or sexually abused by their own parents. Adults possessing the foregoing traits may be at increased risk of abusing their children. The phrase 'battering parent syndrome' was coined to describe the constellation of characteristics observed in some abusive parents.

In the legal context, when an individual charged with physical abuse demonstrates character traits found in the battering parent syndrome, arguably there is an increased likelihood that the person committed the alleged abuse. Prosecutors have occasionally sought admission of testimony designed to establish that a defendant's personality fits the battering parent syndrome (*Sanders* v. *State* (1983)). The purpose of such evidence is to convince the trier of fact that because the defendant fits the profile of a battering parent, the defendant is probably guilty.

Courts have refused to admit evidence of battering parent syndrome because such proof contravenes the rule against character evidence, is highly prejudicial, and is of marginal relevance (*State* v. *Loebach* (1981)). An occasional decision suggests that if further research establishes the validity of the battering parent syndrome, such evidence may become admissible (*Sanders* v. *State* (1983)).

Decisions rejecting the battering parent syndrome are correct. A cardinal principle of American law holds that evidence of a person's character generally is not admissible to prove that the person acted in conformity therewith on a particular occasion. Teitlbaum and Hertz (1983) say it well when they write:

> [The law] makes inadmissible, with certain exceptions, evidence relevant on the following theory: Defendant committed a wrong in the past; defendant therefore has a propensity or a character trait for committing wrongful acts; therefore defendant is more likely to have engaged in the act for which he is on trial than is someone not known to have this character trait.

This maxim finds expression in Rule 404 (a) of the Federal Rules of Evidence, which states that 'evidence of a person's character or a trait of character is not admissible for the purpose of proving action in conformity therewith on a particular occasion'.

Proof of battering parent syndrome violates Rule 404 (a) because the syndrome draws its evidentiary force from the chain of inferences forbidden by the Rule. The syndrome rests on the following logic: (i) People who physically abuse children possess certain character traits, (ii) Defendant possesses such traits, and consequently defendant has a propensity or a character trait for child abuse, (iii) therefore, defendant probably acted in conformity with character on the occasion in question, and committed the charged abuse. This is character evidence, and it is properly excluded when offered by the state to prove guilt.

Unlike the prosecution, the defendant is permitted to offer character evidence to establish innocence. Rule 404 (a) (1) of the Federal Rules of Evidence permits '[e]vidence of a pertinent trait of character offered by an accused . . .'. Theoretically, a defendant charged with physical abuse could offer proof that he or she does not fit the battering parent profile. If the defence offers such evidence, however, the door opens for the prosecution to offer rebutting character evidence.

Regardless of which party offers battering parent syndrome evidence, serious questions persist about the syndrome's reliability. Before admitting such evidence, courts should evaluate the syndrome under the applicable test for determining admissibility of novel scientific evidence. Application of the test will probably lead to exclusion of the evidence.

(b) *Sexual abuse cases*

In the realm of sexual abuse, the clinical and scientific literature discloses that sex offenders are a heterogeneous group with few shared characteristics apart from a predilection for deviant sexual behaviour (Myers *et al.*, 1989). Furthermore, there is no psychological test or device that reliably detects persons who have or will sexually abuse children. Thus, it is appropriate to conclude that under the current state of scientific knowledge, there is no profile of a 'typical' child molester.

Despite the lack of a reliable profile, an occasional prosecutor has offered expert testimony describing the character traits of a 'typical' child molester (*United States* v. *Gillespie* (1988)). The courts have rejected prosecution attempts to prove guilt through profile evidence. Profile evidence violates the rule against character evidence to prove guilt. Furthermore, the relevant literature does not support the existence of a profile that can detect persons who sexually abuse children. But should a different result follow when the defence offers profile evidence? In a number of reported decisions, the defendant offered expert testimony that he did not fit within a profile of a 'typical' child sexual abuser. Under the rules of evidence, a defendant is permitted to offer evidence of a pertinent trait of character to prove innocence. In a child sexual abuse case, the theory of such evidence is that because the defendant lacks the personality traits found in persons who sexually abuse children, the defendant probably did not commit the charged offence.

This theory of proof is defective. The scientific literature does not support the conclusion that there is a reliable profile of a 'typical' sex offender. Despite this fact, however, some mental health professionals are willing to testify that a profile exists. Faced with such testimony, a number of courts have determined that sex offender profiles are a form of novel scientific evidence. Courts adopting this approach correctly conclude that profile evidence has not found general acceptance in the relevant scientific community. Lack of acceptance leads to exclusion of the evidence (*United States* v. *St Pierre* (1987)). Recently, the California Supreme Court approved expert testimony from a defence psychologist that a defendant did not demonstrate any traits of deviance, and was therefore not likely to have committed the charged sexual abuse (*People* v. *Stoll*, 1989).

A NEW CONCEPT: COURT APPOINTED EXPERTS ON CHILD DEVELOPMENT

Children take the witness stand with increasing frequency. It is not uncommon for children as young as three and four to testify. When the individual on the witness stand is a child whose head is barely visible above the rail of the witness box, and whose feet dangle a foot or more from the floor, the judge and the attorneys face unique challenges.

Young witnesses have special needs which must be understood if children are to testify effectively. In some cases, it may be appropriate for the judge to appoint a neutral expert on child development to assist the court in understanding the developmental and psychological needs of particular child witnesses. A developmental expert could assist court and counsel in numerous ways. For example, the expert could advise the court on steps that could be taken to render testifying less traumatic for a child. The expert might inform the court of a child's cognitive and communicative abilities so that the court can control the proceedings to enable the child to communicate effectively.

A court appointed expert on child development should not offer testimony on the substance of allegations of child sexual abuse. The expert should remain strictly non-partisan. The expert's role is not to prove or disprove abuse, but to assist the court in executing the difficult responsibility of ensuring a fair trial, protecting vulnerable witnesses, and fostering complete and accurate testimony.

CONCLUSION

Expert testimony plays an important role in child sexual abuse litigation. Such testimony can assist the jury in many ways. Yet, the issues raised by expert testimony are exceedingly complex, and clinical and scientific understanding of child sexual abuse is still developing. Courts should proceed cautiously when considering the admissibility of expert testimony on child sexual abuse. It is vitally important that professionals offering such testimony are highly qualified. Courts should insist on a thorough showing of expertise before permitting individuals to testify as experts. Furthermore, courts should require the proponent of expert testimony to lay a thorough foundation so that the court understands precisely how the evidence is relevant. When appropriate caution is exercised, qualified experts can assist in attaining justice.

REFERENCES

American Academy of Child and Adolescent Psychiatry (1988). Guidelines for the Clinical Evaluation of Child and Adolescent Sexual Abuse, *J. Am. Academy Child & Adolescent Psychiatry*, 665, 657.

American Medical Association (1985). Diagnostic and Treatment Guidelines Concerning Child Abuse and Neglect, *J.A.M.A.*, 254, 798.

Commonwealth v. *Ianello* (1987). 401 Mass. 197, 515 N.E. 2d 1181.

Commonwealth v. *Baldwin* (1985). 502 A.2d 253, Pa. Super. Ct.

Conte, J., Sorenson, E., Fogarty, L., and Rosa, J. (1988). 'Evaluating children's reports of sexual abuse: results from a survey of professionals', unpublished manuscript.

Faller, K. C. (1988). 'Criteria for Judging and Credibility of Children's Statements about their Sexual Abuse', *Child Welfare*. 657, 389.

Finkelhor, D. (1979). *Sexually Victimized Children*. New York Free Press.

Goodman, G. S., Bottoms, B. L., Herscovici, B. B. and Shaver, P. (1989). *Determinants of the child victim's perceived credibility*. In: S. Ceci, D. Ross and M. Toglia (eds.) *Perspectives on Children's Testimony*..

Jones, D. and McQuiston, M. (1988). *Interviewing the Sexually Abused Child*. 3, The C. Henry Kempe National Center for the Prevention and Treatment of Child Abuse and Neglect.

Jones, D. and McGraw, J. M. (1987). Reliable and Fictitious Accounts of Sexual Abuse to Children, *J. Interpersonal Violence*, 2, 27.

McCord, D. (1986). Expert Psychological Testimony about Child Complainants in Sexual Abuse Prosecutions: A Foray into the Admissibility of Novel Psychological Evidence', *J. Crim. L. and Criminology*, 1, 77.

Melton, G. and Limber, S. (1989). Psychologist's Involvement in Cases of Child Maltreatment. *American Psychologist, 44, 1225.*

Myers, J. (1987). *Child Witness Law and Practice*. Wiley, 5.36.

Myers, J., Bays, J., Becker, J., Berliner, L., Corwin, D. and Saywitz, K. (1989). 'Expert testimony in child sexual abuse litigation', *Nebraska Law Review*, 68, 1.

Owens v. *State*, (1987). 514 N.E. 2d 1257, Ind.

People v. *Gray*, (1986). 187 Cal. App. 3d 220, 231 Cal. Rptr. 658.

People v. *Mendibles*, (1988). 245 Cal. Rptr., 553, 562.

People v. *Roscoe*, (1985). 168 Cal. App. 3d 1093, 215 Cal. Rptr. 45.

People v. *Snook*, (1987). 745 P. 2d 647, 649 n. 4, Colo.

People v. *Stoll*, (1989). 783 P. 2d 698, 265 Cal. Rptr. 111.

Sanders v. *State*, (1983). 251 Ga. 70, 303 S.E. 2d 13.

Seering v. *Department of Social Services*, (1987) 194 Cal. App. 3d 298, 239 Cal. Rptr. 422.

Sgroi, S. M., Porter, F. S. and Blick, L. C. (1982). 'Validation of Child Sexual Abuse',. in: S. Sgroi ed. *Handbook of Clinical Intervention in Child Sexual Abuse*. 72, Lexington Books.

State v. *Black*, (1988). 537 A. 2d 1154, Me.

State v. *Butler*, (1986). 256 Ga. 448, 349 S.E. 2d 684.

State v. *Galloway*, (1981). 304 N.C. 485, 284 D.E. 2d 509.

State v. *Heseltine* (1984). 120 Wis. 2d92, 352 N.W. 2d 673 Ct. App.

State v. *Lindsey*, (1986). 149 Ariz. 472, 720 P. 2d 73, 75-76.

State v. *Loebach*, (1981). 310 N.W. 2d 58, Min.

State v. *Moran*, (1986). 151 Ariz. 378, 728 P. 2d 248.

State v. *Tanner*, (1983). 675 P. 2d 539, 544, Utah.

Teitelbaum, L. F. and Hertz, N. A. (1983). Evidence 11: Evidence of Other Crimes as Proof of Intent, *N.M.L. Rev.*, 428, 423-24.

Townsend v. *State*, (1987). Nev. 734 P. 2d 705.

United States v. *Azure* (1986). 810 F. 2d 336, 8th Cir.
United States v. *Barnard,* (1973). 490 F. 2d 907, 9th Cir.
United States v. *Gillespie,* (1988). 852 F. 2d 475, 9th Cir.
United States v. *St Pierre,* (1987). 812 F. 2d 417, 420, 8th Cir.
White, S. and Santilli, G., (1988). 'A review of clinical practices and research data on anatomical dolls', *Journal Interpersonal Violence,* 3, 430-442.
Wigmore, J. (rev. edn. 1978). *Evidence in Trials at Common Law* 1923. Chadbourn.

9

SOURCES OF STRESS FOR CHILD WITNESSES IN COURT

RHONA FLIN

IN BOTH ENGLAND and Scotland, attempts are being made to improve the legal procedures encountered by child witnesses (many of whom are victims of sexual abuse), who are required to give evidence in a criminal trial. (See chapters 8 and 9 for a full description of the current proposals and reforms.) These changes have been precipitated by a growing public and professional awareness that our criminal courts are imperfectly designed for hearing children's evidence. For many child victims the necessary court appearance proves to be a highly traumatic experience, and for some children an insurmountable hurdle to their evidence being heard or a successful prosecution being achieved.

Effects on the child

Despite the weight of anecdotal and expert opinion that the trial could result in a re-victimization of the child (Avery, 1983) and in failure to prosecute in valid cases, there is very little published research which unequivocally supports this belief. In fact, two other viewpoints have been reported. First, that children are not affected or that any distress caused to children, according to a senior Scottish judge, is of a temporary nature and what one would expect of a witness before a court (Irvine and Dunning, 1985). (That opinion perhaps raises questions about the feelings of adult witnesses and the extent to which these interest the legal profession.) Thus, one view is that any distress caused to children is either temporary or, in fact, does not exist. The second view is that children may actually be helped or be empowered by their experience in the courtroom (Berliner and Barbieri, 1984). This belief tends to be qualified by the rider, if the case is handled well, and any therapeutic benefits may well depend on other factors, such as the final outcome of the prosecution.

Hence, there are three views: (i) the child is affected by the court appearance in a negative way; (ii) there is no effect on the child; (iii) the child is helped by giving evidence in court. One of the problems facing those who argue that courts are unnecessarily stressful for child witnesses and that changes should be made to the rules of evidence and the procedures for hearing children's evidence, is that there is virtually no medical or scientific proof that children are actually harmed by going to court. (Many professionals who work with child victims believe that this is so obvious that it hardly merits debate, but from the resistance to the proposals for reform, it must be deduced that not all lawyers share their concern.) Nor is there any clear definition of which aspects of the trial proceedings cause most distress to child witnesses.

This chapter proceeds on the assumption that courts are unnecessarily stressful, perhaps not for every child, but for the majority of child witnesses. Adult victims can find attending court to be a stressful experience, (N.A.V.S.S., 1988) as can regular witnesses, such as police officers (Davidson and Veno, 1980). The original studies of the effects of court on child witnesses, one English (Gibbens and Prince, 1963), the other American (De Francis, 1969), both suggested that child victims are affected by having to attend court. Their conclusions are weakened by methodological flaws, nevertheless more recent research appears to confirm the basic finding (Runyan *et al.*, 1988; Tedesco and Schnell, 1987). Gail Goodman and David Jones (Goodman *et al.*, 1988) have been assessing the long-term effects of a court appearance on child witnesses. They compared child victims of sexual abuse who gave evidence with child victims of the same kinds of incidents who did not testify. Preliminary findings indicated that three months after the trial 'the children who testified in court show a marginally significant increase in overall behavioural disturbance' (p. 51). This study, the first of its kind, was conducted in Denver and there are no comparable British data although two new research projects are looking at the response of the legal system to child victims in England (Morgan and Plotnikoff, 1990) and child witnesses in Scotland (Flin and Bull, 1990).

One of the problems in attempting to measure the psychological effects of giving evidence is that for child abuse victims, it is very difficult to disentangle the reaction to court from post-traumatic stress effects caused by the abuse, from the parental reaction, or the investigation (Vizard, 1988). In the Scottish project (Flin and Bull, 1990) mentioned above, the researchers are studying a sample of child witnesses who attend court in Glasgow to give evidence in criminal trials. By comparing the reactions of children who have merely observed a crime as a bystander, with child victims, it may be possible to distinguish the effects of attending court from effects attributable to the child's involvement in a criminal incident.

Sources of stress

The forerunner to the Glasgow study was completed in Aberdeen in 1988 (Flin, Davies and Tarrant, 1988), (both projects were funded by the Scottish Home and Health Department). This investigation examined various psychological aspects of children's evidence, namely reliability, credibility and the child's experiences in court. The research concerned all types of crimes involving child bystanders as well as child victims. One major area of interest focussed on the causes of stress for child witnesses. Using a postal questionnaire, a sample of about a hundred professionals who had experience of working with child witnesses in criminal courts (police officers, procurators fiscal, social workers, psychologists and judges) were surveyed. They were asked what they believed to be the main sources of stress for children cited as witnesses.

In summary, some respondents believed that everything was stressful, others thought that cross-examination was particularly difficult, stress was also attributed to seeing, identifying and standing near the accused. Other aspects of giving evidence that were felt to be stressful include the formality of the courtroom itself, standing up in a large room and speaking out in front of an adult audience. Waiting is said to be stressful on two counts: waiting for many months before coming to court and, once called to court, waiting for hours or days for the trial to commence. The legal terminology was thought to present problems: children have difficulty in understanding aspects of the proceedings and what is said to them in the courtroom.

In order to identify the stressful aspects of being in a courtroom, respondents were invited to state anything about the layout and design of the courtroom that might be especially difficult for child witnesses. Experts were of the opinion that the dimensions of the courtroom tend to be unsuitable, being for the most part large, and in the eyes of a child, separating the participants by vast distances. If a young child is allowed to sit while giving evidence, there is unlikely to be a suitable chair. The layout of a typical courtroom is very formal and probably quite alien to a small child. Another problem mentioned was the isolation of the witness box, sometimes children stand there alone with no support person nearby, and the child may wonder exactly who is on trial. The elevation of the judge is not particularly helpful when the witness is a child, nor is the proximity of the dock to the witness box. Finally, poor acoustics and a lack of microphones may result in the child being repeatedly asked to speak louder, a request which is guaranteed to increase the witness's anxiety if the evidence concerns a sexual assault.

The results of this pilot study confirm the findings of an earlier survey of American professionals who worked with child victims, which was conducted by Debra Whitcomb (1985). The stress factors which appear to be present in English and Scottish courts were also present in the United States.

It cannot be assumed that what adults think are the main causes of stress are in fact the real stressors for children, and there is no published research into children's feelings about going to court and their perceptions of what is stressful. In an attempt to remedy this default, the Aberdeen study (Flin *et al.*, 1988) included a small sample of child witnesses attending criminal trials. They were interviewed in the waiting room before the trial, they were observed giving evidence in the courtroom, and were interviewed after the trial. The parent or guardian accompanying the child was also interviewed before and after the trial. Obviously children could not be questioned about the case being heard, but they were asked how they felt that morning about coming to court. The majority of children said that they were worried, scared or nervous. Not all children, but the majority, were clearly anxious about being there. Those who expressed negative emotions, were asked what it was about being in court that morning that produced these feelings. One of the major factors identified was a fear of the unknown. Child witnesses do not know what will happen in the courtroom, they do not always understand their role in the proceedings, nor do they comprehend the roles of the various professionals who are involved in the trial. This result was confirmed by a subsequent study which measured 6, 8 and 10-year-old children's (non witnesses) and adult's knowledge of legal terminology and of court proceedings (Flin, Stevenson and Davies, 1989). The subjects were asked a series of questions about various aspects of criminal law; for example, "Do you know what a jury is?" "Do you know what a judge is?" This survey revealed significant gaps and misunderstanding in children's knowledge of the law. In addition their answers indicated some alarming misconceptions about the roles of participants (including the witnesses) and of the purpose of a trial.

Children are not well prepared for court, they have a rudimentary knowledge of what will happen there and often misunderstand the true meanings of legal terms which they claim they know. Their lack of knowledge is matched by a significant level of legal ignorance in adults. Parents frequently reported having great difficulty in explaining to their children that would take place in the courtroom. This is not to minimise the importance of the work being done by those social workers, police officers and prosecutors who carefully prepare children for criminal trials, but there are no general guidelines or standard procedures (Morgan and Plotnikoff, 1990). In Scotland, the procurators fiscal in Glasgow, in conjunction with the Crown Office, have designed an explanatory leaflet (Crown Office, 1989) which is now being issued to all children cited as witnesses. This kind of practical approach will certainly help to reduce one stressful aspect of a child's visit to court.

The other factors which were mentioned by the child witnesses and their parents had also been identified in the survey of professionals. Facing the accused and fear of retribution was a source of concern for child bystanders as well as child victims. Children were worried about giving evidence and having to speak out in front of many unfamiliar adults. Parents were sometimes concerned about their child's ability to cope with the cross-examination; the children did not necessarily know that they would be questioned in this way. A recent Australian study has shown that children often do not understand the language used by defence lawyers in cross-examination (Brennan and Brennan, 1988), and being wrongfully accused of lying is a traumatic experience for most children (Yamamoto *et al.*, 1987).

The long delays experienced by witnesses were generally regarded as stressful. In the Aberdeen sample, children waited from one to 17 months between witnessing the incident and the date of the trial; the average delay period was six months. There are many reasons for these delays in bringing cases to trial, but a long delay seems to increase the difficulty for both parent and child. Another problem mentioned was waiting on the day of the trial, sometimes in unsuitable surroundings, with the risk of seeing the accused, and the presence of uniformed police officers and begowned lawyers who may look rather frightening to a young child. These sources of stress for witnesses are not peculiar to criminal trials but are also encountered by witnesses in civil trials (Smith, 1988).

Possible solutions

Possible methods of alleviating witnesses' anxieties without threatening the rights of the accused range from radical reforms such as the admission of prerecorded interview material to very minor changes designed to reduce the formality of the courtroom. The ultimate responsibility for the witness's well being rests with the judge, although the degree to which they are prepared to intervene during hostile questioning or to modify courtroom procedures appears to vary quite significantly. In the trial scene in Alice in Wonder land the Judge offered the following encouraging advice to the Mad Hatter:-

> "Give your evidence," said the King; "and don't be nervous or I'll have you executed on the spot." (Carroll, 1865.)

The experts surveyed by Flin *et al.* (1988) were asked to offer suggestions for possible solutions to the problems they had described. Many respondents believed that video-recordings should be used but there appeared to be different conceptions of the way this technique would operate in practice. For example, one possibility would be to use the live video-link system currently being evaluated in England, whereas another option would be to admit as evidence pre-recorded videotaped interviews with the child. There is little doubt that a visual record of a young child's non-verbal behaviour would be informative, as would the record of the questions used to elicit the child's statements. The competence of the interviewer is a major determinant of the reliability of a child's evidence (Spencer and Flin, 1990).

A number of experts suggested that a child supporter or child advocate should be appointed to support the child in court, or recommended that a parent or trusted adult should be allowed to sit with the child when she or he was giving evidence. There are occasions when children are expected to enter the courtroom alone and this can be very alarming for the child. Other proposals included the following: to reduce the formality of the courtroom, for example, by the lawyers removing their wigs and gowns; the introduction of screens to prevent the child seeing the accused; and improved waiting facilities. Parents do not expect to have to wait, sometimes for several hours, before their child is called to give evidence and consequently do not arrive prepared to amuse their child during a delay. Glasgow Sheriff Court must be one of the few which can actually boast of its excellent creche facility.

Many of these suggestions for reducing unnecessary stress would not require complex legal reform or the introduction of expensive equipment. These changes might only alleviate stress to a minimal degree but are worth considering in the short-term while child victims continue to be traumitised by the necessity of giving evidence in open court, in the presence of the accused.

REFERENCES

Avery, M. (1983) 'The child abuse witness: potential for secondary victimization', *Criminal Justice Journal*, 7, 1-48.

Berliner, L. and Barbieri, M. (1984) 'The testimony of the child victim of sexual assault', *Journal of Social Issues*, 40, 125-137.

Brennan, M. and Brennan, R. (1988) *Strange Language*. Wagga Wagga: Riverina Literacy Centre.

Carroll, L. (1865) *Alice's Adventures in Wonderland*. London: Blackie.

Crown Office (1989) *Going to Court*, 5/7 Regent Rd., Edinburgh.

Davidson, M. and Veno, A. (1980) 'Stress and the policeman', in C. Cooper and J. Marshall (Eds.) *White Collar and Professional Stress*. Chichester: Wiley.

De Francis, V. (1969) *Protecting the Child Victim of Sex Crimes Committed by Adults*. Denver: Humane Association.

Flin, R. and Bull, R. (1990) 'Child witnesses in Scottish criminal prosecutions', in J. Spencer, G. Nicholson, R. Flin and R. Bull (eds.) *Children's Evidence in Legal Proceedings*.

Flin, R., Davies, G. and Tarrant, A. (1988) *Children as Witnesses*. Final Report to the Scottish Home and Health Department, Grant 85/9290.

Flin, R., Stevenson, Y. and Davies, G. (1989) 'Children's knowledge of court proceedings', *British Journal of Psychology*, 80, 285-297.

Gibbens, T. and Prince, J. (1963) *Child Victims of Sex Offences*. London: Institute for the Study and Treatment of Delinquency.

Goodman, G., Jones, D., Pyle, E., Estrado, L., Port, L., England, P., Mason, R. and Rudy, L. (1988) 'The emotional effects of criminal court testimony on child sexual assault victims: A preliminary report', in G. Davies and J. Drinkwater (eds.) *The Child Witness — Do the Courts Abuse Children?* Leicester: British Psychological Society.

Irvine, R. and Dunning, N. (1985) 'The child and the criminal justice system', Journal of the Law Society of Scotland, 30, 264-266.

Morgan, J. and Plotnikoff, J. (1990) 'Children as victims of crime', in J. Spencer, G. Nicholson, R. Flin and R. Bull (eds.) *Children's Evidence in Legal Proceedings*. London: Hawksmere.

National Association of Victim Support Schemes (1988) The Victim in Court, Report of a Working Party.

Runyan, D., Everson, M., Edelsohn, G., Hunter, W. and Coulter, M. (1988) 'Impact of legal intervention on sexually abused children', *Journal of Paediatrics*, 113, 647-653.

Smith, P. (1988) 'Families in court — guilty or guilty?' *Children and Society*, 2, 152-164.

Spencer, J. and Flin, R. (1990) *The Evidence of Children: the Law and the Psychology*. London: Blackstone.

Tedesco, J. and Schnell, S. (1987) 'Children's reactions to sex abuse investigation and litigation', *Child Abuse and Neglect*, 11, 267-272.

Vizard, E. (1988) 'Child sexual abuse — The child's experience', *British Journal of Psychotherapy*, 5, 77-90.

Whitcomb, D., Shapiro, E. and Stellwagon, L. (1985). *When the Victim is a Child*. Washington: Department of Justice.

Yamamoto, K., Soliman, A., Parsons, J. and Davies, O. (1987) 'Voices in unison: Stressful events in the lives of children in six countries', *Journal of Child Psychology and Psychiatry*, 28, 855-864.

10

LEGAL AND CLINICAL ISSUES IN VIDEOTAPING

HARRY ELIAS AND KEE MACFARLANE

THE USE OF videotechnology in court proceedings to alleviate the trauma for the child witness has given rise in the United States to legal and clinical issues similar to those emerging in the United Kingdom. Video equipment is used in the United States in three ways: videotaped interviews, videotaped hearings and closed-circuit or contemporaneous television (Dziech & Schudson, 1989).

A videotaped interview is not admissible in court in lieu of live testimony in any of the American states. Videotaped hearings, on the other hand, are commonly used in some jurisdictions. They can take the form of a deposition or of an actual courtroom proceeding, such as preliminary examination before trial, which is adversarial in nature. The attorneys for both sides pose questions and they may or may not be officiated by a judge, so that evidentiary issues can be ruled upon. The whole proceeding is videotaped. In contemporaneous closed-circuit television, one party is separated physically from the courtroom to which they are linked by a live television beam. The defendant can observe and hear the witness's testimony but the witness can neither see nor hear the defendant. Alternatively the witness and the defendant can view each other. The proceeding is also videotaped and used in the event of a later review in the higher courts.

Although most of the issues around videotaping have arisen in relation to criminal proceedings it is a widespread view both in Britain and in the United States that the use of videotechnology is equally pertinent in civil proceedings and, in Scotland, in proof hearings in the sheriff court.

Videotaped interviews

Videotaped interviews have many limitations in the legal setting, and generally they are inadmissible in lieu of a child's live testimony in criminal trials. Where they have been admitted (either in addition to testimony or with the concurrence of the defence) the attention of the court has tended to focus on the style and conduct of the interviewer rather than on the content of the interview with the child.

There are some advantages to videotaped interviews. First, they can be very useful when dealing with young children (in the United States the children are frequently four, five and six years old whereas in the UK the children are more likely to be aged eight, nine and ten years). Because small children have limited reading skills, they have difficulty reviewing their previous statements before going into court. Showing the videotaped interview can refresh the child's memory as to what was said in the past. Showing the videotaped interview to the defendant is a technique which has been used to obtain guilty pleas, thus eliminating a confrontational court proceeding. Videotapes can also be used with advantage in court to demonstrate some of the child's affect when disclosing what transpired.

However, one disadvantage may outweigh the advantages. The attack on the style, conduct and content used by the interviewer may be used to discredit the taped interview, while at the same time giving the interview a central position in that evidence. Consequently, the court does not adequately consider the full amount of evidence from the child.

Pre-trial recorded hearings

The deposition hearing can be held outside the courtroom and, although adversarial, need not be so austere or as hostile an environment as the courtroom setting. However, generally no judge presides. Since each side has the opportunity to ask questions, receive responses, direct examinations and cross-examinations, the rights of neither side are denied. The tape can be used later at trial in lieu of the child's testimony so that the child need only go through the process on one occasion.

The statutes of several states provide that the preliminary hearing testimony of child witnesses may be videotaped. A growing number of states permit trial judges to authorise video depositions of child witnesses. In California, for example, the preliminary hearing is presided over by a judge who will conduct the proceeding. This has the advantage that the child who still has to testify at trial can review the tape in advance. Since in California 'probable cause' is the only issue in the preliminary hearing and there is no jury present to be offended by the attorney's questions, the examination of the child can be much more harsh and aggressive than would occur at trial. This may intimidate children and their parents. If the attorneys know that they are being visually and audibly recorded they may be less likely to adopt a harsh approach. Hence videotaping, by reducing the hostile nature of the atmosphere, results in better protection for the child.

Closed-circuit contemporaneous television

Although in California there is a statute in force which allows the child's evidence to be heard by two-way closed-circuit television, it has been used only with reluctance. Because it must be shown that testifying in open court is likely to harm the child, expert witnesses are called by the prosecution to support this claim: the defence also may call on expert witnesses to say whether in their view the child will suffer trauma. Hence, ascertaining whether closed-circuit television is necessary can result in the child having multiple interviews with experts and is one reason for resisting its use. It should be noted that the issue of whether court testimony via two-way closed circuit television complies with a defendant's Constitutional right to face-to-face confrontation with the accusor has not yet been determined by the highest courts in the United States. The US supreme Court is expected to make a ruling on this issue sometime in 1990.

Another reason for resisting its use is the prohibitive cost. In order to make it effective, the law in California requires expenditure on six cameras, four monitors and four recording systems, that is, a monitor for each of the attorneys, the judge and the jury and two monitors for the child, one to see the person who is asking the questions and one to see the offender. In addition, all of that must itself be recorded. It has therefore been found to be cost prohibitive. For example, in Los Angeles it has cost a thousand dollars a day to set up, a thousand dollars for each day the equipment was in operation, not including the taping itself, and another thousand to dismantle the equipment.

Another practical concern is that many people do not believe much of what they see on a television screen. Many practitioners fear that if the jurors see the defendant and other witnesses in person and the child only by way of a television screen, it may be more negative to the nature of the case. The balance between prejudice to the case and the effect on the child is extremely difficult to strike, but is something that needs to be constantly under review when considering the use of closed-circuit television. While alternatives to live testimony certainly should be explored, a great deal might be achieved by making adjustments to the courtroom and seeking alternative forms of testimony before looking to videotechnology. Of course, the prosecutor may have legal and tactical reasons for choosing a particular approach that is not based on the best interest of the individual witness but relates to the outcome of the case.

Clinical advantages of videotaping

Videotaping has a number of distinct advantages clinically. By reducing the number of duplicate interviews it can lessen the trauma for the child. It also captures the initial emotions and spontaneity and provides a verbatim account of the interview.

Videotaping also can be useful as a medium for translating the interview with the child to the parents and, in particular, to parents, who have difficulty accepting the idea that their child has been molested. Often children are threatened not to disclose the abuse to parents or may be fearful of their parents' reactions. The videotape can provide a bridge between the child, the interviewer and the parents. For example, the parents might be shown the interview in front of the child with the tape being stopped at significant points in the interview. They might then be invited to react by the clinician making a comment, such as, 'That seems pretty hard for you to talk about but it's important for your parents to hear it too'. While the parents watch the videotape, the child usually watches their reactions. If this technique is used, a great deal of time must be given to preparing the parents for viewing the tape and, in particular, working on their reactions to what they will see and hear so that they can remain as calm and neutral as possible in front of the child. This technique should not be used with caretakers who cannot contain their reactions or with anyone whom the child may implicate in the abuse.

The videotape is also an excellent bridge between the initial interview and the therapist who will be responsible for on-going treatment. If the child can share the initial disclosure on videotape with the therapist, or if the therapist at least has access to the tape, it can provide a baseline of information, a picture of the child's reactions to questions and possibly prevent the need for repetitive questioning.

Disadvantages of videotaping

Videotaping can be a distraction which can have an effect on both the child and the interviewer that can never be overcome. Some children and a small percentage of interviewers become self-conscious and distracted by the camera and, even when it is not in the same room, they may become preoccupied with the idea of being filmed.

A further problem with videotaping an initial interview is that a single interview is in no way the whole picture of what has happened in a case or in a child's life. If the interview has been videotaped at a very early stage in a case (especially if it is the first interview with a non-disclosing child), the interview may be difficult and the disclosure process a long one. If the child has been molested in secrecy and threatened or warned not to tell (as is often the case), he or she will be unlikely to disclose the abuse easily or voluntarily, but instead will be very reluctant and may initially deny that abuse occurred. Such a child may go through a process that has been called, 'The No-Maybe-Sometimes-Yes Syndrome' (MacFarlane and Krebs, 1986): a very slow disclosure that takes the form of small steps toward acknowledgment, provides limited amounts of information, and may be overly sensitive to perceived negative reactions of the interviewer. The result of videotaping such an interview could be a recording of denials and of 'yes' or 'no' answers to very specific questions without recording the whole story in the child's own words which he or she may feel safe enough to expand upon later. On the other hand, if these preliminary stages are not recorded the interviewer may be accused of deception, bias or suggestiveness and the videotape can be criticised for being incomplete.

There is also the problem of who is the person best qualified to do the interview. Every discipline believes it has a monopoly of skill and a priority reason to be the interviewer. A comprehensive videotaped interview made available to other disciplines will go some way toward preventing multiple interviews but it does not guarantee that other professionals will make use of it. An agreement as to who will do the videotaped interview, how it will be conducted and what information will be gathered should be established in advance if the interview is expected to serve multiple purposes.

Privacy and confidentiality are also issues of very great importance. Who owns the videotapes, who sees them, who has a right to obtain copies are questions continually being raised. In some states, if criminal charges are filed, a videotaped interview might be considered part of the evidence and the defence would have a right at least to see it. Access as opposed to possession of tapes is a related issue. This can become a considerable problem, for example, in cases where there are multiple victims or defendants and a large number of videotapes circulating in the community. Furthermore, if the tapes were made by a medical or clinical treatment agency which has an obligation to maintain the privacy or confidentiality of its clients who do not want the tapes released, it may be the responsibility of the agency to try to protect them. This usually entails retaining lawyers to petition the courts on behalf of the agency and its clients. The issue of confidentiality of tapes has been before the California Supreme Court on a number of occasions. Similarly, in Britain thousands of pounds have been spent fighting over the possession of clinical material and there has been opposition to anyone other than parents and professional advisers seeing videotapes, unless in the context of a professional relationship. The issue of who owns and who may view the material is complex as well as important.

The erasure of videotapes is an additional concern. If a subpoena is issued, a piece of clinical data in the form of a videotaped interview may suddenly become a piece of legal evidence. Most courts frown very highly on erasure at that point since the act of erasure is regarded as destruction of evidence in a case. The length of time that tapes must be preserved is also a critical question in the United States, particularly in view of the storage problem they may present. Parents also may feel they have a right to own the videotape or at least to receive a copy of the child's recorded interview. In San Diego, California, the Children's Hospital makes two original videotapes simultaneously. One is kept by the hospital, the other is retained in the office of the prosecuting attorney.

Regardless of how carefully done or powerful an interview may be, there are few tapes that do not provide some grist to the defence lawyer with regard to interviewing techniques or the conduct and style of the interviewer. The tape may be transcribed rather than played so that the entire interaction with the child is lost and any non-verbal responses are eliminated. If a lawyer simply reads the transcription without the proper punctuation or totally out of context, it can be very misleading. In the United States, everything that has been said and done by the interviewer is closely scrutinised, often by individuals who are hired specifically for that purpose. Criticising the techniques, method and style of interviewers has become a full-time occupation for some defence 'experts' and has cost the courts, the insurance companies and the tax payers hundreds of thousands of dollars in cases involving videotaped interviews.

One of the most problematic uses of videotaped interviews is to see them introduced in court for purposes of impeaching a child witness. It may be pointed out that what a child said in an earlier interview is inconsistent with his or her present statement, and the point may be emphasised by playing the tape back to the child or by reading the transcript. The child may then be asked to state whether he or she was lying then or is lying now. Since young children usually do not have the maturity or communication skills to explain their own inconsistencies they feel caught and trapped by such tactics. This line of questioning has so disturbed some children and parents that they come out of court saying that, although the videotapes were made with the purpose of trying to protect children, the worst feature of the whole case was not having to testify in court, but the use of the videotape to discredit the child.

Finally, there are ethical considerations with regard to obtaining informed consent by children being interviewed or by those who can consent on their behalf. The issues are somewhat more clear-cut when videotapes are made by members of law enforcement since their purpose is more self-evident (although a child or family might not agree with the purpose if they were fully aware of its potential outcome or ramifications). Regardless of the original purpose of a videotaped or clinical interview or treatment session, it is becoming impossible to predict what other purposes it ultimately may serve. No promise should be made that the accused will never see the tape; indeed the accused may hear every word spoken by the child. It goes without saying that revealing this possibility to a child prior to videotaping might strongly affect the child's willingness to disclose. Yet if the child is not told, the issue of consent remains unresolved. David Finkelhor (1979) has said that the basic objection to sex between adults and children is that children do not have the ability to provide informed consent for things whose potential negative effects they cannot understand. The issue of consent is therefore also a consideration for those who videotape interviews with children. The location of the tapes in ten years time and how children will feel about them being played in court, in public or to the abuser are often unknown. All of these are difficult ethical issues which should be considered before video equipment is put into use.

Summary

The use of video equipment in legal proceedings is in an experimental stage at this point in time. It is anticipated that many of the legal and technical dilemmas associated with its various uses will be resolved over the next few years. Despite its practical and financial considerations, the potential for a victim to testify out of the presence of the defendant and/or the public remains an important alternative for children who, otherwise, would be too frightened or traumatised to present evidence.

The issues associated with videotaping clinical or investigatory interviews have become increasingly controversial in the United States as well as in Great Britain. As we have seen, many of the disadvantages relate to their use (or misuse) in legal proceedings. This is not to say that carefully conducted video interviews with children who freely disclose the circumstances and details of the abuse are not of benefit in a criminal trial. To the contrary, some such videotapes have been credited as the primary cause of guilty verdicts or for guilty pleas prior to actual court proceedings. Clearly, some of the issues that must be taken into consideration before videotaping interviews or clinical sessions are: the point in time that the videotape is made, the way in which the interview is conducted, the psychological and disclosure process of the child, the nature of the case and potential uses of the videotape, and the privacy issues of all concerned parties. These are difficult issues to anticipate, particularly in the early stages of a case, and particularly because the interviewer does not always have control over future uses of videotapes once they are made.

One inadvertant disadvantage of a videotaped interview in relation to legal proceedings is that it puts an unrealistic or unwarranted focus on a moment in time which may not be representative of the child's experience or demeanour since that time, and may not be an advantageous focus for the case. While a 'good' videotape can serve to counter-balance a 'bad' performance by a child on the witness stand, the influence may work in the other direction—causing judges or juries to discount children's testimony in court because of their perceptions of what occurred during earlier, taped interviews. Of equal concern are the ways that videotapes can contribute to the 'defence by distraction' approach to defending child sexual abuse cases. Because they raise so many clinical and legal issues, are subject to so many interpretations and can be so easily broken down into out-of-context pieces, videotapes have been used successfully to side-track cases onto the issue of what occurred during the interview and away from the question of what actually happened to the victim.

The issue of how and when (or whether) to videotape child interviews will probably remain the subject of debate for some time to come. Clearly interviewers are becoming more sophisticated about how to conduct interviews in ways that can minimise legal criticisms, just as prosecutors are beginning to understand and present clinical explanations for why therapists and victims act and respond in certain ways. Nonetheless, we must always keep in mind that legal and clinical purposes in child abuse cases are often quite different, and cannot always be resolved to everyone's mutual satisfaction. Furthermore, as clinicians struggle to avoid being attacked in court and to comply with the demands of the legal system, they should remember that only a small minority of child sexual abuse cases ever go to criminal court. Therefore, protocols or interview and videotaping guidelines must be developed in relation to their likely purposes, rather than tailoring an approach to the majority of cases to the minority of 'worst case' example.

Finally, we must all recognise that practices or policies that are in the best interest of the child victims are not always in the best interest of a legal case, and vice versa. This is not necessarily a terrible thing or even a preventable thing; it is just the way things are sometimes. Recognition of this fact argues all the more strongly for clinicians and legal professionals to work together to determine which cases belong in which arena, and how best to accomplish the purposes of one side without sacrificing the priorities of the other.

REFERENCES

Dziech, B. W. & Schudson, Judge, C. B. (1989) *On Trial: America's Courts and Their Treatment of Sexually Abused Children.* Boston: Beacon Press.

Finkelhor, D. (1979) 'What's wrong with sex between adults and children?', *American Journal of Orthopsychiatry*, 49, 692-697.

MacFarlane, K. & Krebs, S. (1986) 'Techniques for interviewing and evidence gathering,' in MacFarlane, K. & Waterman, J., *Sexual Abuse of Young Children.* London: The Guilford Press.

11

HEARSAY EVIDENCE

JOHN E. B. MYERS

NO ASPECT OF the law of evidence is more complex or obtuse for lawyers than the doctrine of hearsay. *Hearsay* can be defined as an out-of-court statement offered in evidence at trial to prove the truth of the statement. An example will help to clarify that definition.

Suppose that the task is to prove that an individual had toast and jam for breakfast. If a few hours after breakfast a police constable is sent to get the shirt worn by the individual and it is besmirched with jam stains and crumbs, the shirt can be confiscated and used as physical evidence to prove that the individual had toast and jam for breakfast.

But suppose that the individual is a tidy eater and the shirt or blouse is perfectly clean. There is then no physical evidence. But the waiter or waitress who served the individual with toast and jam and saw him or her consume it, might be called to the witness box. They would be an eye witness to the event. Unfortunately, the waiter or waitress has left for Australia and is no longer available: no eye witness.

The individual might be called to the witness box and simply asked whether it were true that he or she had toast and jam for breakfast that morning. But the response may be a refusal to answer because of the danger of self-incrimination. In the United States this is known as 'taking the Fifth'. Hence, there is no evidence: no eye witness, no physical evidence and the individual refuses to answer.

If after breakfast, the individual visits the bank and there says to the teller that he or she had a wonderful breakfast that morning consisting of toast and jam, that would be evidence that the individual had toast and jam for breakfast that morning. The bank teller can be called to the stand and sworn as a witness. He can be asked whether he was in the bank as a teller on a particular date. If he says he was, he can be asked if the individual came before him to transact some business. If he says he remembers distinctly that the individual did, the teller can then be asked if the individual said anything to him about what he had for breakfast. An objection would be raised since the question calls for hearsay in response. If the judge sustains the objection the bank teller would not be permitted to answer the question. The case is likely to be dismissed because there is no evidence of what the individual had for breakfast that morning.

To the lay person it would seem perfectly logical that the bank teller ought to be able to come to court and repeat what the consumer of the toast and jam had said to him. Unfortunately, when the consumer's out-of-court statement is offered in court to prove what he had for breakfast, the statement is hearsay; that is, an out-of-court statement offered in court to prove the truth of the statement. Hearsay is not admissible unless within an exception to the hearsay rule.

It can be readily seen how this applies in child sexual abuse litigation. Only rarely is there physical or medical evidence of child sexual abuse, very seldom are there eye-witnesses to this crime, and usually the defendant does not relate what happened. Parallel to the bank teller, a teacher, psychologist, physician, parent, other relative, or friend may have heard a child say what happened to him or her in distinctly clear terms. Because of the rule against hearsay, however, none of these people may be put on the witness stand to repeat the victim's out-of-court statement, if the statement is offered in court to prove the abuse. Unless the statement falls within an exception to the hearsay rule it is not admissible.

In the United States, there are sufficient hearsay exceptions that very often an out-of-court statement which is hearsay can nonetheless be used in court to prove abuse because it fits within one of the exceptions. Four or five exceptions to the hearsay rule are of particular importance in child sexual abuse litigation. In the United States, the hearsay exceptions relevant in child sexual abuse litigation appear to be greater in number and also more liberal than those applying in the jurisdictions of either Scotland or England.

One hearsay exception that is used daily in the United States is the so-called 'excited utterance' exception. An excited utterance is a statement made by a child shortly after a startling or a traumatic event, and which relates to the event. Another use of out-of-court statements is as a 'fresh complaint of rape'. A statement made by the victim of a sexual crime following that crime may be admissible as a fresh complaint. A further exception to the hearsay rule in the United States refers to statements made for purposes of medical diagnosis or treatment. A statement to a physician, a psychologist, or a psychotherapist for purposes of acquiring treatment, may be admissible in evidence. Hearsay evidence is generally excluded because it is considered to be unreliable. But where a statement is made to a doctor or a psychologist, there is an incentive to tell the truth. In some cases a person's life may depend upon the reliability of what that person tells the doctor. Hence, in most jurisdictions in the United States, statements to a practitioner for purposes of treatment are admissible because of the incentive to tell the truth. Interestingly, there is a real question whether a three-year-old understands the need to tell the doctor the truth and whether the rationale for reliability underlying the exception exists with very young children.

The hearsay exception which the Scottish Law Commission studied and considered but decided not to propose is called a 'child hearsay exception'.

Beginning in 1982 in the United States, Washington State enacted a special hearsay exception which says that any *reliable* hearsay statement by a child which does not fit within another exception is admissible. Other states quickly followed suit, and now in a majority of states there are special hearsay exceptions which apply to children usually under the age of ten or twelve. Under these exceptions, the judge considers on a case-by-case basis the reliability of statements made by children, and permits the jury to hear those statements that are reliable. For example, a vivid and graphic description of abuse made a few days following the abuse which does not qualify as an 'excited utterance' because it is too long after the abuse, but which has a ring of truthfulness about it, may be admissible under a child hearsay exception. Such statements, made closer in time, when memory is fresh, may be more reliable than statements made six months or even a year later, in a trial of a matter.

One of the untapped areas in the United States, and worth exploring in the United Kingdom, is the training of non-lawyers in the recognition and the documentation of important out-of-court statements by children. Too few professionals in the United States realise that precisely what a child says and the context in which a child says it, may have tremendous forensic and evidentiary importance. Hearsay evidence in the United States plays a very important role in child sexual abuse litigation. Training mental health and medical professionals in what to watch for in what children say, in what to document of what children say can be of unparallelled assistance to attorneys responsible for preparing a case for court. There is a whole world of opportunity for medical and mental health professionals to assist in the protection of children by becoming aware of the forensic implications of what children say. In conclusion, the recommendation of the Scottish Law Commission to admit all statements of children who testify in certain proceedings seems to be eminently reasonable and just, and is one that might be pursued. Hearsay evidence is important, and non-lawyers have a major role in gathering that evidence.

12

DIVERSION IN AMERICA AND ENGLAND

I. Diversion in the American Legal System

PATRICIA TOTH

DIVERSION PROGRAMMES FOR child sexual abuse offenders are not extensively used in the United States. They now seem to have reached their peak and the trend towards less frequent implementation in new localities is likely to continue in the future. The primary feature of a true diversion programme is avoidance of the criminal justice system for offenders and victims. No criminal sanctions are applied to offenders; there is no trial or adjudication of guilt when a person successfully completes a diversion programme; and, in effect, there is no public record of the offence committed by the abuser.

Types of schemes

There are three general types of diversion, two of which truly 'divert' offenders from the criminal justice system: (1) Pre-charge or pre-prosecution diversion occurs when the decision to divert is made prior to the filing of criminal charges. Except in very rare situations, judges and courts are not involved in these programmes. (2) Pre-plea or pre-trial diversion occurs after criminal charges have been filed and allows a defendant to avoid pleading guilty or going to trial. This differs from a negotiated plea agreement in which a defendant ultimately pleads guilty to some charge and has a criminal conviction. (3) Post-trial diversion is a term used to describe a situation where an individual has been convicted of a crime, either by guilty plea or guilty verdict, and the judge orders the sentence to be deferred. Basically this is a probationary sentencing alternative and, since there is a conviction, it does not qualify as true diversion.

People considered to be good candidates for diversion programmes are generally those who have been evaluated and found amenable to existing community treatment alternatives, who have admitted and taken responsibility for the abuse, and have acknowledged the need for treatment. Diversion is usually not available to violent offenders who have inflicted extreme physical harm on victims, or used weapons to threaten them. Requirements of the treatment programme are normally specified in advance and the candidate must be willing to comply with all of them.

Advantages of diversion

In the United States, there is widespread disagreement about the underlying philosophy of diversion and its policy implications. Those who support diversion argue that it achieves a number of objectives: (a) it reduces court congestion; (b) it reduces trauma for the victim; (c) it takes the process out of the public view. Proponents also argue that diversion offers better predictability for offenders, victims and families.

Another argument advanced in favour of diversion is that it leads to a reduction in the scale of abuse because the opportunity to avoid an adjudication of guilt and creation of a public record motivates offenders to volunteer for treatment. As a practical matter, the offender escapes criminal sanctions such as jail time and it is less likely that friends, neighbours, relatives and employers will be aware of the abusive behaviour. The theory is that offenders will have greater incentive and opportunity to become involved in treatment, which is presumed to lower the risk of re-offence. The effectiveness of treatment for child sexual abusers is still a subject of great debate however. It should also be noted that offenders who complete a diversion programme will be able to claim and take advantage of the fact that no criminal conviction exists for these crimes if and when prosecuted for future crimes. This is of special significance in the increasing number of American states which have adopted mandatory or 'determinant' sentencing schemes which reduce a judge's discretion regarding sentencing and specify sentence ranges based primarily on the defendant's record of prior criminal convictions. Arguably, a defendant who has gone through diversion and commits new crimes would not receive an appropriate amount of punishment.

Arguments against diversion

Those opposed to the concept of diversion believe that less serious crimes should be used to accomplish the goal of reducing courtroom congestion. They also challenge the suggestion that criminal prosecution will necessarily traumatise the child while the diversion process will not. Before an offender becomes involved in a diversion programme, there will almost certainly be a disclosure of abuse by a child. A thorough investigation should be conducted in any event, including investigative interviews with the child and a medical examination, to determine the frequency and nature of the abuse and the extent to which the offender accepts responsibility. Even those who become involved in diversion do not generally tell the complete truth about the extent of the abuse at the outset of the case. This process itself will impose trauma on the child. Furthermore, a good candidate for diversion should be the kind of person, usually in a familial situation, who would want to avoid forcing the child to testify in court and, in the absence of diversion, would be willing to plead guilty and assume the consequences of their behaviour.

Those opposed to the idea of diversion also regard a public proceeding identifying the offender as a deterrent to re-offence. But the identity of victims is generally not revealed by the media and in some American states special statutes have been passed which require that victims' names not be included in public documents. Thus the public nature of the criminal justice system need not necessarily subject the victim to public embarrassment.

In answer to the argument that diversion encourages abusers to volunteer for treatment, opponents counter that this assumes that fear of prosecution alone keeps them from doing so. The dynamics involved are probably not that simple. The American experience regarding mandatory reporting provides a basis for comparison. Prior to the passage of mandatory reporting laws in the United States, therapists were not required to report abuse they learned about in the course of treatment. Thus a sexual abuser voluntarily in treatment was not risking discovery and potential prosecution. However, very few offenders voluntarily sought treatment under those circumstances. Only since mandatory reporting and the resulting influx of offenders court-ordered to undergo treatment have large numbers of offenders entered treatment. It is likely, therefore, that the absence of diversion does not discourage abusers from seeking treatment on their own.

Another troublesome aspect of diversion is the notion that perpetrators of child abuse are rewarded with the opportunity to be involved in diversion programmes while other criminals are not. They receive the message that somehow child abuse crimes are less serious than other crimes, such as burglary or car theft or those involving adult victims for which there are generally no diversionary alternatives.

With few exceptions, such as California and Colorado, most diversion programmes are operated without specific statutory authority. For example, in Washington State it has been considered to be within the prosecutor's discretion to offer such an alternative. This is accomplished by means of a formal written contract between the offender and the prosecutor's office. The offender agrees to undergo and complete treatment as well as comply with other detailed conditions regarding things such as restrictions on contact with children and the use of alcohol or drugs. The prosecutor's office in turn agrees not to prosecute the offender so long as these conditions are fulfilled.

Problems have arisen in existing diversion programmes when offenders fail to comply and are terminated from the programme. This can occur two or three years later, by which time even the strongest case has become weak. Prosecution of such cases is extremely difficult and there exists the very real possibility that not only will the offender have failed to complete treatment but will have escaped other consequences as well. Unless there is an aggressive policy of prosecution for those who fail in diversion, offenders will have little incentive to comply.

Problems can also arise when people admit to an offence against a child solely for the purpose of being considered for the diversion programme and avoiding prosecution. If they subsequently fail to complete the programme, it is unlikely that their previous admission can be used in the prosecution process. This can be solved by requiring that offenders confess in a legally admissible manner before they will qualify to be considered for the diversion programme. Then if a trial is later necessary, there will be an admissible confession available from the offender.

Treatment and punishment are not mutually exclusive. Many of the aims of diversion can be accomplished within the criminal justice system and indeed, if treatment is to be effective, it must go hand in hand with accountability. To the extent that diversion alternatives reduce the accountability of offenders, it is essential to scrutinise their impact very closely.

II. Diversion in the English Legal System

JOHN R. SPENCER

WHEN A SEXUAL offender is likely to respond to treatment it is obviously better that he should be treated than that he should be jailed — a course which will do him harm rather than good, and break up his family in the process. Assuming that we could identify those child-abusers who would be likely to respond to treatment; and assuming facilities for treatment were available; and assuming that the treatment available offered a good chance of success: would the English legal system provide adequate means for seeing suitable offenders have treatment rather than a spell in prison?

There are two things about diversion upon which all diversionists seem to be agreed. One is that diversion into treatment is useless unless the offender admits what he has done and accepts responsibility for it. The other is that there must be legally effective means for ensuring the treatment is carried through, so that defendants do not agree to a course of treatment simply in order to avoid the usual punishment, and having avoided the punishment then get out of the treatment too. Unfortunately, it would be surprisingly difficult within the English legal system to achieve any regular system of diversion which combined both of these requirements.

A prosecution for child abuse is likely to go through three preliminary stages: first a social worker discovers what has happened and tells the police; then the police investigate, and charge the person concerned with an offence; then the file goes to the Crown Prosecution Service, where someone decides to go ahead rather than to drop the case. In theory a 'diversion' could be organised at any one of these three stages. The social worker could agree not to inform the police if the offender agrees to go for treatment. This would be quite legal, because contrary to popular belief there is no general obligation under English law to inform the police of an offence. The police could agree not to charge the offender in return for his undertaking to undergo treatment. This too would be legal, because the police are under no obligation to charge every person against whom they have sufficient evidence to do so, and are officially encouraged to let certain categories of offender go with a 'caution'. Alternatively, the Crown Prosecution Service could agree to drop proceedings in return for a similar undertaking. This too would be legal, because a Crown Prosecutor has by law the power to drop a case, and is allowed to exercise an intelligent discretion as to when to exercise it. The trouble with each of these courses, however, would be the absence of any real means of seeing the offender kept his side of the bargain. In theory he could be prosecuted for the original offence if he refused to follow the treatment, but in practice it would be hard to produce enough evidence to convict him by the time he had abandoned his course of treatment. If he had confessed to the offence his confession could sometimes be used in evidence against him; but the confession would usually have been extracted by a combination of a threat and a promise, and section 76 of the Police and Criminal Evidence Act 1984 makes confessions legally inadmissible in evidence where they have been obtained in circumstances tending to make confessions unreliable — like threats and promises. By now the evidence of the child, if admissible in the first place, would probably be getting stale; and it would often be unfair to expect the child to give evidence after a considerable interval. (If the child's statement on videotape was admissible in evidence in criminal proceedings matters might be different, because the evidence would be preserved as good as new for future use; but as we have seen, videotapes are not as yet admissible in evidence.)

If we want to make sure that our divertee takes his psychiatric medicine, the diversion has to be done at the final stage when the case eventually comes to court. Where a defendant has actually been convicted of a sexual offence against a child, one of the options available to the court as an alternative to a fine or imprisonment is to make a probation order containing a condition that the offender has psychiatric treatment under section 3 of the Powers of Criminal Courts Act 1973 — or an order with a condition of residence at an named hostel or participation in a specified scheme under other sections of the Act. If a person breaks the terms of his probation order he can then be punished: if he is lucky, the order will remain in force and he will only be punished for breaking it, and if he is unlucky the court may discharge the probation order and sentence him for the original offence.

The difficulty with diversion at the sentencing stage is that diversion is no good except where the defendant admits what he has done and accepts responsibility for it. Unfortunately, when a child sexual abuse case has got as far as the criminal courts the incentives are not very strong to persuade a man to plead guilty, and thereby show that he accepts responsibility for what he has done. Under current sentencing practice, anyone who is convicted of a more than trivial sexual offence against a child stands a good chance of being sent to prison, even if he has pleaded guilty (Glaser and Spencer, 1990). If he is a first offender of previously good character he might get away with a non-custodial sentence; but he would be one of the lucky ones. An additional problem is that there is no way in which he can discover this in advance of the trial and his decision to plead guilty. In the USA there is a well-developed system of 'plea bargaining,' under which the prosecution and defence agree with the judge that if the defendant pleads guilty, a certain type of sentence will be passed. In England, however, it is considered quite improper for the defence to make any approach to the judge about the sentence before the accused has been convicted or pleaded guilty, and improper for the prosecution to make any representations to the judge about sentence at all, whether in court or out of it. In England a limited amount of plea-bargaining is permitted between the prosecution and the defence, but it is strictly forbidden to make any attempt to involve the judge in the process (see *Turner* [1970] 3 QB 321). So the prosecution cannot bargain a plea of guilty in return for the promise of a 'diversionary' sentence, because the prosecutor is not in a position to deliver his part of the bargain. The guilty defendant who knows that he stands a good chance of going to prison even if he pleads guilty, and who certainly cannot be sure in advance of pleading guilty that he will not, is strongly tempted to fight the case. He is likely to be reinforced in his decision on learning from his lawyer that the rules of criminal evidence work strongly in his favour, and give him a good chance of acquittal if he fights.

The American style of plea-bargaining is unlikely to be introduced in England, whatever advantages it may offer in child abuse cases, because in other respects English lawyers generally regard it as an abomination. On this side of the Atlantic it is generally seen as a system under which wicked people who are powerful escape their just deserts, whilst people who are weak are pressured into pleading guilty to offences they did not commit.

So the only way to build up a vigorous system of diversion at the sentencing stage is to improve the incentives for guilty defendants to plead guilty. For this, we need both stick and carrot. The stick is an alteration of the more irrational of the rules of criminal evidence, so that the chances of guilty men being convicted are increased. And the carrot is an alteration of the sentencing policy of the courts so that it becomes generally accepted among the judges that certain types of sexual offender are appropriate to receive diversionary sentences if they admit what they have done and plead guilty. Such a change in sentencing policy can only be brought about if those who are in favour of diversion are able to convince the legal profession, and particularly that part of the legal profession consisting of the judges in the Court of Appeal (Criminal Division), that diversion programmes can work and are therefore a worthwhile alternative to sending offenders to prison.

REFERENCE

Glaser, D. and Spencer J. R. (1990) 'Sentencing, evidence, and children's trauma', *Criminal Law Review*.

13

TREATING THE EFFECTS OF SEXUAL ASSAULT

LUCY BERLINER

VIRTUALLY EVERY PROBLEM that a child could experience has been identified in some population or somewhere in the clinical literature relating to sexually abused children. This has been important in raising professional and public awareness that sexual assault is associated with disturbance in children, and in drawing attention to the need for prevention and treatment. However, the lack of clarity as to the processes leading to the various reported effects of abuse has hindered attempts to provide appropriate treatment.

SHORT-TERM EFFECTS OF ABUSE

A group of systematic studies using direct assessment of children has aimed to provide a clearer picture of the range of psychological disturbances experienced by sexually abused children. Many recent studies have used comparison groups to assess the relative effects of abuse on children. The collected data include behaviour or symptom check-lists completed by parents, direct psychological measures of children, such as results of projective tests, or any specific distress such as depression, anxiety, or lowering of self-esteem.

The results of the studies show that sexually abused children as a group are different from children who have not been sexually abused but there is considerable variation and overlap in the extent of these differences. For example, in a study by Conte and Berliner (1988), children were assessed on a symptom check-list derived from the clinical literature which contained all of the problems reported as effects of sexual abuse. The study found that 21 per cent of the children known to have been abused did not display any of these symptoms. This does not mean that these children would never have problems, nor that they had no other problems, but it does demonstrate that many abused children do not present with external signs of great distress. It is therefore extremely important that, at an initial assessment, behavioural or emotional problems in children are not relied on as a basis for diagnosing sexual abuse.

While abused children as a group are consistently found to have more problems than children who have not been abused, in general they do not have as many problems as children who are identified in psychiatric populations. In all of the recent studies, not even 50 per cent of the children achieved clinically significant levels of distress on the direct assessment measures. There were some variations between cases: for example, not surprisingly, boys tended to have more conduct disorders than girls. Across the sample, sexual problems seemed to increase although the inadequacy of the measures has made this difficult to quantify (Friedrich, Urquiza and Beilke, 1986).

Other studies have attempted to identify the variables associated with more negative consequences in children (Conte and Schuerman, 1987). Researchers have examined abuse variables such as the type of abuse, what happened, who did it, and for what length of time. The general finding is that the closer the relationship, the longer the duration, and the more intrusive the sexual behaviour, then the more negative the outcome. Interestingly, these factors were not always found to be associated with worse outcomes. For example, several studies have not found that the closer the relationship to the offender, the worse the outcome. Even in studies where all these abuse-related variables were statistically significant in predicting negative later outcomes for the child victims, the variables did not account for very much of the variation in these poor outcomes (Mannarino and Cohen, 1988). Knowing that a child who has been assaulted by a family member or subjected to long-standing abuse is at greater risk may be helpful in predicting unfavourable outcomes. It gives no indication of how best to help the child victim, as the abuse variables are impossible to change after the abuse has occurred. Of more practical significance is the finding of Conte and Schuerman (1987) that the variance in outcome for the children was closely related to the available support from a non-offending parent or from siblings, or to the capacity of the family to respond to the child in a supportive way.

Effects of intervention

As well as scrutinizing the effects of the abuse itself, some studies are beginning to examine the effects of intervention. Although it is almost impossible completely to disentangle the different sources of trauma experienced by the children, the studies are trying to determine whether there is a relationship between the consequences for children of reporting abuse and the negative impact. Conte, Berliner and Schuerman (1986), examined the relationship between a range of intervention variables and impact. They found that whether or not the children had been interviewed, whether or not they had been placed out of the home, whether or not they had attended a legal proceeding, and whether or not they had testified in court were not related in any way to outcome. Runyon and colleagues (1988) followed children's progress through the system and also found that children placed out of the home, which many assume to be a very intrusive type of intervention, improved to the same extent as children not placed. Although Runyon found no differences in outcome between cases that had or had not gone into the legal system, children who were awaiting the outcome and resolution of their cases experienced significantly greater distress than other children. Another finding was that children who testified in court (juvenile court in these cases) had, contrary to the researchers' hypothesis, actually improved relative to those who did not testify.

Goodman and colleagues (1989) also compared children who testified in court with children who did not testify. They found that while the former manifested higher levels of distress shortly after testifying, the differences disappeared over time. It was children who testified more than once who were most negatively affected. This supports the general conclusion that on current evidence there are no clear effects of intervention. There are certainly no clear negative effects of the kind that have persuaded professionals to argue that it is best not to intervene because the intervention itself is harmful to children.

LONG-TERM EFFECTS OF ABUSE

Studies of the short-term effects of abuse have shown that some children are very disturbed but, in all, sexually abused children are only moderately disturbed shortly after the abuse experience. Subsequently, the levels of distress abate. Indeed, Frederich, Luecke, Beilke and Place (in press) have shown that in the short-term about 60 per cent of children improve, 10 per cent deteriorate and 20 per cent remain unchanged. However, in general population studies of adults there are significant long-term effects. Reputable studies of general community samples, using standard measures of psycho-pathology and distress, have consistently found that even many years after the event, abuse survivors have elevated levels of symptomatic distress and significantly greater risk of developing psychiatric disorders, in fact, two to eight times the risk in certain diagnostic categories. (Bagley & Ramsay, 1985; Gold 1986; Saunders, Villaponteaux, Kilpatrick & Veronen, 1987; Briere & Runtz, 1988.)

The psychiatric disorders most commonly associated with an abuse history are depression, anxiety, substance abuse, sexual dysfunction and suicide. In the Charleston study (Saunders *et al.*, 1987), twenty per cent of the abuse survivors had made a suicide attempt as compared with 5 per cent of non-abuse survivors. When a fifth of survivors are attempting suicide, clearly the health consequences of sexual abuse are not in any way being overstated. This does not mean that survivors inevitably have psychiatric disorders but simply that they are at greater risk of such disturbance. Approximately 80 per cent of cases in the research studies do not result in psychiatric diagnosis in adult survivors. These survivors may have been seriously affected by the sexual abuse but their recovery was sufficient for them to escape diagnosable psychological disturbance.

The important issue for the development of treatment strategies is how childhood experiences, such as the traumatic experience of sexual abuse, lead to these adult disorders. From a mental health standpoint, it is crucial to make sense of the processes between childhood and adulthood because these constitute the window for treatment. The difficulty of trying to unravel the causal pathways leading to long-term effects, when these effects may only appear indirectly, is well illustrated by the finding of a recent American study (Walker, 1988) of chronic pelvic pain. There was no difference between a group of women with chronic pelvic pain and women without pain in terms of physical pathology. What distinguished the two groups was that the women who had pain had been sexually abused. Perhaps this pain was an effect of the sexual aspect of an abuse experience.

One of the best known theoretical models for understanding the effects of abuse is the hypothesis of 'post traumatic stress disorder' (PTSD) which is an anxiety disorder produced by exposure to an extraordinary and frightening experience. The physiological response of fear becomes conditioned or associated with aspects of the abuse situation. A wide range of stimuli may then induce fear and prompt intrusive recollections or nightmares, disturbing thoughts and flashbacks, avoidance and withdrawal behaviour. A primary coping strategy is cognitive affective, and behavioural avoidance to reduce anxiety. The result may be a temporary adjustment, but unresolved trauma. The condition is diagnosed at a very much higher rate amongst abuse survivors, but there is considerable debate about whether or not 'post traumatic stress disorder' is the most appropriate way to think about the effects of sexual assault.

David Finkelhor (1988) argues that most abused children do not have post traumatic stress disorder, that it leaves a great deal to be explained, and that diagnostic criteria are not a central issue in the assessment of abused children. However, it may still be useful in considering some of the effects of abuse on children, because forms of anxiety are the most commonly reported and observed symptoms. It may be that only relatively few abused children have severe levels of post traumatic stress disorder, which could be related to the degree of intensity of fear or anxiety that occurs in the abuse experience. The majority of sexually abused children probably do not feel that they are in a life threatening situation, and do not have extreme levels of fear. But since they probably do have increased anxiety and nervousness, they may experience a low intensity or mild degree of post traumatic stress disorder. Because they were not as anxious when the abuse happened, their level of conditioned anxiety will be somewhat lower, although anxiety is still clearly a part of the direct effects of the trauma of abuse. Two studies confirm PTSD as a major effect (McLeer *et al*, 1988; Wolfe *et al.*, 1989).

David Finkelhor (1988) maintains that there is clearly more to the effects of sexual assault than anxiety: other effects include the cognitive and behavioural adjustment to the meaning of the experience. The experience of being a victim of sexual abuse is likely to affect people's self-perceptions as they try to ascertain the implications of being a victim of abuse for their perceptions of themselves, of their role in the world and their relationships with others. One approach to organising those kinds of effects is to use the four traumagenic dynamics model developed by Angela Browne and David Finkelhor (1985). They hypothesize that an experience of sexual abuse might affect four different areas of human experience. These are traumatic sexualisation, betrayal, powerlessness and stigmatisation. Children, by being abused, learn things in these four areas, either by direct learning through reinforcement and modelling, or cognitive learning in terms of making sense of their experience.

Many of the effects that are seen in these children are produced by the cognitive meaning of the abuse to them. In other words, how they explain what happened to them may lead to whether or not they feel guilt, anger or other feelings and reactions. The coping strategies used by children may be very adaptive and necessary in the contexts in which they are living. However, these short-term strategies may become maladaptive in the long-term. They may obstruct normal development, and interfere with other parts of their lives. For example, the coping strategy of dissociation has been identified quite consistently in abuse survivors. In dissociation the child psychologically separates herself from the abuse as if it were not happening to her body. Gelinas (1983) in her paper, 'The Persisting Negative Effects of Incest' describes how dissociation might be a common adaptive response for a child victim when there is no alternative, when it is the child's father in the bed and the child's only means of escape. However, if over time this becomes a primary way of dealing with adverse life experiences, it will prevent the development of more instrumental and effective coping strategies. Adult survivors who have made sense of, or developed an explanation for what happened to them have been shown to be less distressed than those who are still searching for a meaning for their experience.

Another example of the generalising effects of sexual abuse is provided by self-blame. The victimisation literature suggests that some kinds of self-blame are adaptive because they allow feelings of power or influence over what may happen in the future (Janoff-Bulman, 1986). The alternatives open to child victims are to believe that the abuse is either their fault or the fault of the person who abused them. Because the abuser is someone they depend on and care for, someone whose job it is to take care of them, children are likely to find it a painful realisation that that person hurt them and used them on purpose. Rather than believe that the adults are bad it might be simpler for a child to believe that 'I'm bad and that's why this happened to me'. The implications of believing that the adults on whom one depends are bad are so devastating that it is scarcely surprising that children avoid or do not deal directly with the experience. Furthermore, the strategies that are most available to children have to do with not dealing either with the painful affect (which adults also tend to avoid) or with the painful meaning of the experience. By the same argument, it is not surprising that many survivors frequently present problems of dissociation, withdrawal, avoidance, running away. Indeed, all sorts of abuse disorders might be categorised as ways to avoid meaning and pain. These strategies may then be generalised to all parts of the survivors' lives and over time may lead to personality disorders or to other serious problems.

TREATMENT

The impact on the child of the sexual abuse experience clearly has implications for treatment, particularly as many of the referred children have either no or very mild symptoms. It raises questions about what is being treated and whether professionals should be treating children who have no overt problems. Many people, including parents, might suggest that there are dangers in over-emphasising the importance of abuse in the children's lives when it would be better left alone. However, all general population studies that have found many survivors experiencing serious long-term problems, identify abuse retrospectively in individuals who have never received treatment. Not receiving treatment does not therefore seem to be the answer. However, it may be necessary to adjust the treatment approach not only to respond to the symptoms of referred children, but also to prevent the development of short-term reactions that are likely to result in more severe problems. The most important part of treatment is not necessarily just helping children to feel better in the short-term, but to provide the opportunity in therapy to develop and use adaptive skills and coping strategies, and to develop a cognitive adjustment to the abuse experience that is less likely to result in negative attributions or destructive behaviour.

Coming to terms with the abuse

If treatment is necessary, even in the absence of symptoms, what should be its goal? Firstly, anxiety needs to be addressed, including confronting the source of that anxiety. Rather than avoid the source of the anxiety, it is better to reduce anxious responses by means of organized strategies such as systematic desensitization or habituation. This means associating an anxiety evoking stimulus with a non-anxiety provoking situation or simply repeating, thinking or talking about the source of anxiety in order to limit its power and effect.

One way to assess the effectiveness of all treatment in sexual abuse is to measure or gauge the child's success in managing the anxiety produced by the above. The abuse experience itself must be addressed in therapy and children must be taught how to manage their anxiety, both the anxiety of thinking about the abuse or being reminded of it and the situational anxiety that is generalised from the original abuse situation. All kinds of strategies are available. In addition to having children talk in a group or alone, where they learn how to recall the experience without suffering anxiety, there are also techniques such as thought stopping, cognitive restructuring, covert rehearsal and various relaxation strategies. These skills can be acquired by children in therapy and applied in other anxiety provoking situations. This is not to suggest that children should be forcibly exposed to things that make them anxious. On the other hand, non-directive therapies are unlikely to be effective, because the patient or client will direct the therapist away from the pain of the abuse. There is a great danger in talking to children about many other things without any reference to the anxiety that they feel when they think about what happened to them. It is normal to avoid anxiety, and part of the therapist's task is sensitively and perhaps gradually to insist that directly confronting the experience itself is one of the requirements of treatment.

The cognitive aspect or the learning part of treatment, whether or not the child is manifestly disturbed, is to help the child toward an acceptable and harmless explanation of events. Most professionals do not find this is simple to achieve in practice. For example, telling children that they are not to blame does not achieve the goal of children believing it. It is therefore necessary to be much more creative by learning more from the children about why they believe that it is their fault, why they believe it happened to them, and not inhibiting them by dictating to them what they ought to think. By allowing children to explore and explain the self-blame more fully, professionals may find that opportunities for change become more apparent.

Sometimes children believe it was their fault because, for example, they should not have asked their father where babies come from. Corrective information might help in that type of case. But it is more complicated when children believe it was their fault because they wanted affection and felt lonely but did not tell anyone. Every child who did not report the abuse after the first time it happened learns and realises that they could have told. If they had told, the abuse probably would have stopped in most cases. One approach is to have them go back and look at this a little differently, to change how they think about what they did and how they chose not to tell. It was the better choice at the time, or they did not know that they had alternatives. Since they now know them they can make different choices. In part, this allows opportunities to ventilate affect in the therapeutic setting because, as children come to grips with what it means, they experience intense feelings of guilt, anger or grief that they have lost something — whether this is a relationship, an idea of their childhood or a 'real' father.

Traumatic sexualisation

Another area for treatment is traumatic sexualisation. It is quite clear that whether or not children conceptually understand the sexual nature of it, they experience abuse in part as a sexual experience. Even if they learn later that it was a sexual experience, without some corrective learning they may be left associating sexuality with other inappropriate and destructive things.

If children demonstrate sexual behaviour problems of any kind — sexual pre-occupation, sexual acting out with other children, precocious sexual interest, sexual aggression — it is not sufficient to hope that, if ignored, these behaviours will go away. Those behaviours need to be addressed directly, for example, by talking to children about their sexual fantasies and sexual thoughts.

Sexual dysfunction in adult women is a major outcome of abuse. Of course, therapists experience great difficulty in talking to little children about their sexual thoughts and their sexual feelings, beyond just telling children where babies come from. Physical aspects of pregnancy and birth is not the most important element in the children's therapy. It is much more important to offer the opportunity to develop sexual value systems which involve consent and mutuality, and which do not associate sexuality with meeting needs that are more properly met in other ways, such as, needs for affection, needs for closeness, needs for power.

Another problem is in providing children with ways to manage sexual feelings that are not going to lead to trouble because of their particular background and attitude to sexuality. What individual therapists might believe about society's attitudes to sexual behaviour will not necessarily be relevant in helping a child who lives in a fundamentalist religious home. Children who may be taught at home that they will go to hell if they masturbate, may then be told by a therapist that there is nothing wrong. Therapists often perceive masturbation, pre-marital sex and homosexuality as variations in normal sexual behaviours. But many people disagree and it is very complicated to deal with sexual issues without conveying to children a confusion about these different values.

Powerlessness

In the area of powerlessness, it is important to increase the children's perceived self-efficacy. An important component of treatment for all children is conveying to them the chances of being able to avoid future victimization. This is a real risk to the children and not just something they happen to fear as a reaction to abuse. Preventive education ought therefore to be an integral part of all treatment for sexually abused children. More can be done with children who have already been abused than with children who have not yet been abused, because they understand the process of victimization in a way that non-abused children do not. They understand the gradual progression, the selection and isolation of victims from other support systems, the rationalisations and justifications used by offenders. The knowledge they derive from their experience can help them to identify and avert potentially dangerous situations.

Stigmatization

Stigmatization refers to the feelings of children that there is something bad about them, because the abuse happened to them. One way of reducing such negative self-perceptions is to increase the number of people who know that the child was sexually abused, with whom the child feels free to talk and behaves normally. In the past, there was a tendency to discourage children from talking to others about their victimization because of the potential negative effects, but it is better to encourage children to choose whom they wish to tell and then to work on how to deal with the potential negative consequences. This is one of the more obvious ways of removing stigmatization because it makes the negative abuse something the children can share with their friends and with other significant people.

Betrayal

The abuse of the child may have involved the direct betrayal of trust by someone close to the child, or the inability of a loved and trusted person to protect the child from abuse. The abuse can therefore have a negative effect on the child's perception of relationships with people in general and with close, trusting and supportive relationships in particular. An obvious way of altering disturbed cognitions about relationships with other people is to help children develop skills in relating with people. Group therapy is commonly used to enable children to learn such skills. In addition, the child's relationship with the therapist is an opportunity to let the child experience a new relationship with a responsible caring adult who sets boundaries, who does not take advantage and is genuinely concerned and interested. The importance of the therapeutic relationship in counteracting the negative effects of the abuse experience should not be underestimated. Nowhere is this more obvious than in the adult patient who suffers from more serious long-term effects, such as borderline personality disorder. These individuals are likely to put the therapist through the test of staying in a relationship with them. This inability to relate to other people is one of the effects of sexual abuse that each intervention should aim to prevent.

The importance of families

Since the majority of children live in families, one cannot treat children without working with their families. Parents and families have so much more influence on children than a therapist that part of the work with children always should include their families. First and foremost, parents should know enough to understand their child's experience and to assist in carrying out many of the therapeutic strategies discussed in this chapter. For example, the parent's help is required to assist the child in learning strategies to manage anxiety or to avoid feeling stigmatized, to observe the child relating to others and to give them opportunities for relationships.

Although the parent must be a partner in treating the child victim, things also have to be done for and with the family in order to overcome the obstacles standing in the way of parents being able to help the therapist help their child. These have to do with their potential problems with regard to learning and knowing that their child has been victimized. There are many painful realizations for parents, including coming to terms with the fact that they have not been able to protect their child from abuse. It can evoke aspects of their own childhood which could well include a history of child abuse. Parents might choose to de-emphasise the victimization or, alternatively, they might focus too much on the victimization as a way of evading other family problems. Parents therefore need help to deal with their own issues, perhaps encouragement to seek therapy for their own abuse histories so as to ensure there is no collusion between family and therapist not to acknowledge other problems, such as domestic violence or emotional abuse or neglect of children. Family therapy should not be reserved for incest situations where the offender continues to be part of the family. It has been unfair that the presence or not of the offender tended to determine whether or not the family deserved and should have treatment, whereas children in any family where there is sexual abuse deserve to be viewed and treated a family.

A particular form of family treatment applies to offenders who will be coming back into the home. The victim would receive treatment for the victimization experience itself. The offender would be in a programme such as that advocated by Becker (this volume). Family treatment that is geared towards the offender coming back would be a gradual process. It would begin with the intact family which would be the mother and the children, and eventually would include the offender. Beginning away from home, the visits gradually, over approximately six months, could allow re-entry into the family life. Upon re-entry the restructured family would never be the way it was before. As the family situation was previously unacceptable, the person returning to the home will be treated like a person with a weakness. The family will be restructured so as to prevent mistakes being repeated, which will include restricting his access to children, limiting the enforcement of discipline, not permitting initiation of physical contact with children, prohibiting involvement in certain family activities, such as discussions about sex or hygiene. The family therapy will include teaching the members to live with and adjust to this new structure. When the family members have learned to solve problems, to negotiate and communicate under these conditions, they may well function in a much healthier way than many other families in the community.

REFERENCES

Bagley, C. and Ramsay R. (1985). 'Sexual abuse in childhood: Psychosocial outcomes and implications for social work practice.' *Journal of Social Work and Human Sexuality*, 4, 33-47.

Briere, J. and Runtz (1988). 'Symptomatology associated with childhood sexual victimization in a non-clinical sample.' *Child Abuse and Neglect*, 12, 51-60.

Cohen, J. and Mannerino, A. (1988). 'Psychological symptoms in sexually abused girls.' *Child Abuse and Neglect*, 12, 571-578.

Conte, J. and Berliner, L. (1988). 'The impact of sexual abuse on children: Empirical findings.' In L. Walker (eds.) Handbook on Sexual Abuse of Children: Assessment and Treatment Issues, (pp. 72-93) New York: Springer.

Conte, J., Berliner, L. and Schuerman, J. (1986). 'The Impact of Sexual Abuse on Children,' Final technical report NIMH Grant 37,133, Department of HHS, Washington, DC.

Conte, J. and Schuerman, J. (1987). 'Factors associated with an increased impact of child sexual abuse.' *Child Abuse and Neglect*, 11, 201-211.

Einbender, A. and Friedrich, W. (1989). 'Psychological functioning and behaviour of sexually abused girls.' *Journal of Consulting and Clinical Psychology*, 57, 155-157.

Finkelhor, D. and Browne, A. (1985). 'The traumatic impact of child sexual abuse: A Conceptualization.' *American Journal of Orthopsychiatry*, 55, 530-540.

Finkelhor, D. (1988). 'The trauma of child sexual abuse: two models.' In G. Wyatt and G. Powell (Eds.) Lasting Effects of Child Sexual Abuse. Newbury Park, CA: Sage.

Friedrich, W., Luecke, W., Beilke, R. and Place, V. (in press). 'Group treatment of sexually abused boys: an agency study.' *American Journal of Orthopsychiatry*.

Friedrich, W., Urquiza, A. and Beilke, R. (1986). 'Behaviour problems in sexually abused young children.' *Journal of Pediatric Psychology*, 11, 45-57.

Gelinas, D. (1983). 'The persisting negative effects of Incest,' Psychiatry, 46, 312-332.

Gold, E. (1986). 'Long term effects of sexual victimization in childhood: An attributional approach.' *Journal of Clinical and Consulting Psychology*, 54, 471-475.

Goodman, G., Taub, E., Jones, D., Port, P., Rudy, L. and Prado, L. (1989 under review). 'Emotional effects of criminal court testimony on child sexual assault victims.' Available from the first author at the Department of Psychology, State University of New York at Buffalo, Park Hill, Buffalo, NY 14620.

Janoff-Bulman, R. (1986). 'The aftermath of victimization: Rebuilding shattered assumptions.' In C. Figley (ed.) 'Trauma and Its Wake: Study and Treatment of Post-traumatic Stress Disorder' (pp. 15-36), New York, Brunner-Mazel.

McLeer, S., Dellinger, E., Atkins, M., Foa, E. and Ralphe, D. (1988) 'Post traumatic stress disorder in sexually abused children.' *Journal of the American Academy of Child and Adolescent Psychiatry*, 17, 650-649.

Mannarino, A. and Cohen, J. (1988). 'Psychological symptoms in sexually abused girls.' *Child Abuse and Neglect*, 12, 571-578.

Runyon, D., Everson, M., Edelsohn, Hunter, W., Coulter, M. (1988). 'Impact of legal intervention on sexually abused children.' *Journal of Pediatrics*, 113, 647-653.

Ryan, G. (1989). 'Victim to victimized: Rethinking victim treatment.' *Journal of Interpersonal Violence*, 4, 325-341.

Saunders, B., Villeponteaux, L., Kilpatrick, D. and Veronen, L., (1987). 'Child sexual assault as a risk factor in mental health.' Paper presented at annual meeting of National Association of Social Workers, October, New Orleans, LA.

Tufts New England Medical Center, Division of Child Psychiatry (1984). 'Sexually Exploited Children Service and Research Project.' Final report of Office of Juvenile Justice and Delinquency Prevention, U.S. Department of Justice, Washington, DC.

Walker, E., Katon, W., Harrop-Griffith, S. (1988). 'Relationship of chronic pelvic pain to psychiatric diagnoses and childhood sexual abuse,' *American Journal of Psychiatry*, 145, 75-80.

Wolfe, V., Gentile, C. and Wolfe, D. (1989). 'The impact of sexual abuse on children: A PTSD formulation.' *Behaviour Therapy*, 20, 215-228.

14

WORKING WITH PERPETRATORS

JUDITH V. BECKER

THE HEIGHTENED SENSE of public concern about the sexual abuse of children has led to the idea that the people who perpetrate these offences can be identified from their particular characteristics. To anyone working in this field it soon becomes clear that perpetrators form an extremely heterogenous group. Most offenders are male, but they do not come from any particular part of society and have no obvious socio-economic or demographic profile by which they can be identified. They include the unemployed, manual workers such as drivers and mechanics, and various types of white collar workers such as physicians, clergymen, social workers, attorneys and judges. Indeed, the majority of sex offenders can be characterized by only two common features other than their gender as males. First, they all have committed a deviant sexual act and, second, they have beliefs which permit or support their behavior.

The heterogeneity of sex offenders suggests that there are many reasons or many paths by which they come to commit a sexual crime. It is distinctly possible that an extremely small percentage are organically brain damaged, psychotic or otherwise psychiatrically ill and that their sexual crime is a direct result of that individual impairment.

A second and larger group of offenders have suffered major personality damage and commit a sexual crime as just one part of other anti-social activities. They may, for example, break into a house with intent to rob and then opportunistically rape someone asleep in the house. The primary motive may not be rape but these offenders take advantage of every available opportunity and sometimes this includes the sexual abuse of children.

There are other offenders who prefer to engage in consensual sexual activity with adult partners but if those partners are not available, or do not agree to engage in sexual activity, then the offenders may coerce another person to do so. Many 'date rapes' fall into this category as do some cases of incest. It is surprising that non-availability of willing sexual adult partners should be a reason for sexual offences when there are so many potential adult partners in the general population. It is particularly strange that offenders turn to children rather than to other adults when they experience any sexual or other difficulty within their marriage. For some of these men it is the power and control which they exert over their victims that serves to eroticize.

The fourth and final group prefer to have consensual or coercive sex with children. These offenders have deviant sexual urges, fantasies and activities and therefore are classified, according to the DSM-III-R Classification (American Psychiatric Association, 1987), as having paraphilias. That is the group most frequently seen by the author in her clinic and is the main focus of this chapter.

Human behavior is very complex and is never determined by a single variable or factor. Consideration has to be given to the ways in which individual and family characteristics and social, economic and environmental circumstances interact with macro-societal and cultural variables. Unfortunately, it is far from clear how the various factors operating at different levels of explanation interact and lead to instances of abuse. This is highlighted by the variation in the number of offences committed per offender. Some offenders commit a single act of abuse and then never commit another act. Some offenders on their own stop committing the abuse. Others are identified as perpetrators and the various consequences are so severe that they never repeat the offences. Some continue to re-offend as one feature of an anti-social behaviour pattern. Others continue to re-offend because of their deviant sexual interests.

Speculation about the causes of abusive behavior frequently is based on survey findings of clinical and legal samples that perpetrators have a number of background factors and life experiences in common. The most frequently reported factors include a history of sexual or physical victimization; an early childhood devoid of loving, caring relationships; negative sexual stereotyping and dysfunctional peer relations. Physiological explanations have also been formulated. A study by Dr Fred Berlin at John Hopkins University found that approximately three quarters of a sample of offenders had either high testosterone levels, brain dysfunction or other types of physical abnormality.

The factors identified by correlation studies do not denote simple causation. Many people have been sexually or physically victimized, have grown up in families or with peers who are not good role models, have been exposed to sexually explicit material, have organic problems, live in a society where there is gender disparity, have dysfunctional peer relations, and still they do not hurt other people sexually. Although the relative importance of these factors and the manner in which they interact are obscure, an individual's early sexual experiences are currently viewed as very likely the most critical. Probably the most influential experiences are whether the sexual fantasies of childhood that are reinforced through masturbation are deviant or non-deviant; whether early sexual experiences were pleasant or unpleasant; whether they involved anxiety and whether or not coercion was used so that the child became a victim of abuse.

Sexual experience during puberty and early adolescence may be particularly important. Adolescents spontaneously develop erections to all forms of stimulae, and adolescent males learn to control their erection responses. For some young people who fail to control that erection response, sexual arousal may become associated with inappropriate stimuli.

Sex offenders often have cognitive distortions. They fail to recognize their wrongdoing and the norms prohibiting that type of behaviour. They permit themselves to do whatever they want sexually to other people, either by prior justification or by rationalization after the event. Healthy early sexual experiences consist of consensual sex or masturbation that feels good and does not cause harm to others. The sexual activity is repeated because of its positive consequences, including its appropriateness socially. Similarly, deviant behaviour patterns are self-reinforcing. Acts of sexual abuse are rarely associated with negative legal consequences and the offenders misperceive or are unconcerned with the harm caused to the children. Because they are doing only what to them feels good, there is little reason to cease the abuse. The crucial research and practice issue is how these deviant interest patterns develop.

The clinic sample

It is difficult to obtain information on sex offenders because they get little advantage from identifying themselves or from providing details of any offence that they are either suspected of or convicted of committing. For the current sample, the National Institute of Mental Health issued a 'Certificate of Confidentiality' which prohibited members of staff from giving testimony in any court in the land against any of the men seen at the clinic. The certificate was issued to our clinical research project to allow us to solicit full disclosure regarding past sex offences from our clients without their being threatened with prosecution. Without the certificate, clients might have refused to share the full extent of their deviant behaviors.

The men are offered treatment at an out-patient clinic for sex offenders and therefore live in the community. Indeed, because prosecutions for sexual offences against children are very difficult to achieve, 85 per cent of known sex offenders are commonly resident in the community. The clinic sample is based upon cases of known or suspected abuse and therefore is unrepresentative of the total offender population. However, the Certificate of Confidentiality encourages a wider representation of cases than normally can be achieved.

Although treatment is voluntary, the patients are required to sign a consent form outlining the evaluation and treatment. The offenders who are not self-motivated may have other reasons for coming forward for treatment. For the adult offenders in the clinic sample, approximately 5 per cent were self-motivated, the others were motivated by family, by therapists or by the criminal justice system.

A total of 561 men were interviewed. Of that sample, 153 men had the primary diagnosis of male paedophilia. These men had committed 43,000 sexual crimes against young boys while the 224 men who primarily molested young girls had committed 5,197 sexual crimes. It seems that men who become involved with young boys do so at much greater frequency than men who become involved with young girls (Abel, Becker, Mittelman, Cunningham-Rathner, Rouleau and Murphy, 1987).

Offenders were asked about their other deviant sexual interests, such as other crimes they had committed without telling anyone. Forty-six per cent of the exhibitionists reported that they had either urges or fantasies or some involvement sexually with other people's children. Twenty-five per cent of the exhibitionists reported urges to engage in hands-on sexually coercive behavior. Forty-nine per cent of incest offenders involving female children reported an interest in other people's children. In sum, most offenders reported two or three paraphilias and some as many as ten paraphilias.

Until recently, it was thought that offenders each exhibited only a single type of deviant sexual behavior. The clinical task was to discover an offender's true single diagnostic category. It is now clear that this is not the case and that multiple paraphilias are more common than single paraphilias. It seems that for a subgroup of incest offenders, what determines whether offenders molest children inside or outside of families is the availability of a child of the sex and age that is of interest. The data show that this was true for 49 per cent of the clinic sample. It is also clear that offenders start to develop their deviant sexual interest patterns at a young age. Approximately 58 per cent of the sample reported that the onset of deviant sexual behavior for all forms of paraphilia was in the teenage years. That so many offenders start to abuse children when they are themselves so young has important implications for preventive work. By early intervention it may be possible to prevent the victimization of many children.

The majority of the adolescent sex offenders seen at the clinic had been arrested for sexual crimes, 78 per cent had been arrested once, but almost 9 per cent of the youngsters had two or three prior arrests for sexual crimes and were still within the community. There is a myth that anything an adolescent does sexually can be explained as sexually exploratory behavior. If, for example, a 17-year-old sodomizes a 3-year-old boy, it is understood as an attempt to learn about sex. It was therefore common to find a previous arrest but with no treatment, no history of clear intervention or attempts to prevent re-offending. The most detailed data are available for the first 160 adolescents seen in the clinic. There are three main groups: incest offenders, boys who have molested their own sisters, brothers, or cousins; mixed offenders, that is, boys who have molested relatives and non-relatives; and boys who have molested only non-relatives. The majority are non-incest offenders (58 per cent).

The age and sex of the victims varied according to these groups. For the 42 incest offenders there had already been 56 victims. Most of the victims were female and were less than 8 years of age, with a mean age of about 5 to 6 years. The acts committed against these 56 victims ranged from one to 224 crimes. For the 91 non-incest offenders, who victimized non-relatives, there were 134 victims. Fewer acts were committed against these people because of easier access to relatives compared with non-relatives. Most of the victims were also female and less than 8 years of age. For the 27 boys who molested relatives and non-relatives, there were many more victims; almost three per boy. Most of the victims were less than 8 years but almost an equal number were male and female. Between one and 994 deviant acts were committed against these children.

The prevalence of abuse also varied between groups. Fifty-two per cent of the mixed offenders had been sexually abused as children compared to 17 per cent of the juvenile incest offenders and 18 per cent of the juvenile non-incest offenders. These data are taken from the initial interview with the boys. The same question is repeated at the final interview, on exit from the programme. For the whole sample, the figure reported at initial interview was 23 per cent and the figure from final interviews is likely to be 40 per cent of the boys reporting that they had been sexually abused as children. There was also variation in who committed abuse against the boys for the 7 incest offenders who had been abused; four reported having been abused by females and only three reported having been abused by males. The boys did not report the experiences as abuse, but gave other descriptions. For example, one boy reported that at 8 years of age a 25 year old aunt engaged him in sexual activity. He described it as an initiation into sex. However, it would be sexist if this were not labelled as sexual abuse because the youngster could not consent and did not initiate the activity. Most of these boys also reported that they had never felt able to tell anyone about the abuse and that the interview was the first disclosure of its occurrence. At the time of the offence, the boys knew nothing about sex, they were little and vulnerable compared to the powerful adult man or woman. For non-incest offenders and mixed incest and non-incest offenders, most of the abusers were male.

There is a statistically significant relationship at the one percent level between having been sexually abused as a child and the number of victims. Boys who were sexually abused themselves as children had more victims than boys who had not been sexually abused. Furthermore, boys who had been abused were as likely to select male victims as female victims. Many boys also reported a prior history of physical abuse. Mixed category offenders had experienced the most problems: 67 per cent reported being physically abused as children compared with 33 per cent and 25 per cent in the other two groups. There is again a highly significant relationship between a prior history of physical abuse and number of victims. The boys who had been physically abused had many more victims.

Only 38 per cent of youngsters reported that they did not use alcohol, 49 per cent said it had no effect on their offences and an equal number said it increased or decreased their sexual arousal. There is, however, a statistical relationship between the use of alcohol and the number of victims. Those individuals who used alcohol and said it increased their arousal had more victims. There was no such relationship between drug use, which was not high in the sample, and the number of victims. Many of the offenders did use sexually explicit material (89 per cent) but this was not child pornography nor violent sexual material and there was no relationship found between the use of sexually explicit material and the number of victims.

It is difficult to ascertain why the boys had felt motivated to abuse other children. Twenty boys in the clinic sample were asked this question. Two reported that it was due to their personal experience of being abused; two said that they acted on impulse and one boy said home conditions were bad and he knew that if he abused a child he would get out of the house. Another said that he did not realise that it was wrong; another that he picked up the idea from hearing his friend talking about sex. Eight of the boys said they did not know it was a crime and a further four denied having committed a crime, even though they had been found guilty of a crime. Few of the boy offenders had been arrested for other types of crime. When there was a history of other crimes these were often robbery or burglary and were usually carried out by the rapists in the sample.

The boys started to engage in normal (non-deviant) sexual activity at an early age, some starting as early as 6, 7 and 8 years of age. Although there were behavioural differences among these offenders, in general they showed relatively little evidence of psychiatric disturbance as classified by DSM-III diagnostic categories (Kavoussi, Kaplan and Becker, 1988). The largest category was conduct disorder, then marijuana abuse and alcohol abuse. Using a broader definition of evidence of any of the criteria for DSM-III, there is more evidence of conduct disorder and about one-third of the sample has some form of attention deficit disorder. Dividing the sample into rapists and non-rapists (child molesters) shows that 75 per cent of the rapists met full criteria for conduct disorder compared to 38 per cent in the non-rapists. It is likely that a proportion of those rapists in the future will be labelled as anti-social personality disorder.

Assessment and treatment

Although all of the adolescent offenders volunteered to attend the clinic, only 26 per cent admitted to the abuse in the initial interview. The challenge is how to enable the total deniers to admit to what they have done or to admit that it is still sexual abuse even if the victim had clothes on, or if there was only minimal genital contact. Denial is a major issue in assessing what the offender actually did and their attitude towards it, and also for providing a basis for a therapeutic relationship. Often pressure comes from other professionals and from the criminal justice system to clarify what has occurred, and because it can be difficult to find this out from the victims, many people are focusing on an evaluation of the perpetrator of any possible offence. However, there is no psychological test nor any combination of tests that can determine whether or not an offender committed a specific sexual crime, although some people profess to be able to do this. The only way to know what happened is for the perpetrator to admit to the offence or for the victim to disclose abuse and be believed.

The treatment offered in the clinic is a multi-component treatment, based on a cognitive behavioural model. The major goal is to achieve a change in the way offenders think about their behaviour as well as actually to change the behaviour. It does not cure offenders but teaches them control and provides the requisite skills to relate to people in a functional, caring manner. Single case research studies were used to evaluate the effectiveness of individual components of treatment which have now been assembled into a complete treatment programme. Therapy is carried out in groups because it is most cost effective. Individual therapy would be equally good and it is a myth to believe that group treatment should be the sole form of intervention for offenders.

Each offender is assessed in terms of their assets and deficits. The first component of therapy is called 'satiation' which targets the individual's fantasies. Sex offenders are asked to repeat their fantasies out loud, over and over again for a prescribed period of time. The goal is to make these highly erotic deviant fantasies become boring and aversive through verbal satiation. Adolescents are given eight half-hour sessions of satiation, while the adults have a minimum of 20 hours of satiation. These treatment procedures are described in detail elsewhere (Abel *et al.*, 1984).

Component 2 of therapy is called 'cognitive restructuring' which targets distorted beliefs. Sex offenders sometimes report that they had sex with their child because they wanted the child to have information about sex and to learn about sex from a very experienced loving person. These seemingly altruistic men are so concerned about what teenage boys in the community are going to do to their daughters that, instead, they had sex with their daughters themselves. Similarly, some sex offenders argue that women really want to be raped and that when women stop resisting a rape, it indicates consent to the activity. Cognitive distortions such as these are listed on a scale and the client is asked to indicate his level of agreement or disagreement. Treatment involves role-playing where male and female therapists adopt the belief systems. The offenders are assigned roles as members of society and attempt to persuade the therapists of the inappropriateness of the belief systems. Persuading others is a powerful tool for cognitive restructuring and in developing empathy with victims.

Those offenders who have been victims of abuse are also asked to share what it was like, to tell group members whether or not they initiated the behaviour, and how much they enjoyed the behaviour. Of course, none of them initiated it, and in part they have become offenders because of that behaviour. The therapeutic strategy is covert sensitization or 'risk and consequences' therapy, since it teaches offenders the risks or risk situations to avoid and the consequences of engaging in the deviant behaviour. Each offender is assessed from the chain of events that leads up to them committing a crime. This is fed back to them so that they learn that there are different links in the chain where they can stop themselves from committing abuse. They learn that they do not have to go all the way and, when they find themselves on a certain link so to speak, they are reminded of the consequences of that behaviour to themselves and to the victim.

The treatment also involves education relevant to social skills. Much of this is provided using standard techniques of social skills training such as role-playing to enable offenders to meet and sustain relationships with peers. Developing and maintaining relationships are not helped by the fact that the majority of the offenders believe that the use of force and aggression is a major way of resolving interpersonal problems. Assertiveness training and anger control are therefore provided for the adults and adolescents respectively. Sex education is also important and in a short course offenders are taught how to communicate their sexual wants and needs to a consenting partner.

The therapy programme for adults involved 30 weeks, one and a half hour sessions, in a group format.

Treatment outcome

Outcome data on the treatment of adult offenders are available at one year follow-up. As these men were seen under the certificate of confidentiality there were no consequences from reporting to the programme any new offences.

Thirteen per cent of the adult offenders reported new offences and eighty-seven per cent reported that they did not re-offend. Twenty variables were examined to determine what factors correlated with successful outcome; three were predictive. The first was marital status; those men who were married were less likely to reoffend than those men who were not. The second factor was multi-target offenders, men who molest boys and girls, and molest relatives and non-relatives. The third predictive factor was treatment goals. Men who attended because they wanted to acquire control over their deviant behaviour were less likely to reoffend than those whose stated aim was to develop self-awareness and personal growth (Abel, Mittelmain, Becker, Cunningham-Rathner and Rouleau, 1988).

Of the men who entered into treatment, 40 per cent dropped out before completing the program. This is disappointing but is comparable to studies of treatment outcome in other areas of mental health. The amount of pressure to participate was predictive of drop-out. The more pressure a person was under to participate, the greater the chance of drop-out. Groups of men who were self-motivated were more likely to stay in therapy than others. A second predictive factor was a diagnosis of anti-social personality disorder. This is not surprising as these men rarely stay involved for very long with anything but crime. The third factor was being a multiple target offender. These men appear to be the most dangerous to society.

There is also limited follow-up data on the adolescent offenders. Three of the seventy-seven completing the treatment programme have re-offended.

Recidivism was expected in all three cases as it was thought that they all needed more therapy but they were no longer on probation and it was impossible to persuade the boys or their parents to agree to more therapy. The parents were told never in any circumstances to leave their children alone with another child. In one case, the boy revictimized the same child and in the same situation, while acting as a baby sitter. In the second case the parent let their boy baby sit for a child whom he then molested. In both of these cases it could be argued that the parents neglected their care of the adolescents in allowing them to be in situations where they were likely to re-offend.

The sexual abuse of children is a major problem in our societies and it is therefore necessary to identify who abuses children and for what reasons. One way forward is to ask children and adults about their sexual fantasies and urges. Whether the purpose is prevention or treatment it is necessary to enquire about a history of abuse. This will enable the early identification of those with deviant interest patterns and with a greater potential to become perpetrators of abuse. Every time there is a victim, professionals need to provide counselling services to the victim. Treatment must also be made available to the offender.

It is also necessary to have treatment options at a number of levels: therapy in prisons; residential facilities in the community where treatment can be provided; group homes for those men who can remain in the community but who, having been removed from their homes, need a place to live, in order to continue to support their families. We also need sociologists and anthropologists to help make the social and environmental changes that are necessary to combat this major public health problem.

REFERENCES

Abel, G., Becker, J., Cunningham-Rathner, J., Kaplan, M. and Reich, J. (1984), 'Treatment Manual for Child Molesters.' Unpublished manuscript.

Abel, G., Becker, J., Mittelman, M., Cunningham-Rathner, J., Rouleau, J., and Murphy, W. (1987), 'Self-reported sex crimes of non-incarcerated paraphiliacs.' *Journal of Interpersonal Violence*, 2, 3-25.

Abel, G., Mittelman, M., Becker, J., Cunningham-Rathner, J. and Rouleau, J. (1988), 'Predicting child molesters' response to treatment.' In R. A. Prentky and V. L. Quinsey (eds.), *Human sexual aggression: current perspectives* (pp. 223-234). New York: New York Academy of Science.

American Psychiatric Association *Diagnostic and Statistical Manual of Mental Disorders (Third Edition, Revised 1987)*, Washington, D. C.: American Psychiatric Association.

Kavoussi, R., Kaplan, M. and Becker, J. (1988), 'Psychiatric diagnosis in juvenile sex offenders.' *Journal of the American Academy of Child and Adolescent Psychiatry*, 27, 241-243.

15

PARENTS UNITED PROGRAMMES

ESTHER GILLIES

PARENTS UNITED IS a complex, highly sophisticated model of treatment for children and families where intrafamilial sexual abuse is the presenting problem. The term Parents United in this context is synonymous with 'The Giarretto Approach' to treatment of intrafamilial sexual abuse. The term 'Parents United' is also frequently used to refer to the self-help component of the programme which is only one part of treatment. The discussion that follows will look at both Parents United as a model of treatment and Parents United as the self-help component of a complex treatment programme.

THE PARENTS UNITED TREATMENT MODEL — THE GIARRETTO APPROACH

The Parents United Treatment Model is a comprehensive treatment response to the problem of intrafamilial sexual abuse. The model was developed in the early 1970s by Henry Giarretto, PhD in conjunction with the California Santa Clara County Department of Probation and a network of community agencies. The model is comprised of three separate parts —

(1) A professional treatment component, the Child Sexual Abuse Treatment Program, (CSATP);
(2) a self-help component, Parents United (PU);
(3) and, a network of community agencies including, for example, child protective services, probation services, law enforcement, and the courts (see Figure 1 overleaf).

The model is victim oriented. Because children generally tend to thrive better in their own homes and should be allowed to grow up with their own families, efforts are directed to keeping the children with their families. At the point of disclosure, when child protective services and law enforcement intervene, the offender is expected to leave the home. All efforts are made to keep the child at home if it appears that the child will be safe there. Treatment is then directed to all members of the family — child victims, siblings, non-offending parents and offenders. Reunification of offender with the family comes only after significant progress in treatment. Reunifi-

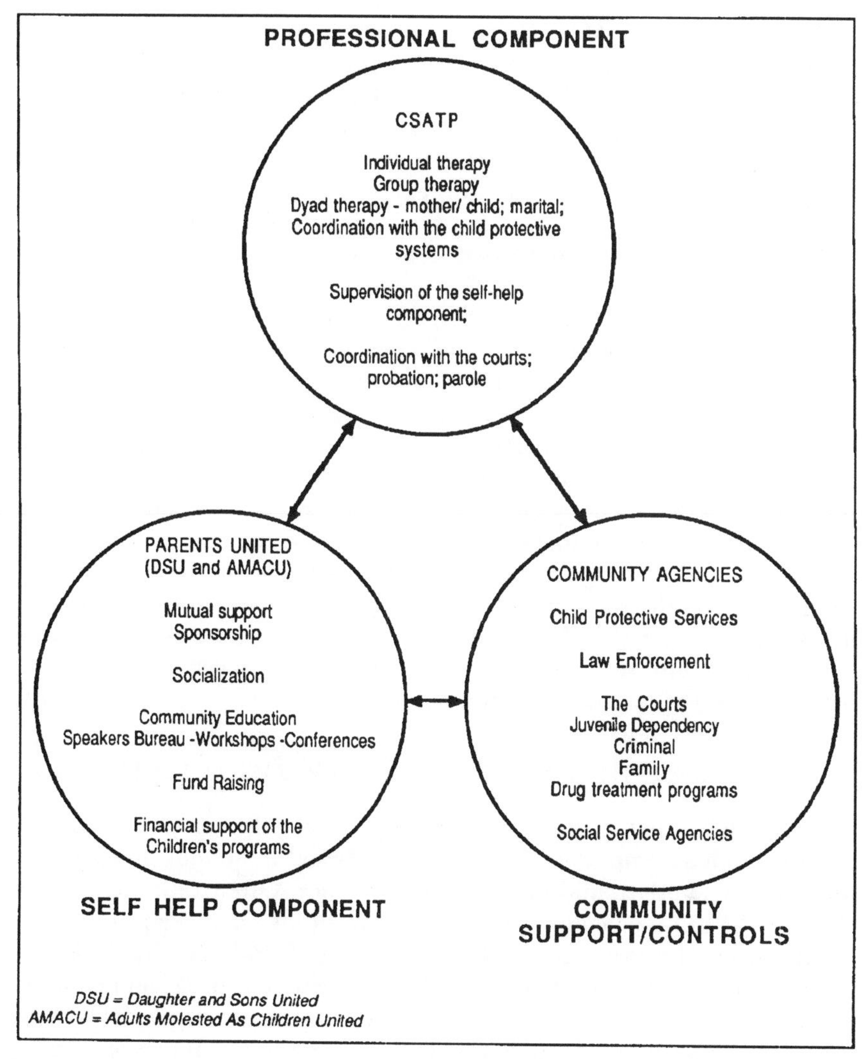

Figure 1: The Three Components of the Comprehensive Child Sexual Abuse Treatment Program.

cation is based first of all on the ability of the child to tolerate the return of the offender parent, secondly on the ability of the non-offending parent to protect the child from future abuse, and lastly on the indicated changes in behaviour of the offender.

The CSATP is responsible for providing all direct professional treatment services to children and families, including individual and group therapy and dyad (Mother/daughter; mother/father) and family therapy. The CSATP also co-ordinates support services within the community network.

Parents United is the self-help component of the treatment programme and also includes Daughters and Sons United (DSU) and Adults Molested as Children United (AMACU). The primary function of this component is to provide mutual support for the members of the programme. Other functions include community education, socialization opportunities for members and fund raising activities. This component is an integral part of the treatment model and cannot exist separate and apart from the professional component or apart from community agency involvement. All PU activities are supervised and monitored by the Professional Co-ordinator of the CSATP. In recent years, the Parents United component has been referred to as 'Guided' self-help.

The Network of Community Agencies provides the environmental controls necessary for effective treatment. The problem of intrafamilial sexual abuse does not lend itself well to voluntary treatment. The Parents United Treatment model was built on the premise that the most effective treatment takes place with families where a criminal filing against the offender has occurred and court action resulted in a minimum of probation supervision of the offender, and where juvenile court action has been taken on behalf of the child so that supportive services can be offered to the child and non-offending parent. Court ordered treatment for the offender, the child, the non-offending parent and siblings is preferred to voluntary participation in treatment. The network of community agencies includes at a minimum: law enforcement, child protective services, juvenile court, criminal court, probation, and sometimes parole.

PARENTS UNITED: THE SELF-HELP COMPONENT

Parents United is the title given to the self-help component of the Parents United comprehensive community based treatment programmes for sexually abused children and their families. Often referred to as a chapter, this self-help component must always be attached to a professional CSATP which has within its ranks qualified professionals with sufficient experience and skill to run a mental health treatment programme. Some people find it surprising that professionals are involved, particularly as there is a widely held misconception that the programme is one of autonomous self-help, akin to Alcoholics Anonymous, Overeaters Anonymous and other anonymous groups. In an authentic Parents United programme, Parents United self-help is only one component of an integrated treatment programme that is dominated by qualified professionals with expertise, experience and education in mental health.

The purpose of the self-help component is to provide mutual support, increase public enlightenment through educational activities, to offer an opportunity for socialization activities and to support the treatment programme through fund raising activities.

Mutual support: sponsorship

One of the strongest features of the self-help component is Sponsorship. When adult family members have completed at least six months of working through their own issues and have completed the initial phases of the treatment programme they may become a sponsor. This is not unlike the sponsorship in Alcoholics Anonymous. Sponsors assume the role of supporting new family members as they come into the programme. Sponsors are trained to provide lay counselling, a service clearly differentiated from professional therapy. In the sponsorship programme, parents are trained to listen. Mothers talk with mothers. Fathers talk with fathers. Parents, therefore, provide each other with the opportunity to talk about their problems and to ventilate their feelings at times of crisis.

Crises tend to arise not during working hours but late at night, on weekends and when professional services are generally inaccessible. Groups of parents are trained to provide crisis counselling to each other and to the new families on a twenty-four hour basis. Occasionally face-to-face contact occurs in the sponsorship process. But, generally, services are provided by way of a telephone network. Should a specific sponsor not be available when a need arises, most chapters have established a back-up system which provides parents in crisis with someone to respond to their need.

Support for mothers

Another powerful aspect of the self-help in Parents United is the hope that it offers families. Professionals who work with these families know that as the disclosure occurs, families go into crisis. The children become confused and scared. Parents also are very disoriented and fearful. Mothers in the programme report that initially they feel they are going crazy. The crisis is so intense that they are not only thinking about how to get through the next week but are anxious about surviving from one hour to the next. They feel that they have lost all control of their lives.

Sponsors in Parents United programmes offer support to mothers in crisis by listening to them and sometimes by sharing some of their own past experiences with them. Because the sponsors have been through the crisis themselves, they are more able to understand and empathize with the mother's feelings. They are also more likely to be respected and trusted by the new mothers entering the programme. The sponsors do not tell the mothers how to behave nor do they predict possible outcomes. Rather they provide someone to whom the mothers can talk and can explain what happened and how they coped and reacted. By being healthy and competent in their own lives, the sponsors offer the mothers hope. Indeed, the sponsors are living proof that it is possible to survive

Benefits to sponsors

Both for the recipient and for the client offering the service, self-help is a powerful and impressive remedial force. On entry to the programme, many of the family members, particularly the mothers, feel extremely inadequate and have never had any real sense of accomplishment in their lives. By providing support, sponsors are able to play an important role and to show their competence in effectively assisting others at a critical point in their lives. Giving to others in such a meaningful way, therefore, has in itself an important therapeutic value. Sponsors are able to feel good about themselves and to identify a healthy place for themselves within the organization. Secondarily, sponsors learn a great deal about themselves in the process, providing material for their own therapy.

Support for offenders

The use of parents who have been in the programme for some time is also highly important in the treatment of offenders. Confronting denial is one of the most difficult tasks in working with offenders and few can do this better than other offenders. The sponsor who has been an offender can confront the new offender with the fact that he used similar denial on entry to the programme. Sponsors can clearly define the limits of the programme by indicating that persons who have abused their children will save time and energy if they admit to it and start working toward change. Offenders know the tactics and denial systems of other offenders. New offenders learn very quickly that their rationalizations and projections are not likely to be believed. They also recognize that it is possible to survive, even after admitting the abuse.

At first, offenders are likely to deny the abuse. People with healthy egos are likely to resist disclosure. They are being self-protective. If they admit to abuse they risk becoming totally lost and experience a fear of annihilation. They know there is a chance of being sent to prison where they may be persecuted by other prisoners. They often have unrealistic fears of the duration of a prison sentence, seeing themselves spending a lifetime in jail. However, the longer the denial remains, the harder it is to engage in meaningful treatment. The sponsorship programme attempts to move the offender quickly towards acceptance of some level of responsibility for the abuse, including some level of understanding of the impact of abuse on the victim.

The new offenders are not protected from the real consequences of their behaviour, nor are they offered misleading information about what is likely to happen. The programme is straight-forward and honest and attempts to avoid violating the sense of new-found trust that the offenders are expected to begin developing in the programme. The offender's sponsors will often disclose that they have spent time in jail and that they know what it is to be in jail. Even this information, properly framed, can be therapeutic. It can be reassuring to the new offender to know that even though jail may be part of the future, it can be survived and can lead to living a life as full and healthy as that of the present sponsor. The sponsors thus provide the most powerful force available to penetrate the offenders' defence systems.

Support to the child

The self-help components of the treatment programme provide powerful indirect support of the child victim. Programme requirements plus the peer pressure within the self-help component require that the offender leaves the home. Where possible, the child remains in the home. Sponsorship supports mothers in acting as mothers to their children and not abandoning them in favour of a relationship with the adult offender. Sponsorship supports offenders in quickly moving to some level of acceptance of responsibility for the abuse. This often opens a door for the child to begin to release the responsibility that she has assumed for the abuse. Programme requirements and peer pressure prohibit any action by the offender that would allow denial of the abuse, and the child as a result having to testify in court against the parent. This removes the potential of systems abuse of the child.

Educational activities

The Parents United Self-Help component actively works with the professional co-ordinator of the CSATP to develop and provide educational programmes for the community. Many chapters have developed a Speakers Bureau consisting of senior members of the programme who have been trained to speak in public about their experiences with intrafamilial sexual abuse. Many chapters engage in organizing and/or sponsoring conferences in the community to increase the level of awareness about sexual abuse issues and improve the quality of response to child sexual abuse victims and their families. Most Parents United programmes encourage members of the community to visit the programme and sit in on Parents United meetings to develop an increased sensitivity to the issues of child sexual abuse.

Socialization activities

Social skills and the opportunity to test out newly developed social skills is one of the primary needs identified in families coming into the Parents United programmes. All Parents United programmes provide opportunities for parents to socialize on a weekly basis. About once every three months, a special social activity is arranged for the parents by the parents under the direction of the CSATP co-ordinator.

Many parties, play activities and trips are organized for the children by the professional staff. Social activities for the family as a group may occur but with careful attention to the needs of the children and appropriate separation of victims and offenders. Knowledge of current court orders becomes critical for supervising professional staff in appropriately managing these activities.

Fund-raising activities

Within the structure of the chapter, each Parents United self-help chapter charges fees to its membership. (About $2.00 per week.) Funds raised are used to support the cost of the meeting site, social activities, snacks and tools to be used in the children's treatment programme, attendance at regional Parents United conferences, attendance at the national

Parents United conference, and subscriptions to the National Parents United Organization.

Some chapters use fund-raising as a tool for developing group cohesion and offering members an opportunity to test and develop their leadership skills. Large fund-raising activities may occur in these instances. Often these funds are used to pay for services for the children.

CONCLUSION

A programme using the Parents United Treatment Model is composed of three basic parts: 1) the professional component; 2) guided self-help; 3) and a network of community agencies, including law enforcement, child protective services and the courts. The guiding philosophy of the programme for children who have been victims of intrafamilial sexual abuse is that children do not grow up in isolation. And, out of home care has generally not proved successful with victims of sexual abuse. Therefore, attempts will be made to make the family a safe place in which children can grow up without having to permanently leave home.

At disclosure, the family will probably experience a severe crisis. Parents United sponsorship programmes can be activated immediately to offer support to families, minimize the initial crisis and maximize the potential for engaging in effective treatment. It takes powerful external controls to create the environment in which the family can engage in effective therapeutic treatment. The majority of Parents United programmes prefer that cases go through the court systems: juvenile court to provide for the protection of the child; criminal court for the control of the offender. The suspected offender is asked to leave the home in order to allow the child to remain at home.

The criminal court system continues to be involved to give support to the case plan and to make it obligatory that the offender remains out of the home until it is therapeutically sound for him to return. When reunification is considered, the situation must have sufficiently changed so that his return home is in the child's best interests. This is not simply a matter of the offender accepting responsibility and superficially changing his behaviour. Offenders can be adept at working out quickly what therapists want them to say. They can be remorseful and admit responsibility and give verbatim everything that is required of them within a short time in treatment. Questions of reunification should not, therefore, be based primarily upon the performance of the offender. The real central issues when considering reunification are: is the child able to cope well with the family reunification; is the non-offending parent now able to protect the child? Family reunification is rarely considered appropriate in less than a year. If it is not possible for the offender to return home, then what constitutes a 'family' must be redefined.

A Parents United programme co-ordinates activity with all other systems in the community involved with the family. It responds to the needs of the entire family system. It attends to needs of every individual within the family system. The child is the identified victim. The mother is seen as needing tremendous support to change her role within the family and to carry many of the responsibilities she has previously never assumed. She has to learn to protect her children. Not only does she have the support of traditional group and individual therapy, but through the sponsorship programme of the self-help component, she will have access to other mothers who can assist in this difficult area.

The programme provides a non-judgemental acceptance of the offenders. They are not seen as sexual molesters but as parents who have molested their children. Treatment is offered in the hope that over time, with support and with therapy, the offender will be able safely to return to the home. The home will be changed and the dynamics of the family interactions will be different. If a family is reunited, we should not be seeing the family that presented at disclosure. It should appear to be a different family with rules and regulations for interacting within the home that are specific to their needs. It will become a reconstituted family with ever vigilant family members ensuring that the identified problem of sexual abuse will not be repeated.

In the majority of cases referred to Parents United programmes, the offender is male and the identified father figure. The non-offending parent is female and the mother. For the sake of clarity, offenders were here referred to as male; non-offending parents as female; victims as female. There are situations, however, where the offender may be female and the non-offending parent male. More and more victims are identified as both male and female.

A Parents United programme is a powerful treatment response to child sexual abuse combining professional therapy, community systems and self help.

REFERENCES

Giarretto, Henry (1982), *Integrated Treatment of Child Sexual Abuse.* Palo Alto, California: Science and Behavior Books, Inc.

Gillies, Esther H. (1984), *Los Angeles County Department of Children's Services Child Sexual Abuse Program Biennial Report.* Los Angeles, California: unpublished report.

Parents United International (1987), *Chapter Development Packet.* San Jose, California.

16

PREVENTIVE EDUCATIONAL PROGRAMMES FOR CHILDREN

DAVID A. GOUGH

CONSIDERABLE EVIDENCE EXISTS that the sexual abuse of children is widespread within western societies (Finkelhor, this volume). It is not a problem that can be dismissed as small-scale involving a few pathological adults and children in abnormal families, nor is it isolated incidents of children being sexually assaulted by psychologically disturbed strangers. To the extent that all children are potentially at risk of becoming victims, society needs to develop a special interest in preventing abuse.

Araji and Finkelhor (1986) have listed some of the factors associated with adults becoming perpetrators. These are : emotional gratification from relating sexually to a child; sexual arousal to a child; blockage from other sources of sexual gratification; and lack of disinhibition from having sexual relations with a child. For the adults possessing these pre-conditions the translation of the potential for abusing children to the actual engagement of children in sexual activity depends on the children's availability for assault. One strategy for restricting that availability is to ensure that children are not left unsupervised and therefore open to approaches from strangers. There are two problems with this. Firstly, it is neither possible nor even desirable for children to be supervised at all times. They need their own freedom, not only as a basic right but also to enable them to grow into independent adults. Second, it is often those with supervising responsibilities who assault the children, whether these be parents, other relatives or professional workers, such as nursery staff (Finkelhor *et al*, 1988).

An alternative approach is to improve children's ability to protect themselves. If they can develop strategies for avoiding situations of risk, acquire skills for avoiding assault, and learn how to summon assistance from protective adults then the children may be less likely to become victims. Not surprisingly, this approach has been criticised because it places the responsibility for preventing abuse on the potential victims and the least powerful people involved. Instead, the responsibility should be upon the perpetrators of abuse and on society to protect children, and not allow a situation to develop where sexual abuse is a common experience for children. But because human values are difficult to change, even those who ultimately prefer societal or structural solutions believe that in the absence of such changes, children should be offered skills and knowledge to help them protect themselves (Hindman, undated).

An awareness of the extent of the sexual abuse of children developed in the United States several years ahead of Britain. Since, as a result, preventive educational programmes have a longer history in the United States, we should consider what can be learned from that experience.

DEVELOPMENT OF PREVENTIVE EDUCATIONAL PROGRAMMES

The State of California has been at the forefront of the development of child sexual abuse prevention programmes in the United States. Recently, Gilbert and colleagues (1989) have documented how these programmes were established. In the early 1980s, there was growing concern about child abuse and pressure for action by the State government. In 1984, the Child abuse Prevention Training Act (CAPTA) bill was one of 28 pertaining to child abuse presented to the State legislature. Gilbert and colleagues (1989) explain how intense lobbying was used to distinguish the CAPTA bill as a priority to the other bills. Whilst the bill was being considered by the legislature a new scandal broke that concerned allegations of mass sexual abuse at the McMartin School, a middle-class pre-school in Manhattan Beach (Crewdson, 1988). The timing of the scandal meant not only that 'The bill had been intensively lobbied and persuasively argued' but also 'The issue of child abuse was politically uncontestable' (Gilbert *et al*, 1989). Furthermore, the bill was concerned with helping children to protect themselves from such abuse. The Child Abuse Prevention Training Act which was fully implemented in 1985 now offers children preventive training five times in their nursery and school careers at an annual cost of $11 million (Gilbert *et al*, 1989).

Although California has played a leading role in the development and the formal implementation of these programmes by education authorities, similar developments were also occurring across North America. This has spawned the growth of companies, foundations, and campaigning groups whose sole purpose is the development of educational materials and programmes for use by private and state schools. A large industry has been created, likely to be influenced by financial pressures to market and sell its products. The educational programmes differ in length, content and presentation (for programme descriptions see Nelson & Clark, 1986, and Gilbert *et al*, 1989). Some are single half-hour sessions and others occupy several days or weeks (Wurtell, 1987). Despite these variations the programmes share the same general philosophies and specific aims outlined by Finkelhor (1986):

General Aims

— to educate children about the responsibilities and boundaries of parental care, of other caretakers, and of other adults;
— to educate them about their own bodies and the nature and appropriateness of different relationships;
— to teach them the extent and nature of their own rights and self-worth;
— to develop their self-confidence, knowledge, and skills in order to empower them to assert and protect their rights and to seek the assistance of others when necessary.

Specific aims

— to teach children about the existence and nature of child sexual abuse;
— to broaden children's awareness of who potential abusers may be, including people that they may know and like and members of their own family;
— to arm children with strategies to avoid abuse or to receive assistance if they are abused or at risk of abuse. To encourage them to have confidence in taking such action.

EVALUATION

The growth of the industry in preventive educational programmes has been paralleled by the development of research evaluation. Monitoring and evaluation have often been built in from the start. The developers of these programmes have sometimes included evaluation as part of the justification for the funding of their programmes and the funding agencies have desired that effectiveness be demonstrated. Furthermore, the programmes have opened up new areas of research enquiry for academics. Evaluation studies have been the subject of a number of major reviews (Berrick, 1989; Conte & Fogarty, 1989; Doherty and Barrett, 1989; Finkelhor and Strapko, in press; Wurtele, 1987). One review (Gough *et al*, in preparation) reports that child sexual abuse prevention programmes represent more than 10 per cent of all research evaluations of child abuse interventions. Despite the interest in the prevention of the sexual abuse of children, however, there is a dearth of programmes (let alone evaluative studies) to assist children in the primary prevention of physical or emotional abuse or neglect.

As with the programmes themselves, most of the evaluation studies have been carried out in the United States. To date there are at least three British studies (Adams and Llewelyn, 1989; Doherty and Barratt, 1989; Hamilton, 1989), but Kidscape the most widely used programme in Britain has not been formally evaluated, although a study is underway in Scotland.

A common problem for the evaluations discussed in the research reviews is the choice of outcome measures for assessing programme effectiveness. For example, it is difficult to directly test the child's ability to resist assault as it would be inappropriate to put a child in a situation that fully corresponds with an attempted assault. On the other hand, it is difficult to devise indirect measures for testing a child's ability to avoid assault. Different strategies have been attempted by researchers, such as those described by Conte and Fogarty (1989) in their division of studies by outcome measure.

Knowledge gains

Most programmes attempt to teach children the concepts and skills that the authors consider relevant to self protection from sexual abuse. Evaluation studies therefore often assess the impact of programmes by testing for changes in children's level knowledge of prevention, using tests and questionnaires. This is usually accomplished by an oral interview with pre-school children and by pencil and paper tests with school-age children. The tests are applied before and after the programme to check for any changes in score. Some studies include a control group of children who did not receive the programme in order to ensure that any change in scores is due to the programme rather than chance variation or some other uncontrolled factor.

Studies of pre-school children have produced disappointing findings. These suggest that the children are too young to learn the concepts that are taught in the programmes (Gilbert *et al*, 1989). In contrast, older children perform significantly better on tests after receiving the programmes (Finkelhor and Strapko, in press). The latter findings have been replicated by the few existing British studies (Adams and Llewelyn, 1989; Doherty & Barrett, 1989; Hamilton, 1989). Some authors report that these knowledge gains are maintained at three and six month follow up, though Plummer (1984) found that children are likely to forget that abusers may often not be strangers and that some things should not be kept secret from trusted adults. These concepts are known to present particular difficulties for children (Doherty & Barrett, 1989; Finkelhor and Strapko, in press).

Appropriate Touch

Distinguishing between the types of touch that are appropriate for people in different roles and relationships is one way of explaining to children what types of physical contact are acceptable. However, these are difficult concepts to operationalise. Many programmes attempt to teach children to distinguish between 'good' and 'bad' touches. But should this allow a young child to complain and seek help in response to physical punishment from their parents (Gilbert *et al*, 1989)? This may not be a problem for those staff who disapprove of physical chastisement of children, but such views, despite being enshrined in law in Scandinavia and Austria (Newell, 1989) are not generally accepted in North America and Britain. A similar problem concerning the appropriateness of different types of touch arises from the specification in the programmes of the genital area as being private and not to be seen or touched by others. In many programmes parents are excluded from this rule. However, incestuous perpetrators are known to use the excuse of bathing, toileting, and health care for initiating sexual contact. Fortunately, a study by Adams & Llewelyn (1989) has shown that the dangers from adults in toileting can be taught to children through puppet videos. The result in a significant change in children's descriptions of what is a good touch.

In reviewing the published studies, Conte and Fogarty (1989) conclude that children do show knowledge gains about the appropriateness of different touches, but that more concrete forms of teaching the abstract concepts produce better results. Clear rules for what is or is not appropriate were easily understood by children and more effective than encouraging them to rely on their intuition (Wurtell, 1989). Gilbert and colleagues have demonstrated that even young children can associate different touches with different emotions, but that they find difficulties with ambiguous touches. The problem is that perpetrators are highly manipulative and likely to use deliberately ambiguous and confusing touches with children. Role play of inappropriate touches of genital areas are more easily taught than abstract concepts of 'confusing touch' (see Conte and Fogarty, 1989). This leaves few options for the preventive programmes but to instruct children about the inappropriateness of genital touches to which the ambiguous touches may lead.

Avoiding assault

Many programmes attempt to teach children strategies for verbally (and in some cases physically) resisting assault and summoning assistance. These strategies can be taught in a standard format as in other knowledge-based parts of programmes, but there is more potential for them also to be taught as skills that can be modelled, role-played, and rehearsed. Another difference is that there is greater potential for skill-based outcome measures. The most common method used to date has been the presentation of vignettes of different scenarios to children who are then asked how they would respond in such situations. Many of these vignettes are no more than one line statements whilst others more fully describe situations to which the child can respond. Even more realistic is the use of dolls, puppets, or videos of various scenarios. These measures require the child to state how the character in the scenario should act or how the child would act if he or she were in that situation. This approach has been taken further by Doherty and Barrett (1989) who asked the children to role-play the potential victim of a bully. Although the scenario related to bullying rather than sexual abuse, it allowed the children actively to demonstrate the skills that were available to them both before and after the programme.

The most direct measure of children's skills in avoiding abuse involves the use of research confederates who approach the children and ask for their assistance in a way which could lead to the children's abduction (Poche *et al*, 1981; Fryer *et al*, 1987). Both of these studies at post test reported encouraging increases in children's skills at resisting abduction, even for pre-school children in the study by Poche. Not all of the children, however, showed improvement, and in the study by Fryer and his colleagues, it was the children with the lowest self-esteem scores who benefitted least from the intervention. Thus the children who benefitted most from the intervention were those with higher self-esteem, and the appropriate behaviour of these children on the simulation test was matched by an increased understanding and awareness of the issues involved. On the other hand, the least able children showed no evidence of any increase in appropriate behaviour or understanding. Such a result might give rise to questions about the value of widespread programmes, as they may only be effective for those groups most able to protect themselves and less likely to be exposed to risk. Interventions may only speed up the learning of skills and concepts that the more able children are anyway about to learn.

RELEVANCE OF THE STUDIES

Whether the increased knowledge displayed by children receiving the programmes generalises to actual behaviour in abuse situations, with the exception of the stranger abduction studies, is virtually unknown. The abduction studies are limited to approaches by strangers rather than the more difficult and more common problem of abuse by persons known to the children.

Much depends on the context in which children are victimised. Recently researchers have begun to interview victims and perpetrators to examine the realities of the sexual abuse of children. These studies have revealed the insidious nature of sexual abuse: perpetrators deliberately seeking out children who are a bit 'lost', in need of affection and receptive to attention (Berliner & Conte, 1990; Budin and Johnson, 1989; Conte Wolf and Smith, 1989). The perpetrators 'groom' (Berliner and Conte 1990) the children by giving them attention and affection so as to engag them in a relationship before slowly initiating sexual contact for which tl child is then made to feel responsible. Secrecy is maintained by encour ing the children's self-blame and by threatening that disclosure will resul withdrawal of the perpetrator's affection, and in dire consequences to children, their families, and the perpetrators. These descriptions of social contexts in which children are sexually abused raise important q tions about the relevance of school based programmes that teach chil about appropriate touch or how to seek help when assaulted. At the least, it is necessary to understand which individuals assault which children and in what circumstances before it is possible to determine how best to arm children to defend themselves.

A second problem of relevance or generalisability of the studies concerns the emphasis that programmes tend to put on abuse by non-family members. Whilst the programmes aim to teach children concepts or skills relevant to avoidance of sexual assault by all types of perpetrators, it is not surprising that programmes often do not dwell upon the possibility of abuse by parents, particularly when parents and schools may have reservations about the programmes being implemented.

The focus on strangers as perpetrators is particularly clear in the evaluation studies by Poche and by Fryer (Poche *et al*, 1981; Fryer *et al* 1987) which used real life simulations to test the impact of the prevention programmes. Both were behavioural in approach. Poche and colleagues emphasised teaching the correct response to potentially abusive situations, rather than conceptual awareness of child sexual abuse and potential perpetrators. In one sense, this seems a more appropriate approach, given that 't is so much easier to train young children to exhibit certain behaviours ıan it is to teach them concepts. But would children know that these sponses could also be used with Daddy or Uncle? The message that ısers are strangers may well be reinforced by using strangers in the real- ;imulations. The children have not been made so aware of the distinc- between good and bad touches or that abusers can be friends or es. Fryer *et al* (1987a) reported an increased conceptual awareness ght generalise to intrafamilial situations but this was not retested at month follow-up. There is thus little evidence that behavioural ıes of this kind really equip children to resist intrafamilial abuse.

d issue about the relevance of training programmes is whether help to children who have been abused before, or are abused rogramme. Population surveys of adults clearly indicate that :n become victims of sexual assault (Finkelhor *et al*, 1986). over ten per cent of assaults continue over a period of time, victims of intrafamilial abuse who are also less likely to ıse and seek assistance (Haugaard and Reppucci, 1988).) argues that the educational programmes should put on attempting to identify cases by helping children to pite the potential relevance of prevention programmes fect on disclosure has received little research attention ɔ, in press). Disclosure is also relevant when children receiving a training programme. The findings of gest that these children are more likely to disclose n if the programmes help the children to adjust and her ways.

of studies examining the impact of sexual abuse ficult to determine the variables, if any, that who are more rather than less scarred by the experience. One study that has attempted this (Conte and Schuerman, 1987) has found that the strategies adopted by children during the assaults were related to the impact of the abuse. The two different responses of passively submitting and actively resisting abuse were both associated with reduced impact. The authors speculate that the potential adaptability of these responses may relate to the children's general coping strategies in their lives, which suggests that educational programmes need to be tailored to fit the potential variability in the coping strategies of their pupils. Most impact studies do not attempt to demonstrate whether the educational programmes have a significant effect on those children most at risk. Nor do they try to relate effective intervention to the social and psychological characteristics of the children trained, to their internal and external resources for avoiding abuse, or to the situation in which they live that may put them at relatively higher or lower risk of different types of approach by a perpetrator.

WIDER ISSUES

Mention has already been made of one of the most fundamental criticisms of the educational programmes: that they place the responsibility for prevention on the potential victims of abuse rather than on those perpetrating these assaults or upon a society that allows such assaults to be so prevalent. However, to change either the behaviour of offenders or the attitudes and priorities of society is likely to be such a slow process that there is understandably a need to help children to protect themselves (Hindman, undated). The programmes attempting to encourage self-protection can however work towards the changes that are required in adults and society in general in order to prevent abuse. The danger is that programmes shy away from these challenges because of the need to gain acceptance by parents and schools.

A central issue in this debate is the power of children to exercise their rights relative to others. Children, like women, non-whites and the poor, are relatively disadvantaged compared to wealthy white adult males (Ennew, 1986). The proportion of perpetrators of sexual abuse who are white and who have wealth is unclear, but the preponderance of male offenders has been repeatedly demonstrated (Finkelhor, 1986). The power differential between children and offenders is even greater when the offender has parenting or other child care responsibilities. To counter this, prevention programmes often aim to enhance the power of children by providing them with information about what is not appropriate contact with adults, and with strategies for avoiding abuse and seeking assistance. However, several authors have questioned the bases on which these strategies of 'empowerment' are made.

The reality is that adults in many ways do have greater power than children. They have greater physical strength, material resources and knowledge of the world. Furthermore, their views are taken more seriously by others with power, that is, other adults. Children cannot resist the physical strength of an adult male, and to suggest to them that they can, may increase the physical risks to themselves (Crewdson, 1988). In addition, failing to resist more subtle pressures from perpetrators as described by Berliner & Conte (1990) may make children feel responsible for any abuse they suffer. Furthermore, other strategies such as passive submission may seem a more effective coping strategy for some children (Conte & Schuerman, 1987; Kitzinger, 1990). Kitzinger argues that we need to take more notice of the children's view of their situation and the strategies children adopt in practice, such as running away from home, and making themselves physically unattractive or unwell.

Whether or not these are the most useful strategies, they are what children choose to do in response to their situation. The emphasis therefore needs to be on helping children to explore the realities of the power differentials and the strategies that they might use to fully exploit the available resources. Children are very knowledgeable about power and the ability one has to exercise one's rights. They learn about this everyday in the playground, in the classroom and in the family home. It is not a topic, however, that is openly discussed by parents or teachers. If educational programmes were directly to address the realities of being a child and the abusive use of power in sexual assault, the programmes might be more relevant and effective in practice. However, to assess such effectiveness the research studies would need to employ more sensitive outcome measures than those in current use.

A related issue is the attitude taken towards childhood sexuality. Kitzinger (1990) suggests that public concern and reaction to sexual abuse is in itself problematic. Public revulsion against abuse is often stated in terms of children being robbed of their 'sexual innocence' rather than being considered wrong because it infringes a child's right not to be sexually exploited by adults. The concept of sexual innocence is based on an adult definition of childhood which is implicated with difficult issues of sexual attraction, availability, and sexual roles. This is well illustrated in the media portrayal of sexual innocence, such as in virginity, as sexually attractive. Victims who have lost this innocence are therefore seen as 'damaged goods' and 'fair game' for sexual approaches. Kitzinger argues that the most dangerous aspect of this portrayal of children is the way in which it denies them access to the knowledge and power of the adult world.

There is a general tendency for programmes not to directly address sexual issues. For example, many programmes do not even call genitals by their proper names, but instead, refer to them indirectly as 'private areas' or as 'the places underneath one's swimming costume' (Crewdson, 1988; Hindman, undated). One can sympathise with the difficulties programmes may have in being accepted by parents and schools if they address sexual issues, but failure to acknowledge sexuality with children is part of a wider problem of openness and equality in communication. If adults are unable to be frank and honest with children about sexual matters then how can adults expect children to disclose the experience of sexual assault? All that is communicated to children is that sex is not discussed and is somehow shameful. If the realities in society are that children are relatively less powerful than adults, particularly adult males, then prevention strategies need to encourage communication with children. As Hindman (undated) argues, it is the key to disclosure. For this to occur, adults need to respect the views and the rights of children. The way in which many courts reject children's testimony as evidence despite little scientific basis for doing so (Spencer, this volume, Flin, this volume) does not indicate good communication between adults and children nor adult respect for the views of children.

Young children are aware of sexual knowledge and sexual interest. They realise that sexual matters are secret and possibly shameful and so masturbation and same sex sexual exploration, which are probably both very common are not openly discussed. It is, therefore, not surprising that the children who are manipulated into sexual activity by adults feel guilt, responsibility, and are open to blackmail of threats of disclosure by those abusing them.

The tendency of prevention programmes to ignore childhood sexuality is also difficult to reconcile with the fact that perpetrators of sexual abuse were once children themselves, many of whom started offending in adolescence (Becker, this volume). Educational prevention programmes that avoid discussing sexuality are therefore unlikely to be of much help to children who are developing inappropriate sexual preferences and behaviours. This compounds a more general problem of there being few resources available for helping those who admit to inappropriate sex-age preferences. This is unfortunate as such people form the obvious focus for targeting preventive resources and for studying the precursors of abusive behaviour (Finkelhor, 1986; Gilgun & Gordon, 1985).

Finally, the position of children with disabilities may usefully demonstrate the relevance of power and sexuality to the debate on educational prevention programmes for children. Disabled children are often more dependent and are offered fewer relative rights than non-disabled children. When they also have problems of communication, it will be more difficult for them to claim the limited rights that they do have. In addition, society tends to place such individuals in institutions where they are more under the control of others and, as in families, there is limited opportunity for external monitoring of the children's welfare. Institutions differ from families in that they are likely to have a turnover of staff and may attract those with a tendency to sexually abuse children. An extra handicap for disabled children, particularly the physically disabled, is that many adults find it difficult to accept that disabled adults, let alone disabled children, are sexual beings with developing sexual awareness and sexual desires. The resistance to accepting their sexuality is paralleled by a reluctance to see that they are potential victims, who are perhaps at greater risk than other children. In sum, these children may have even less power to exercise their rights not to be sexually abused than non-disabled children (see Brown & Craft, 1989; Senn, undated; Sullivan *et al*, 1987). The lesson we can learn from disabled children is that children are most at risk of abuse when their rights are not taken seriously by adults. Preventive educational programmes therefore need to examine how they may assist children to avoid abuse when they may have little direct power. They need to ensure that they do not compound the lack of power that children already experience.

CONCLUSION

The development of educational programmes to enable children to avoid sexual assault has led to a number of research studies to evaluate them. The programmes have been found to be effective within their limited parameters of teaching children specific skills and knowledge. Less certain is the extent that the programmes actually protect children from abuse. The problem is that the skills which are the easiest to teach children and the easiest to measure in outcome studies are not necessarily the skills most important for self-protection. This is so, particularly when perpetrators are often already known to the children, and adopt subtle, insidious pressures to achieve and maintain their compliance. Furthermore, the children who perform worst on the current programmes may be drawn from the group of children who are exposed to the greatest risk of assault. Also open to question is the effect that the programmes have on children who have already been victims of sexual abuse. Similarly, there has been little attention to the effect of programmes on children who are subsequently abused. Children who cannot avoid becoming victims may be helped by programmes incorporating elements that specifically focus on the problems of reacting and coping to the experience of sexual assault.

A more fundamental issue is the extent that the programmes help to change those attitudes in western societies that have allowed so many children to become victims of sexual assault. By not directly addressing basic issues such as the power differentials between adults and children the programmes may not be as effective as they could be. More seriously, they may implicitly perpetrate and reinforce power imbalances between adults and children and make children more vulnerable to abuse. The reluctance of adults to discuss sexuality between themselves, let alone with children, does not encourage children to be open about these issues. Society seems reluctant to discuss the unresolved ideological questions concerning our attitudes towards children and towards sexuality.

How are we to assess technical solutions to the problem of the sexual abuse of children, whether these be diagnostic criteria for abuse, videotechnology in court, or educational preventive programmes? Their appropriateness can only be assessed by a greater specificty of their aims, their possible outcomes, and of their potential effect on the various ideological debates. Within certain parameters prevention educational programmes can be effective techniques. However, their contribution can only be fully assessed within a wider debate about adult-child relations, gender, sexuality, and power. Such a debate could include discussion of the reasons that children themselves become perpetrators and what we should do to try and prevent this.

Aknowledgements: this review was informed by D. A. Gough, J. Taylor and F. A. Boddy 'Child Abuse Interventions: A Review of the Literature', Report to the Department of Health, October, 1988.

REFERENCES

*British evaluation studies.

*Adams, J. and Llewelyn, A. (1989). 'A puppet video designed to prevent sexual abuse in nursery and infant school children', Unpublished data.

Araji, S., and Finkelhor, D., (1986). 'Abusers: a review of the research' in D. Finkelhor and Associates. *A Sourcebook on Child Sexual AbuseÈ,* Beverley Hills: Sage.

Berliner, L. and Conte, J. R. (1990). 'The process of victimisation: The victims' perspective', *Child Abuse and Neglect,* 14, (1), 29-40.

Berrick, J. D. (1989). 'Sexual abuse prevention education. Is it appropriate for the preschool child?', *Children and Youth Services Review,* 11, 145-158.

Brown, H. and Craft, A. (1989). *Thinking the Unthinkable. Papers on sexual abuse and people with learning difficulties.* London: Family Planning Association Education Unit.

Budin, L. E. and Johnson, C. F. (1989). 'Sex abuse prevention programmes. Offenders attitudes about their efficacy', *Child Abuse and Neglect,* 13, (1), 77-88.

Conte, J. R. and Fogarty, L. (1989). 'Sexual abuse prevention programmes for children', Paper prepared for a special issue of Education and Urban Society.

Conte, J. R. and Schuerman, J. R. (1987). 'Factors associated with an increased impact of child sexual abuse', *Child Abuse and Neglect,* 11, 201-211.

Conte, J. R., Wolf, S. and Smith, T. (1989). 'What sexual offenders tell us about prevention strategies', *Child Abuse and Neglect,* 13, (2), 293-301.

Crewdson, J. (1988). *By Silence Betrayed. Sexual Abuse of Children in America.* Boston: Little, Brown and Company.

*Doherty, N. and Barratt, W. (1989) 'Personal Safety Programme', Report to Cambridgeshire County Council in co-operation with Huntingdon Health Authority.

Ennew, J. (1986). *The Sexual Exploitation of Children.* Cambridge: Polity Press.

Finkelhor, D., 'Prevention: A review of programs and research' in D. Finkelhor and Associates. (1986). *A Source Book on Child Sexual Abuse.* Sage: Beverly Hills.

Finkelhor, D. and Strapko, N. (in press). 'Sexual abuse prevention education: A Review of Evaluation Studies', in D. J. Willis, E. W. Holder, and M. Rosenberg (eds.) *Child Abuse Prevention.* New York: Wiley.

Finkelhor, D., Williams, L. M. and Burns, N. (1988). *Nursery Crimes, Sexual Abuse in Day Care.* Newbury Park: Sage.

Fryer, G. E., Kraizer, S. K. and Miyoshi, T. (1987a). 'Measuring actual reduction of risk of child abuse: a new approach', *Child Abuse and Neglect,* 11, 173-179.

Fryer, G. E., Kraizer, S. K. and Miyoshi, T. (1987b) 'Measuring children's retention of skills to resist stranger abduction. use of the simulation technique', *Child Abuse and Neglect,* 11, 181-185.

Gilbert, N., Berrick, J. D., Le Prohn, N. and Nyman, N. (1989). *Protecting young children from sexual abuse. Does preschool training work?* Masachusetts: Lexington Books.

Gilgun, J. F. and Gordon, S. (1985). 'Sex Education and the Prevention of Child Sexual Abuse', *Journal of Sex Education and Therapy*, 11, (1), 46-52.

Gough, D. A., Taylor, J., and Boddy, F. A. (in preparation) *Child Abuse Interventions: A Review of the Evaluation Literature.* London: HMSO.

*Hamilton, S. (1989) 'Prevention in child sexual abuse — An evaluation of a programme', MSc. Thesis, University of Edinburgh.

Haugaard, J. C. and Reppucci, N. D. (1988). *The Sexual Abuse of Children. A Comprehensive Guide to Current Knowledge and Intervention Strategies*'. San Francisco: Jossey-Bass.

Hindman, J. (undated). *Abuses to Sexual Abuse Prevention Programmes or Ways we abuse our children as we attempt to prevent abuse.* Ontario: Alexandria Associates.

Kitzinger, J. (1990). 'Sexual abuse and the violation of childhood', in James, A., and Prout, A. (eds.). *The Social Construction of Childhood.* Oxford: Oxford University Press.

Kolko, D. J., Moses, J. T., Litz, J. and Hughes, J. (1987). 'Promoting Awareness and Prevention of Child Sexual Victimisation using the Red Flag/Green Flag Programme: An Evaluation with Follow up', *Journal of Family Violence*, 2 (1), 11-35.

Nelson, M., and Clark, K., (1986). *The Education Guide to Preventing Child Sexual Abuse*, Santa Cruz: Network Publications.

Newell, P. (1989). *Children are People Too. The Case Against Physical Punishment.* London: Bedford Square Press.

Poche, C., Brouer, R. and Swearington, M. (1981) 'Teaching Self-Protection to Young Children,' *Journal of Applied Behaviour Analysis*, 14, 169-176.

Senn, C. (undated). *Vulnerable Sexual Abuse and People with an Intellectual Handicap.* Toronto: Allan Roeher Institute.

Sullivan, P. M., Vernon, M. and Scanlan, J. M. (1987). 'Sexual abuse of deaf youth', *American Annals Deaf*, 132, (4), 256-26.

Wurtelle, S. K. (1987). 'School-based sexual abuse prevention programmes: A review', *Child Abuse and Neglect*, 11, (4), 483-496.

17

IMPLICATIONS AND PROSPECTS

KATHLEEN MURRAY AND DAVID A. GOUGH

EARLIER CHAPTERS HAVE reviewed from an American perspective the evolution of the problem of child sexual abuse, the introduction of social and legal processes to deal with reported cases, the issues currently arising in medical evaluation, and the associated changes in professional attitudes and relationships. The aim here is to define those features of American experience that in our opinion may have a particular significance for policy makers and practitioners in the United Kingdom. Inevitably, we have the problem of finding criteria by which the full benefits of particular processes can be evaluated. However, even at the level of descriptive information, there is sufficient in the foregoing chapters to allow us to speculate about the implications of recent trends in the United States for policy and practice in a British context.

Our conclusions begin with the dramatic upsurge of reports of child sexual abuse on both sides of the Atlantic. The numbers of such reports tell us little about the scale of the problem, reflecting as they do the breadth of the definition used, and unknown and largely unknowable variations in the disclosure of an act shrouded in secrecy. There are, therefore, serious constraints on the inferences that may legitimately be drawn from the prevalence figures contained in official publications. Indeed, the Cleveland Inquiry (1988) found it impossible to obtain any reliable measures of the incidence of child sexual abuse in the United Kingdom, and cautioned against accepting the ten per cent figure that is frequently quoted.

Although Finkelhor (this volume) emphasises the importance for public policy reasons of recognising the degree to which child sexual abuse occurs, he regards knowledge of the exact extent of the problem as a lower priority than understanding its nature and causes and how to intervene effectively. The value of simple prevalence studies in determining the exact extent of child sexual abuse is therefore questionable. Nevertheless studies of this kind are useful in providing objective data to show that child sexual abuse is a continuing social problem which we cannot ignore. Beyond the simple statistics of frequency, more specialised studies can throw light on the particular circumstances in which abuse occurs, the social context and the interpersonal factors in abuse, and the kinds of discord, stress and suffering that commonly act as triggers.

Whatever its scale, child abuse and neglect in any of its forms, but especially sexual abuse, clashes violently with our assumptions about the natural entitlement of all children. In both America and Britain an amalgam of many forms of response has emerged whose common denominator is the intention to save children from being abused. Not only are government agencies involved, but parents and children themselves, communities, professional associations and voluntary organisations are all caught up in responding to the problem. While no response is pure, it might be useful, for the sake of analysis, to classify society's reactions as preventive, protective, therapeutic, and cosmetic.

PREVENTIVE RESPONSE

The factors which contribute to the causation of child sexual abuse are still only partly understood. Even if logically and practically we cannot prevent something whose causes are not yet known, this does not remove the obligation to maintain our efforts. Indeed, the adoption of a number of measures can go a long way towards preventing the sexual abuse of children. These may be directed at society in general, or at vulnerable children and families.

To prevent child abuse there needs to be an understanding of the ways in which given social, economic and environmental circumstances affect the quality of family life and the relations between parents and children, and how these in their turn are influential in shaping attitudes and lifestyles of which child abuse may be a by-product. It follows that the traumatic event which brings the child to official attention is the most recent link in a whole chain of causal processes. It also follows that the work done with children and families cannot be sufficient in itself to bring about major changes in the overall level of abuse in society. To say this is in no way to diminish the value of such interventions, but only to argue that they must be fortified by action on another plane to improve the quality of life in our communities (Parton, 1985).

In physically decaying and socially disorganised localities, the challenges faced by parents are especially daunting. The way forward seems to be not only through the development of supportive social services, but through an increasing emphasis on informal care networks, usually family based but sometimes more broadly community based, which aim to alleviate feelings of isolation and to develop community awareness and mutual responsibility. Romantic notions of 'the community' as easily capable of coping with its own problems should realistically be resisted, nevertheless it is a resource to be used creatively, a possible source of support, protection and guidance.

In terms of structural prevention, universal day care is regarded as the single most valuable reform in the field of child welfare (Frost and Stein,

1989). Collective child care not only benefits children in many ways but also allows women to compete equally in the work-place which is an important source of power in society. Such provision should be available in a variety of forms to meet the wide range of need in the community. It is however extremely unfortunate that day care itself has been the context of a large number of sexual assaults against children (Finkelhor *et al.*, 1988).

Attitudes to women and children

The subordination of women and children is deeply embedded in the cultural norms of western society. Largely as a result of feminist writings, it is now widely recognised that the sexual abuse of children, at least in part, is the expression of male dominance and a symptom of the unequal balance of power in the family (J. Ennew, 1986; Frost and Stein, 1989). If this view is valid, major structural changes will be necessary to bring about a reconstruction of masculinity in a way which deflects the need to exercise power over others.

A primary source of concern has been the development of particular role models in childhood (Finkelhor, this volume). Children are seldom offered a range of role models on which to base appropriate attitudes to members of the opposite sex. Finkelhor argues vigorously for the development of preventive strategies which involves *inter alia* policies towards equal opportunity, a general child advocacy programme charged with the maintenance of professional standards, and a planned balance between the rights of parents and children. Schools need to develop a whole-school policy towards equal opportunity and to ensure that this is reflected not only in the experiences of children, but also those of the staff.

During children's school years, the education service can provide opportunities for a variety of learning experience which might help to inculcate basic parenting skills and also create realistic expectations in young people of both sexes about the responsibilities of bringing up children. A course on human psychology, for example, might include lessons on the dynamics of behaviour and human relationships, the use of power, and the development of responsibility and self-assertion, the ways in which people interact and react at a great variety of levels, the role of values and the roots of prejudice. Sex education, family planning, home economics and political education, in addition to first-hand practical experience of babies and young children might form an integral part of the programme.

It would be wrong to convey the impression that children need simply to acquire the technical skills of parenting. Education should influence the perceptions and attitudes of young people so as to increase the quality and effectiveness of parenting, instil in them a concern and responsibility for children's well-being and safety, and generally raise the level of awareness and mutual responsibility for the care of children in the community. There is no reason why education cannot embrace these ideas, but to take them fully into account in thinking about educational provision requires a degree of courage and self-assurance in breaking away from a familiar and traditional concept of the place of education in society.

Assertiveness training

To avoid risk of abuse, children need to acquire assertive and independent styles of behaviour. Strategies of this kind are unlikely to be popular with adults who prefer children to be compliant and conforming. For example, children who challenge parental rules create difficulties which their parents associate with threats to a well-established pattern of discipline and control. Yet, children should have a right to be safe and should be entitled to protect themselves, even if teaching them to exercise their rights might change the balance of power in relation to adults.

The education service is in a unique position to teach children how to protect themselves. In Britain and the United States preventive educational programmes aim to develop in children a greater awareness of their control over their own bodies. The principle is that children who acquire skills in self-assertiveness are more likely to question the situation where an adult tries to impose his or her will on the child. They are also more likely to refuse such approaches and to seek help if necessary. However, alerting children to danger in a way that will guarantee their safety is not at all a straight forward matter (Gough, this volume). Whether the concepts of self-protection that are most easily taught to children actually protect them in practice is still far from clear. Also, the self-protection programmes raise a variety of ideological issues concerning attitudes towards children and towards sexuality that remain unresolved.

Identifying families at risk

The burden of protecting children from sexual abuse should not be placed on prevention programmes alone (Gough, this volume). More responsibility should be taken by adults to be aware and concerned about the welfare of the children they know, and therefore more likely to become alerted when a child is in distress.

Some adults are especially well placed to detect at an early stage those families at risk of violence or neglect in child care. Health visitors routinely screen the population of children under the age of five; teachers see all school-age children and have the support of child guidance workers in monitoring children at risk; school nurses assist with the medical screening of school children; community nurses provide clinical nursing care to patients in their own homes; community midwives routinely follow up women with new babies: they are all potential sources of referral. Medical practitioners in general practice, at health clinics, in accident services and in the maternity service deal with large numbers of children and are in a position to identify possible cases of sexual abuse (Dingwall *et al*, 1983).

Other agencies involved with the child population are the police, probation workers, local voluntary bodies such as family centres and play groups, and also neighbours and relatives. The staff and volunteers of all of these bodies are in a position to identify children at risk, although their ability to do so will depend on their level of knowledge and awareness. Social services departments have powers to intervene in cases where it is clear that children are seriously at risk, and to take them compulsorily into care. However, their work is more likely to involve responding to referrals from other agencies rather than making initial identification of abuse: it is also typically crisis intervention with little follow-up of cases. The unhappy consequence of a heavy emphasis on crisis intervention came to light last year when the Social Services Inspectorate at the Department of Health reported that 600 children on the 'at risk' register in the London Boroughs were unallocated to a social worker.

Recent government policies which aim to keep young people over the age of sixteen dependent on their parents for income support have forced many to remain in family situations where they continue to be abused. Under new social security arrangements introduced in 1988 young people under the age of eighteen who were not usefully occupied in employment, training or education were denied income support and thereby the means to live independently. Young people leaving local authority care were especially vulnerable, since many were forced to return to the families where they had originally been abused. Although the government has made some concessions, many young people continue to experience financial hardship if they decide to leave home rather than continue to suffer abuse.

PROTECTIVE RESPONSE

Referral and investigation

All the American states have child abuse reporting laws which require that specified professionals who are likely to come in contact with children report suspected abuse and neglect to child protective agencies. The reporting laws were designed to prevent evidence of abuse from going unnoticed and to provide child protective agencies with a new and much larger 'cadre of discoverers' than had been previously available (Zellman, 1990). While it has been difficult to find a wholly satisfactory way of identifying who should be on the list of mandatory reporters, some of the states are clearly ignoring the caveat that everyone's responsibility is no one's responsibility. 'The longer the list of reporters, the more encouragement there is to pass the buck.' (Fox, 1982) In many states there are criminal penalties for failure to report by a mandatory reporter and in all places there is a potential civil liability for harm caused to the child by failure to comply with the legal obligation to report. However, criminal prosecutions are relatively rare: civil suits are more common.

In a great many states, the number of reports usually far exceeds the ability of the investigating agency to do an in-depth verification of all reports. This discrepancy is not caused by the mandatory reporting laws. Very few people really believe that the passing of a statute forces people to disclose what comes to their attention. Indeed, empirical data from a variety of studies confirm widespread beliefs that the reporting laws are frequently violated (Davidson, 1988). The large number of reports seems to be a function of public education programmes. The greater the attempt to educate the public about the problem of child abuse, the more focussed are the minds of the professionals and the greater the number of reports received from all sources. Child protection resources are thereby stretched beyond their capacities, and unless there is some coherence in the way that suspected cases are dealt with, public education may be potentially counter-productive.

In the United Kingdom, where there is no mandatory reporting, local authorities have a statutory responsibility to pursue enquiries into suspected cases of child abuse or neglect. In the aftermath of the many child abuse inquiries, the central government departments have given strong encouragement to social services and social work authorities to review their procedures for the administrative management of known and suspected cases of child abuse, and to ensure that responsibilities are clearly defined and understood. Although a leading role is assigned to social services and social work departments in the investigation and management of these cases, the nature of the problem of child abuse and its consequences are such that there can never be any question of these departments excluding all other agencies.

One major objective of the initiatives taken by central government in recent years has been to ensure co-ordinated action between the agencies likely to become involved. The area child protection committees (area review committees in Scotland) are intended as a means to that end. However, a series of tragic cases and ensuing public inquiries have led to much adverse criticism of the arrangements for multi-disciplinary collaboration (Hammersmith, 1984; Brent, 1985; Greenwich, 1987; Lambeth, 1987; Cleveland, 1988). The Cleveland Inquiry (1988) recommended the creation of specialist assessment teams and joint training for police, social workers and medical practitioners. They also recommended alternative models of collaboration which would ensure that the investigation is not seen as the prerogative of any one profession.

In the procedures for the investigation and management of child abuse cases a central place is occupied by the case conference. The case conference is the principal means of ensuring that different agencies share information, agree on the allocation of responsibilities for further action, and make key decisions concerning the management of cases. Case registers are also essential instruments of co-operation when cases come to light or when major decisions have to be made. They exist to provide information as to whether a given child (or another child in the same household) has previiously been identified as a victim of abuse, and to indicate a need for regular follow-up and review of activities by social work staff.

Despite the confidence placed in these procedures, we still know relatively little about the factors influencing the various professional participants in case conference decision-making or in entering a child's name in the register. Research has been undertaken on child abuse cases referred to specialist centres, but the systematic study of the management of routine cases has been relatively neglected. This is currently being rectified by a nationwide programme of research funded by the Department of Health. Such evidence as there is suggests that case conferences are largely dominated by social work (Gough *et al.*, 1987), that there is little clarity in the criteria used for registration purposes (Gough, 1988), and that criteria are not applied consistently (Bacon and Farquar, 1983). It is not surprising therefore to find wide geographical variations in the proportion of children placed on child protection registers (Gough, 1988).

When dealing with alleged sexual abuse, American child protection systems have experienced a number of inherent difficulties which are replicated in the British systems. Except in cases of severe physical trauma or injury, not only are the facts difficult to determine but even within what is known, there is always the further question of whether it is right for the law to intervene. Moreover, one level of identification will not always suffice. There are different stages in child protection procedures and in civil and criminal proceedings, and the identification may serve different functions at each stage. It would be wholly wrong, for example, for the same level of identification to tell the social worker when a child should be taken into a place of safety as tells the judge when a child should be placed in a foster home or parental rights should be terminated.

In England, use of the 'place of safety' order, which provides emergency protection for a child at risk, has in recent years given rise to increasing concern. The length of time a child may be detained prior to judicial scrutiny, the curtailment of access and the stated purpose of the order, which have been the subject of widespread criticism, were recently reformed under the Children Act 1989 (Spencer, this volume). The Scottish system of children's hearings with its independent reporter, the disposition role of the lay panel and statutory referral to the sheriff court for adjudication are reputed to provide a fairer and more effective process (Nicholson, this volume). While the wholesale adoption of the Scottish system has never been seriously considered in England and Wales there are some elements which could be usefully applied south of the Border. For example, the proposed 'officer of child protection', which was recommended by the Cleveland Inquiry and the subject of a detailed paper by the Lord Chancellor (1988), was to have a role similar to that of the Scottish reporter in reviewing local authority decisions. So far, that innovative proposal has not become a reality.

Considerable support has increasingly attached to the possibility of excluding an abuser or suspected abuser from the family home instead of removing the child from the comfort and security of known surroundings, from the support of friends and from the care of a trusted parent. In both Canada and the United States the law allows the alleged abusing parent to be excluded from the family home (Yuille *et al.*, 1988; Myers, 1987). A similar proposal is currently under consideration both in England and Wales and in Scotland (Law Commission, 1989; Child Care Law Review, 1989). Under the Children Act 1989, local authorities have the power to provide alternative accommodation or cash assistance to alleged abusers who have voluntarily left home or promise to do so. The Law Commission proposes that the court should have power to make exclusion orders against alleged abusers in appropriate cases and that these should be enforceable by having power of arrest attached in all cases. It remains to be seen whether the proposals will be enacted by Government. In the United States, the success of voluntary undertakings appears to have substantially reduced the need to resort to an ousting order. One of the factors determining the public acceptance of this approach is the availability of services and treatment agencies for parents suspected of abuse.

Criminal prosecution

The view that criminal prosecution is an appropriate response to child abuse is highly controversial among child protection workers who fear that the arrest and possible prosecution of a parent will impair efforts to treat the parent and re-unite the family. Others argue strongly in its favour on grounds that 'prosecution recognises that children are as entitled to protection under the law as adults, and that offenders — whether parents, other caretakers, or strangers — are accountable for their behaviour' (Peters *et al.*, 1989).

There are no statistics, either in Britain or America, on how many cases of child sexual abuse disclosure ultimately appear in the criminal courts, although it is believed to be only a fraction of the total. The problems encountered in prosecuting parents for offences against their children include the reluctance of the victims to testify against their own mother or father, the competence of very young children to give evidence, their credibility and the emotional stress visited on the children in the course of the trial and pre-trial investigations.

A number of changes in court room practice have already been implemented in the United Kingdom. The introduction of new rules of evidence and procedure has also been recommended. These aim to alleviate some of the stress on the child victim who appears as a witness in criminal or civil proceedings. The main purpose is to avoid the child witness experiencing the trauma of giving evidence in open court in front of the accused. Live closed circuit television, pre-trial deposition procedure, preliminary hearings, video-recorded evidence and prior statements of the child admissible as proof of the facts are some of the new procedures being advocated in the United Kingdom (Spencer; Nicholson, this volume).

In view of the fact that the majority of foregoing chapters describe fifty-five sovereign jurisdictions in the United States, there is a surprising amount of similarity in the laws. It is a number of years since the technological revolution reached the American courts and since then similar innovations have been introduced in many of the states. Yet the law does not appear to have been invoked very often, partly because of constitutional difficulties but also because many prosecutors believe that they have a greater chance of winning the case if the child gives evidence in open court (Elias and MacFarlane, this volume).

The universal adoption of videotaping as an investigative tool is thought to be inevitable (Hechler, 1988). The videotape is a valuable means of preserving evidence, of reducing the number of (often traumatic) interviews a child must submit to, and of sharing information among investigators, lawyers, therapists, and parents. Furthermore, it provides a means not only of evaluating but also of refining techniques. Tapes can be reviewed by those who made them and can also be used to train investigators in proper and improper interviewing methods. Nevertheless, the admissiblity of video-recorded statements as evidence in court continues to be highly controversial in the United States (Elias and MacFarlane, this volume).

Although, when it began, videotaped testimony was favoured by prosecutors as a means of avoiding multiple interviewing of children, and also was seen as a possible alternative to a child's live testimony, ultimately it was taken over by the defence. Videotape ensures that investigators can be held accountable for their techniques. Apparently, the demand for the recording of investigative techniques has become a rallying cry of VOCAL (Victims of Child Abuse Laws) in the United States (Hechler, 1988). Unsurprisingly, professional enthusiasm for introducing videotapes in court seems to have waned considerably. American experience suggests that less may be gained by these innovative measures than by reviewing the arrangements already in place, by careful pre-trial preparation of the child and by comprehensive training for the professionals involved (Elias and MacFarlane, this volume). Furthermore, Berliner (this volume) provides firm grounds for believing that long delays in bringing the case to trial and the uncertainty these create are the most likely cause of the child's suffering. The laws therefore need to assure that trials are speedy in all cases where children appear as witnesses (Murray, 1988).

The successful prosecution of child abuse requires different practices than those used to investigate other types of crime (Toth and Whalen, 1987). One of the major differences is the extent to which information is derived from a variety of individuals and agencies such as police, social work, medical personnel and mental health professionals. The best response, therefore, is a co-ordinated, multi-disciplinary approach. In American jurisdictions the multi-disciplinary approach takes a variety of forms: some are merely a group of concerned professionals meeting on a regular basis, whereas others have fixed teams of agency representatives responsible for investigating cases and recommending action. By the end of 1986, many states had passed laws mandating the implementation of multi-disciplinary approaches to child abuse.

With the development of scientific knowledge concerning children and the effects of trauma on them, information is available for the trial of child sexual abuse cases that should be utilised. To obtain a conviction in these cases, prosecutors increasingly look to the expert evidence not only of physicians but also of mental health and social work practitioners (Myers, this volume). The expert witness can provide essential information to help juries evaluate evidence and provide an informed framework in which to judge the child. Jurors will be able to make more accurate assessments of the credibility of child victims. The jurors' new found knowledge may later be communicated to others, leading to an increased awareness of the realities of child abuse within the community. And finally, judges exposed to experts will become better educated, which should encourage more flexible and sensitive handling of subsequent child abuse cases (Toth & Whalen, 1987).

The pressures are such that the experts are not seen as providing independent assessments of the child and his or her experiences. For each expert testifying on behalf of the prosecution, there is likely to be a defence witness waiting in the wings to give the contradictory 'expert' opinion and interpretation. The experts who routinely testify for the defence are called 'hired guns' by the opposition. The therapists and social workers have been derisively called 'child savers'; their techniques have been characterised as everything from manipulation to out-and-out child abuse (Hechler, 1988). Perhaps this is a necessary consequence of an adversarial legal system. The effect on the lawyers is even more starkly seen. It is their business to intimidate the children, confuse them into withholding information and giving incorrect answers, or seeming untruthful when in fact they are not. Defending those accused of child abuse is now such a common practice that lawyers' organisations are even offering seminars on the fine points of how to confuse children and bamboozle jurors. In order to minimise adversarial sparring and broaden the search for truth in child sexual abuse trials, it has been suggested that judges should appoint neutral expert witnesses (Myers *et al*, 1989). There is much to be said in favour of the inquisitorial legal system, such as that in Germany.

It is also a feature of American experience that the perpetrators of child sexual abuse are resistant to voluntary treatment (Becker, this volume). The justice system and the risk of punishment, which is society's ultimate instrument for enforcing its values, provides a powerful incentive to co-operate with the treatment agency. Therefore, it has been the policy in the United States to promote the prosecution and conviction of child abusers while advocating aggressively on behalf of child victims.

The heavy criticism evoked by disparities in sentencing has led to an interest in mandatory sentencing policies as well as to considerable discussion of the possibility of a middle road, the structuring of judicial discretion by the use of 'sentencing guidelines' — with the latter seen not as gentle advice but interpreted in a fairly strict and formal sense. In Minnesota's guidelines, which are considered a model by experts in the law (Crewdson, 1988), the sentence is based on the ranked seriousness of the offence and the criminal history score of the offender. However, a judge can stay whatever sentence is mandated by the guidelines if he finds doing so to be 'in the best interests of the family'. Although the Minnesota guidelines have worked well during their six years of operation, not many states have yet followed their example. England and Wales are different from Scotland in this respect in that sentencing guidelines have already come into use in the English criminal courts, whereas Scotland has watched and waited and only so far suggested certain minimum sentences.

Compensation

The possibility of compensation for the victims of sexual abuse has recently attracted increasing attention in Britain. Under the Criminal Injuries Compensation Scheme which was set out in a document approved by Parliament in 1964, the physically or sexually abused child not living in the same household as the offender was entitled to claim compensation for injuries suffered. Although since 1979 it has been competent to claim for an intra-familial assault, it appears likely that very few of those eligible for compensation made a claim. For example, the 21st Report of the Criminal Injuries Compensation Board (CICB) (1984/85) stated that applications were received on behalf of only twelve children who were victims of family violence (Brown, 1989).

The scheme was given statutory force in the 1988 Criminal Justice Act. Any applicant who is dissatisfied with the decision made at the hearing is now entitled to a judicial review. Although applications should be made within three years of the incident, a claim that is based on disclosure of sexual abuse made some time after the incident will not be refused on grounds of late reporting. Victims may be entitled to claim so long as they can prove that abuse occurred. There is no need for an individual to be found guilty of an offence. Although the CICB's 1989 Report refers to an increased number of applications on behalf of children, the reasons for failure to take up compensation claims still persist: inadequate publicity, promotion and training, and limited developments in professional practice (Brown, 1989).

Central government has made it clear that local authorities have a responsibility to inform clients of their right to compensation. This is particularly true when a child victim is received into the care of the local authority. If no claim is made, the child can take a civil action against the authority for the monies that the child should have received. The victims of abuse can also take direct civil action for damages against those who perpetrated the abuse.

It would not be altogether surprising to find considerable compensation being claimed from public funds by child abuse victims over the next few years. Not only is it appropriate that society honours the victim's right to financial compensation but it is also important that the child thereby receives society's confirmation that abuse occurred. However, new knowledge with implications for action tends everywhere to percolate established practice fairly slowly. The burdens of many families have for long gone unrecognised. The children themselves have been afraid to speak out and those who represent them have been ignorant or slow to assert their demands, preferring to seek the protection of privacy. It will be a major task to shift significantly the pattern and style of response of child victims.

THERAPEUTIC RESPONSE

The therapeutic response aims to stop sexual abuse by changing or modifying the behaviour of the abuser, and by treating the child victim so as to guard against both short- and long-term damaging effects of the abuse experience.

Perpetrators

The long search for the distinguishing characteristics of abusers has yielded over the years disappointingly few clear-cut and unambiguous findings, although there is widespread agreement that personal, family and social environmental characteristics interact in such a way as to predispose the individual to take the deviant path (Becker, this volume). There is some convincing evidence that a relationship may exist between a history of sexual victimisation and the development of a deviant sexual interest pattern (Becker, this volume). Cognitive distortion, which is another common finding in perpetrators, reflects the fact that there are very few offenders aware that there are norms prohibiting this type of behaviour.

Another widely held view is that perpetrators tend to be drawn with disproportional frequency from persons with an accentuated need for personalised power. A broad range of life situations and cultural processes may make personalised power important or salient (Finkelhor, this volume). For example, where there is a strong cultural emphasis on male strength and daring, and in certain childhood socialisation experiences such as achievement-obedience conflicts. The prevalence of sexual abuse may also derive from a conflict between an accepted cultural demand for masculine assertiveness and any structural restriction of the normally acceptable routes to achievement. These social processes may have a greater impact on males who have been abused themselves and may increase the portion who might indulge in deviant sexual activity (Becker, this volume).

Studies of cultural and social factors go some way to reducing the bias towards the investigation of personal and family factors in relation to abuse. The two sets of explanation are not of course mutually exclusive or contradictory. They can be brought together if it is postulated that sexual abuse is a special hazard for individuals with particular types of early experience. A hazard is not of course an inevitability: a favourable social climate can do a great deal to reduce the risk, even if it does not wholly eliminate it.

In the treatment of perpetrators, the principal emphasis is placed on various forms of psychological re-education. Becker describes a 'cognitive behavioural treatment model' which aims to teach control over deviant sexual impulses and to teach the skills required to relate to people in a functional and caring manner. The seven components that are used according to individual deficits, effectively teach behaviours that are incompatible with re-offending. Preliminary outcome data show a positive finding (Becker, this volume). With a few notable exceptions (Wyre, 1987; Mezey *et al.*, 1990) there is a paucity of services available for the treatment of perpetrators in Britain. Perpetrators found guilty of an offence and sent to prison are particularly unlikely to receive treatment, and prison may even encourage further offences to be committed on release (Coburn, 1990).

The relative effectiveness of different therapeutic methods may depend as much on the social and personal circumstances of the individual as on the type of abuse. Removal of the perpetrator from the family home is favoured in the United States as an alternative to removing the child victim, but we need to assess how much is achieved if the abuser is removed physically but his motivation and desires remain unchanged. Other approaches include the encouragement of either alternative and less damaging modes of expressing personalised power drives, or, more effectively, the socialisation of power drives by encouraging the person to do things for other people. The latter is one of the key working principles of the Parents United programme and of other self-help groups in the United States (Gillies, this volume).

Children and families

Relatively little is known about either the specific consequences of sexual assault on children (Li, forthcoming) or the relative effectiveness of different modes of treatment. Yet few would dispute that all children who have been sexually abused should have the opportunity to obtain treatment, even if the abuse was short-lived or has been denied by a child (Long, 1986).

Although all children are potential victims of abuse, there is a growing belief (Berliner and Conte, 1990) that perpetrators seek out children living in difficult social-emotional circumstances who are more open to exploitation. If such a child becomes a victim, it seems logical to provide as much social support as possible and to use the social interaction of small groups as a medium of treatment. Adult support groups and networks are a further potential support and a useful medium for working towards successful and more rewarding social relationships.

Furthermore, if all sexually abused children actually disclosed that fact, it would be necessary for the available treatment resources to be supplemented by a self-help component which some believe anyway is the most effective means of support. Indeed, the professionals might be more usefully engaged as back-up resource rather than working directly with an individual or group.

As far as individual therapy is concerned, perhaps the most important feature is the gradual building up of a relationship of trust with the child and the family. As Jones (this volume) has indicated, the process can make a start at the first interview, even if this is primarily concerned with gathering legal evidence. Within this relationship defensiveness can be reduced and a sense of security engendered. The child's feelings of guilt, concerns about trust and betrayal, and sexualised behaviour can be brought to the surface and explored. It is not a matter of isolating some crucial childhood event which, once uncovered, both explains and magically eliminates the effects of the abuse. Rather it is a matter of unravelling the victim's perception of the event, the emotional reaction to it and helping him or her to confront and successfully manage the guilt, fear and anxiety aroused by the abuse. In the context of the child's life history and present circumstances, it should be possible to encourage self-awareness, to increase the individual's perceived self-efficiency, to enhance self-esteem and to mobilise the child's inner resources for self-help (Berliner, this volume). Part of the therapist's task is also to assist the child through the contacts with the medical and law enforcement systems as well as through traumatic court testimony.

Family work is also considered an important dimension of treatment. Indeed, Berliner (this volume) takes the view not only that parents are essential partners in any treatment programme for children but that much needs to be done with parents in acknowledging the full implications of the trauma, particularly if it evokes memories of their own victimisation. For the perpetrator to either remain in or return to the family requires skilful management and control. Allowing a perpetrator to return without sufficient controls leaves the practitioner open to the charge of putting the needs of the offender or the desire for a re-united family above the need to ensure a child's safety from sexual abuse.

Other treatment modules have been developed in parallel mother-child therapy groups where the goal is to help mothers and children to express and resolve their feelings regarding sexual abuse; to increase their assertiveness, to heighten the mothers' awareness of their children's need for protection from abuse and to assist them in providing protection (Damon and Waterman, 1986).

Many of our therapeutic responses to perpetrators, victims and families are based on the need to do something rather than on the basis of empirical evidence. This is most clearly demonstrated in the 'birdshot' approach where perpetrators are provided with a range of therapies within a programme in the hope that at least some components will have an effect. The only way to move forward from this position is empirically to assess the efficacy of different interventions. The usefulness of this will multiply if it is linked to theoretical work that hypothesizes certain effects and outcomes. The work of David Finkelhor in proposing theoretical models for pre-conditions in perpetrators and for the effects of abuse on victims is an important step in this direction (Finkelhor *et al.*, 1986).

Treatment context: a multi-disciplinary approach

The context in which treatment takes place is equally important. On this subject, a number of questions come to mind. First, given the range and depth of knowledge and skill that are required of practitioners dealing with child sexual abuse, what are the roles, responsibilities and relationships of the different professional groups? The way in which the professionals interact, their attitudes to each other, their ability to communicate and co-operate are likely to be crucial in determining the presence or absence of abuse and the outcome for the individual child and family. Moreover, pressures may flow from the legal context in which professionals must act, from new legislation and less directly but very powerfully from the non-client public, shaping both the explicit and the unspoken priorities of the professional services.

It is as true in the United Kingdom as it is in the United States that many practitioners in the health and welfare professions worry unduly about the distinctiveness of their own discipline. Perhaps without ever having seriously planned it, we have tended to build up a pattern of services around specific professions and groups of professions. Yet time and again the needs of clients — or patients; even their title is changed when another profession looks after them — cut right across the boundaries between services. The problem of providing a comprehensive assessment and treatment service, which could never be easy in any circumstances, is made very much more difficult by the careful separation of little tracts of professional territory and the entrenched attitudes with which they defend their boundaries. Pleas for more co-ordination or better communication will achieve little. Symbolic joint committees at national level will in themselves bring about few changes unless the practice of joint working can be carried through to local level. Even at national level, there are unfortunately often major discrepancies in the policies advocated by different professional and government departments.

To work effectively at local level may require a different structure of service delivery. Virtually all social workers function within bureaucratic systems, the majority of them in large and complex ones. Major policy decisions are made by committees of elected local authority members, dependent though they may be on the advice of senior officers. In what has rapidly become the most politically sensitive area of social work practice, guidelines proliferate, holding management anxieties at bay as well as offering a framework for better professional practice. The 1989 White Paper on Community Care (HMSO, 1989) places a requirement on local authorities to review those aspects of social welfare provision which could be contracted out to the private or voluntary sectors. These new arrangements will create a very different structure of service delivery which has important implications for child protection.

COSMETIC RESPONSE

The cosmetic or symbolic response can be identified most clearly in those government actions which serve to persuade the public that the problem is being dealt with. They are a means of assuaging our consciences, because we can be seen to be 'doing something', without making any real contribution to prevention or management. Karl Marx once commented very appositely on 'man's eternal hypocrisy — his belief that he is changing things when he is only changing their names'. Equally, man has a belief that things are changing even if that may amount to no more than a set of procedural guidelines, a register of names, reforms to the law of evidence to make it less traumatic for children required to give evidence in criminal court.

In the various documents and guidelines produced by central and local government, relatively little attention is given to the reality of the identification of sexual abuse itself. Emphasis is laid principally upon the more severe cases involving physical trauma, rather than on the other equally serious and more numerous cases where there may be real difficulties in establishing a distinction between what is and what is not sexual abuse. Only a few victims of even extensive sexual assault will have clear physical signs of abuse (Heger, this volume), and it is unlikely that there will be other forms of clear evidence. The reality is that professionals must exercise discretion on the basis of experience and sound judgment. Guidelines which are limited to consideration of administrative and procedural matters are therefore no more than a cosmetic response since they do little to guarantee the necessary professional judgment and good practice. If the guidelines provide no support for professional decision-making and a tragedy occurs, public criticism is likely immediately to be directed at the social workers in the case. Social workers are sometimes presented as if they were more blameworthy than the parents or parent-substitutes who inflicted the fatal injuries.

RECENT TRENDS IN AMERICAN EXPERIENCE

There are a number of issues currently arising in American experience that are only just beginning to emerge in a major way in the British context. They include an increase in cases of different types of abuse, for example, cases of satanic ritual abuse and of abuse in custody proceedings, in children in foster care, in institutional settings and in children with disabilities; and, on the other hand, a backlash against taking child sexual abuse seriously.

Child custody and divorce

Reported cases of child sexual abuse are appearing in growing numbers in the divorce courts on both sides of the Atlantic. In the context of custody and visitation disputes an increasing number of cases has involved an allegation, usually by the mother, that a young child has been molested by a father or step-father. The possible fabrication of sexual abuse by one parent intent on hurting the other has been an additional concern. The timing can look suspicious, especially when raised for the first time in conjunction with disputes over access and property rights or immediately preceding a court hearing. While the possibility of false accusations must always be considered, the research and clinical evidence currently available suggests that it may be a factor in only a small minority of cases (Myers *et al.*, 1989).

Understandably, children may disclose abuse more readily and may have more chance of being believed by the other parent when a divorce is imminent (Berliner, this volume). When parents are moving apart there may be less opportunity for the abusing parent to enforce secrecy since the child may be in contact with parents separately and therefore will have more opportunity to disclose the abuse. As parents lose trust in one another, child abuse by the other parent may appear more feasible.

The stress of parental conflict and the increased opportunity for a child to be alone with a parent may precipitate abuse (Corwin, 1989). Separation and divorce are often accompanied by feelings of bereavement and loss which may lead parents to regressive acting out behaviour, including sexual abuse. Corwin also postulates that the adult character traits and behaviour problems frequently associated with sexual abuse of children are more common in people whose marriages break up, and that this rather than false allegations may be the explanation for the increase in such claims.

Multiple victim and multi-suspect sexual abuse

Multiple victim cases are the types of child abuse allegations that arise in a setting where children are at risk of being victimised by one or more offenders. For example, schools, pre-schools, youth groups, and out-of-home facilities such as group homes. Multi-suspect cases are the types of child abuse allegations that arise where more than one suspect has been named by children as having participated in or been aware of the abuse against one or more children. Examples of this would be sex ring participants, child pornographers, and other offenders who, with each other's knowledge, engage in abusing children.

Sexual abuse in day care facilities is being increasingly reported. In 1983 and 1985 a nationwide survey across the United States identified 1,639 victims in 270 day care centres for pre-school children (Finkelhor *et al*, 1988). The researchers estimated the risk to children is 5.5 children sexually abused per 10,000 children enrolled, compared to 8.9 per 10,000 pre-school children sexually abused in their homes. An active lobby and criminal defence argument has sometimes attempted to blame agencies for creating false cases and abusing children with inappropriate investigative techniques. The scale of the problem is now sufficient to justify the authorities having special guidelines on how to deal with these cases. They recommend a team approach to minimise the risk of contamination, provide for more humane interviews with the victims and assure that investigation is more efficiently and effectively carried out on behalf of the children and families involved in these cases (Los Angeles County, 1988).

The McMartin pre-school case is perhaps the most notorious example of multi-suspect, multi-victim abuse so far documented. It involved 360 children who claimed to have been sexually abused by their teachers and also allegedly involved in satanic rituals. After the longest criminal trial in US history the jury, on 23 January 1990, acquitted the two accused (although going to re-trial on some of the counts). This is an important example of the interaction of legal, social, psychological and medical factors in such cases and the complexity of the professional roles and responsibilities.

Ritual abuse

During the past ten years American society has become increasingly aware of many cases of multi-victim, multi-suspect abuse which are thought to have ritualistic components. Many of these, but not all (Jones, 1990), have a religious dimension and are commonly known as satanic ritual abuse (Kelley, 1989). This has been defined as 'repeated physical, emotional, mental, spiritual assault combined with a systematised use of symbols, ceremonies and use of evil designed and orchestrated to attain harmful effects — to turn the individual against themselves, society and God' (Simandl, 1989).

In spite of the hidden nature of these practices there have been intermittent reports of activities in England, sufficient for the subject of 'occult societies' to be raised in debate in the House of Commons (Hansard, 1988). Nonetheless, ritualistic cases are a small proportion of all sexual abuse cases. The danger is that those who read and hear such bizarre stories involving infanticide, and torturing and killing animals might begin to think that all children who claimed to have been sexually abused, whether by Satanists or not, were lying. One theory is that the masks, potions and dead animals are nothing more than a trick devised by child abusers to discredit their victim's story. Another theory is that rituals, particularly the animal sacrifices are no more than attempts to frighten the children into silence. Others believe the myths are rooted in the collective unconscious. But whatever the explanation the allegations of infanticide and torturing and killing animals as well as sexual abuse has not so far been supported by factual evidence.

The backlash

There are fears in the United States that the efforts to force society to acknowledge the reality of child sexual abuse will be quickly forgotten in a public backlash of disbelief, including accusations of witch hunting. This suppression of the reality involves the belief that child sexual abuse does not occur with any frequency; that children who make such claims are sick or depraved; that whatever the case the children are not to be believed. The impression is that in the United States the backlash is already well under way and gaining strength daily (Myers, 1989). There are indications of similar processes being followed in Britain. For example, a recent newspaper article on the McMartin Pre-school in California case described day-care provision as 'the child dumps of post-liberation maternity', and explained the accusations of abuse as arising from children being 'fed on a diet of Stephen King horror movies . . .', from 'parental guilt at dumping their children', and from the 'strong likelihood of financial profit from the companies who insure such schools' (Botsford, 1990).

In different countries, people have reacted to different issues. In the United States, the prosecutors have been criticised for what has been described as over-zealous actions in prosecuting child sexual abuse cases. In Britain, social workers have been attacked for either failing to remove a child from the home, in spite of danger signals, or for snatching children from their homes without sufficient justification; and physicians have been accused of making hasty diagnoses on the basis of uncertain physical evidence. If the perception emerges that physicians are on a witch hunt, that no one is safe and that any touching of a child will bring down the full force of the law, there will be a public backlash.

During the present campaign in favour of legislating against the physical punishment of children by their parents, many have expressed a fear that it is not safe to touch a child. Eventually people react negatively and the backlash is fuelled. Similarly, a belief that children never lie is difficult for people to accept and invites criticism. Children rarely lie about sexual abuse but they do sometimes fabricate claims and they have been known to be coached by parents into making false allegations (Jones and McGraw, 1987). Over-statements of this kind invite criticism from the entire professional community and scepticism of its knowledge and motives.

A second triggering factor is described by Myers (1989) as 'the knowledge gap'. He maintains that our increasing recognition of the existence of child sexual abuse has not been accompanied by an equal development in our understanding of the problem. There is therefore a danger that the discrepancy between the scope of practice and the trained competence of most practitioners becomes intolerably wide. For example, American research has indicated that very few social workers, police officers, and doctors using anatomical detailed dolls as an adjunct to interviewing are trained in the use of dolls. Consequently, improperly suggestive interview techniques are sometimes employed (Boat, 1987). It could therefore be held that interviewers are planting false allegations of abuse in children's minds through suggestive questioning. One of the problems is the great shortage of reliable information as to the relative merits of various interviewing methods (Jones, this volume). There is a marked tendency for ideas about social and psychological assessment and treatment to be diffused on the basis of superficial attractiveness rather than on the basis of evidence derived from controlled investigation. Furthermore, there tends to be a low level of sensitivity among practitioners and managers to research-based knowledge as a guide to action.

Finally, a strong factor in the backlash phenomenon is 'society's blind spot'. Society is said to be resistant to seeing child sexual abuse and tries to force it from human awareness. John Myers (1989) quotes Roland Summit on the subject.

> Anyone proclaiming [the reality of child sexual abuse] imposes a dismal flaw on our hope for a just and fair society. All our systems of justice, reason and power have been adjusted to ignore the possibility of such a fatal flaw. Our very sense of enlightenment insists that anything *that* important could not escape our attention. Where could it hide? Parents would find out. Doctors would see it. The courts would stop it. Victims would tell their psychiatrists. It would be obvious in psychological tests. Our best minds would know it. It is more reasonable to argue that young upstarts are making trouble. You can't trust kids. Untrained experts are creating a wave of hysteria. They ask leading questions. No family is safe from the invasion of the childsavers. It's time to get back to common sense (Summit, 1988).

Myers also reminds us that it is as well to remember that three times in the past society has suppressed recognition of the reality of child sexual abuse: in approximately 1857, 1896 and 1932. In 1857, the efforts of Ambrose Tardieu to force society to acknowledge the truth of children's complaints about sexual assault were fiercely opposed and ultimately forgotten. When in the 1890's Sigmund Freud identified child sexual assault as a major factor in the aetiology of hysteria, his theories met with such ridicule that he was forced to abandon them. The view that child sexual abuse was a fantasy rather than reality gained the upper hand. The third acknowledgment of child sexual abuse occurred in the 1930s when Ferenczi tried to bring to light what he believed was a very widespread problem. His beliefs about child sexual abuse were wholly rejected, and because he refused to recant, his career ended in ruin. And now at the end of the first decade of the fourth acknowledgement we must ask whether in the enlightened nineties society is prepared to recognise the reality of child sexual abuse and to demand a proper response.

CONCLUDING REMARKS

Intervening in child sexual abuse raises questions of remarkable complexity, in which social, medical, psychological and legal factors are elaborately interwoven. If we are looking for solutions our first concern must be with public attitudes and priorities. For example, the development of an effective co-ordinated approach to assessment and treatment does not happen by bringing the various disciplines together, but must be a planned effort involving all the disciplines at every level of management and practice. Such co-ordination will only occur with the full motivation of the various professional disciplines and, more importantly, with the full backing of society. If society is ambivalent to child protection intervention, then this will be displayed by attacks on professionals from both within and outside the professional agencies. Society needs to face the complexities of the potential conflict between the rights of children and parents. For example, where video-recordings are made of the child's disclosure interview: who owns the tape and what right does the child have to control its use.

Similar problems of values and the purposes of laws and procedures exist in the uneasy gap between the civil child protection proceeding and the criminal prosecution. More thought should be given to the relative strengths of these proceedings. There needs to be a serious examination of the therapeutic support services provided for families. Professional services are unable to respond to all the reported cases let alone provide preventive support services. This has encouraged the deficit model of parenting where informal or formal risk schedules are applied to identify those parents deficient in the care of their children. If we could instead provide a more positive and empowering model of service provision there might be fewer cases requiring the crisis intervention that is resisted by the 'backlash' against child sexual abuse intervention. One way forward is to develop neighbourhood support that will provide the guidance and protection to families when it is needed. The self-help initiatives that have developed in the United States have increased community awareness of the need to care and protect their children. They have also helped to bring together perpetrators to help overcome their problem, and allowed victims and non-abusing parents to benefit from mutual support.

What we still do not know about the characteristics, causes and effective intervention and treatment of child sexual abuse far exceeds what we can be reasonably sure that we know. Yet the urge to intervene is great. The expansion of child protection procedures and legislation increases the need to protect children from those with good intentions, but operating with inadequate skills. It may also raise false expectations of the ability of an overloaded system to respond. At the same time the forces of denial and inertia and the subordination of children are so well organised in society, even institutionalised, that an honest examination of the problem of child sexual abuse is a continuing challenge.

REFERENCES

Bacon, R. and Farquar, I. (1983) 'Child abuse in an English local authority. A descriptive and interpretative study of the identification, definition and social work management and treatment of child abuse cases in a local authority setting', Research Report to DHSS.

Berliner, L. and Conte, J. R. (1990) 'The process of victimisation: the victims' perspective', *Child Abuse and Neglect*, 14 (1).

Boat, B. (1987) Address to the First Annual Conference of the California Professional Society on the Abuse of Children, Los Angeles, December 4. Cited in J.E.B. Myers (1989) 'Protecting children from sexual abuse: what does the future hold?', *Journal of Contemporary Law*, University of Utah College of Law, 15 (1).

Botsford, K. (1990) 'Whiff of Salem in the loony state', *The Independent*, 3 March.

Brent Borough Council (1985) *A Child in Trust*. The Report of the panel of inquiry into the circumstances surrounding the death of Jasmine Beckford. London.

Brown, P. (1989) 'Criminal injuries compensation scheme: compensation for abused children', in: *Criminal Injuries Compensation Scheme: Briefing Papers for Applications for Compensation for Sexually Abused Children*. Scottish Child Law Centre.

Caring for People: Community Care in the Next Decade and Beyond. Cm. 849, London: HMSO.

Cleveland (1988) *Report of the Inquiry into Child Abuse in Cleveland, 1987*. Cm. 412. London: HMSO (Butler-Sloss Report).

Coburn, M. (1990) 'Working with sexual offenders in prison', Paper presented to conference on Child Sexual Abuse, Research and Policy Issues, Institute of Child Health, London, 20 March.

Corwin, D., Berliner, L., Goodman, G., Goodwin, and White, S., (1987) 'Child sexual abuse and custody disputes: no easy answers', *Journal of Interpersonal Violence*, 2.

Crewdson, J. (1988) *By Silence Betrayed, Sexual Abuse of Children in America*. Boston: Little, Brown and Company.

Damon, L. and Waterman, J. (1986) 'Parallel group treatment of children and their mothers', in: K. MacFarlane and J. Waterman, *Sexual Abuse of Young Children*. The Guilford Press.

Davidson, H. (1988) 'Failure to report child abuse: legal penalties and emerging issues, in: A. Maney and S. Wells (eds.) *Professional Responsibilities in Protecting Children*. New York: Praeger.

Dingwall, R., Eekelaar, J., and Murray, T. (1983) *The Protection of Children*. Oxford: Blackwell.

Dziech, B. W. and Schudson, Judge, C. B. (1989) *On Trial: America's Courts and their Treatment of Sexually Abused Children*. Boston: Beacon Press.

Ennew, J. (1986) *The Sexual Exploitation of Children*. Polity Press.

Finkelhor D. and Associates (1986) *Sourcebook on Child Sexual Abuse* Beverley Hills: Sage.

Finkelhor, D., Williams, L. M. with Burns, N. (1988) *Nursery Crimes. Sexual Abuse in Day Care*. Newbury Park, Sage.

Fox, S. J. (1982) *Modern Juvenile Justice*. West Publishing Company.

Frost, N. and Stein, M. (1989) *The Politics of Child Welfare*. Harvester Wheatsheaf.

Gough, D. A. (1988) 'Scottish Child Abuse Statistics', Report for Association of Directors of Social Work.

Gough, D. A., Boddy, F. A., Dunning, N., Stone, F. H. (1987) 'The children who were registered'. A longitudinal study of child abuse in Glasgow, Volume 1. Report to the Scottish Office.

Greenwich Borough Council (1987) *A Child in Mind: Protection of Children in a Responsible Society*. Report of the Commission of Inquiry into the circumstances surrounding the death of Kimberley Carlile. London.

Hammersmith Social Services Department (1984) *Report on the Death of Shirley Woodcock*. London.

Hansard (1988) 'Occult Societies', Debate on 27 April. Col. 485-488.

Hechler, D. (1989) *The Battle and the Backlash*. Lexington Books.

Lord Chancellor's Department (1988) *Improvements in the Arrangements for Care*

Proceedings. Green Paper.

Jones, D. P. H. and McGraw, J. M. (1987) 'Reliable and fictitious accounts of sexual abuse to children', *Journal of Interpersonal Violence*, 2 (1).

Jones, D.P.H. (1990) "Satanic rituals and child sexual abuse', Paper presented to Conference on Child Sexual Abuse, Research and Policy Issues, Institute of Child Health. London, 19 March.

Kelley, S. J. (1989) 'Stress responses of children to sexual abuse and ritualistic abuse in day care centres', *Journal of Interpersonal Violence*, 4 (4).

Lambeth Borough Council (1987) *Whose Child?* The Report of the panel appointed to inquire into the death of Tyra Henry. Chair: Stephen Sedley. London.

Law Commission (1989) *Domestic Violence and Occupation of the Family Home.*, Working Paper No. 113.

Li, C. K. (Forthcoming) 'Adult sexual experiences with children: a study of personal accounts', in C. K. Li, D. J. West and T. P. Woodhouse (eds.) *Sexual Encounters between Children and Adults.*

Long, S. (1986) 'Guidelines for treating young children', in K. MacFarlane & J. Waterman, *Sexual Abuse of Young Children.* The Guilford Press.

Los Angeles County (1988) 'Protocols developed by the multi-victim, multi-suspect child sexual abuse subcommittee', Inter-Agency Council on Child Abuse and Neglect.

MacFarlane, K. (1986) 'Challenges for the future', in K. MacFarlane & J. Waterman, *Sexual Abuse of Young Children.* The Guilford Press.

Mezey, G., Vizard, E., Hawkes, C. and Austin, R. (1990) 'A community treatment programme for convicted child sex offenders: a preliminary report', Unpublished paper available from E. Vizard, Child Guidance Unit, 84 West Ham Lane, London E15 4PT.

Murray, K. (1987) *Evidence from Children.* Research report. Scottish Law Commission.

Myers, J.E.B. (1989) 'Protecting children from sexual abuse', *Journal of Contemporary Law,*, University of Utah College of Law, 15 (1).

Myers, J., Bays, J., Becker, J., Berliner, L. Corwin, D. and Saywitz, K. (1989) 'Expert testimony in child sexual abuse litigation', *Nebraska Law Review*, 68 (1).

Parton, N. (1985) *The Politics of Child Abuse.* Basingstoke: Macmillan Education Ltd.

Peters, J., Dinsmore, J. and Toth, P. (1989) 'Why prosecute child abuse?', *South Dakota Law Review*, 34 (3).

Simandl, R. J. (1989) 'Identification and investigation of ritualistic criminal activity', Paper presented at a Conference on Ritualistic Abuse, University of Dundee, 22 September.

Summit, R. (1988) 'Hidden victims, hidden pain: societal avoidance of child sexual abuse', in G. E. Wyatt and G. J. Powell eds. *The Lasting Effects of Child Sexual Abuse.* Newbury Park: Sage.

Toth, P. and Whalen, M. eds. (1987) *Investigation and Prosecution of Child Abuse.* American Prosecutors Research Institute.

Waterhouse, L. and Carnie, J. (1989) 'Child sexual abuse: a Scottish perspective', in A. Brown and D. McCrone, *The Scottish Government Year Book 1989.* Unit for the Study of Government in Scotland.

Wyre, R. (1987) 'Working with sex abuse', Conference and workshop papers. Perry Publications, Oxford.

Wyre, R. (1989) 'Gracewell Clinic', in S. Rogers, D. Hevey and E. Ash, *Child Abuse and Neglect: Facing the Challenge.* The Open University.

Zellman, G. (1990) 'Influences on the reporting behaviour of mandated reporters', Paper presented at conference on Health Science Response to Child Maltreatment, The Center for Child Protection, San Diego.

INDEX